Against the Philosophical Tide

Essays in Popperian Critical Rationalism

DANNY FREDERICK

Critias Publishing
Yeovil, UK

ISBN: 978-1-5272-6628-5

CONTENTS

IV MISCELLANY

ACKNOWLEDGMENTS

Chapter 1 is a revised version of 'A Regimented and Concise Exposition of Karl Popper's Critical Rationalist Epistemology,' which was published in *Cosmos + Taxis* 6 (6+7): 49-54 (2019). I thank the publisher for permission to re-use here some of the material contained in that earlier paper. All the other papers in this volume are previously unpublished.

I PHILOSOPHY OF SCIENCE

1 A REGIMENTED AND CONCISE EXPOSITION OF KARL POPPER'S CRITICAL RATIONALIST EPISTEMOLOGY (VERSION 3)

Abstract. Criticisms of Karl Popper's critical rationalist epistemology are often confused and misleading. In part that is due to Popper's somewhat lax use of language, in which technical terms are used in more than one sense. I attempt to clarify Popper's views by regimenting his terminology. The result is offered as a clear and concise exposition of the main points of Popper's epistemology.

Keywords. Ad hoc; critical rationalism; epistemology; falsifiability; metaphysics; Karl Popper; pseudo-science; rationality; science.

1. Introduction

Discussions of Karl Popper's epistemology typically exhibit a range of confusions. To some extent that is Popper's fault. He disdained meaning or linguistic analysis as trivial and scholastic. But that reasonable disdain engendered in him a reluctance to be fussy over terminology; and that reluctance led him to speak loosely, often using terms ambiguously, thereby leaving his expositions unclear overall and wide open to misinterpretations. To exhibit the value and coherence of Popper's epistemology it is therefore necessary to restate it in a clear and concise way that regiments the terminology that Popper uses. I ended my first attempt at that task with the words "I propose that this regimentation should become standard until it is improved upon" (Frederick 2019b, p. 54). I offered an improved regimentation in Version 2 of my paper, published online on 17 May 2020.

This new paper is my attempt to improve upon Version 2.

The main improvements in Version 2 were the addition of a non-redundancy condition to the explanation of a scientific statement, (S), and of a redundancy condition to the explanation of a purely metaphysical statement, (PM); the re-description of basic statements as 'observation statements' (to avoid the suggestion that theories are *based on* observations); some clarification of the falsifiability of observation statements; and the replacement of talk of the impossibility of *establishing* the truth or falsity of a statement by talk of the *absence of any indicators* of truth or falsity. The main improvement of this new version over Version 2 is the clearer separation of scientific statements (direct or indirect) and merely empirical statements.

As before, I recommend that the following exposition should be accepted as standard until it is improved upon. The regimentation differs from the terminology I have used in some earlier expositions of Popper's ideas (Frederick 2010; 2015). The fact that those expositions differed among themselves in the ways in which Popper's terminology was explained was itself a testament to the need for a standard regimentation. The references to Popper's work given below show some places in which will be found his relevant views but, plainly, not necessarily the same terminology.

It may be helpful, before launching into the regimented exposition, which may be a little dry, to give a less formal sketch of Popper's epistemology so that its broad outlines can be comprehended. On Popper's view, the growth of knowledge begins with a problem, which is usually an inconsistency discovered either within an inherited theory, or between inherited theories, or between an inherited theory and an accepted observation statement. We attempt to solve the problem by proposing new explanatory theories. These new theories are not derived from observations and they are not conclusions of a process of reasoning; they are conjectures, guesses, albeit guesses informed by our analysis of the problem. We criticise these theories in various ways and we evaluate them as better or worse solutions to our problem. That criticism and evaluation involves deductive reasoning. So, the theory comes first; the reasoning comes afterwards. As a result, we usually come to understand the problem better, which leads us to suggest further new theories, which are in turn criticised and evaluated. It may be that we eventually settle on one theory as clearly better than its available rivals, as happened in the case of Newton's theory in the eighteenth century. That dominant theory may then become a main focus for our criticism, identification of new problems and further development of theory. The attempt to resolve the problems that the criticism of the dominant theory generates may lead to new conjectures which are rivals to that theory and which manage to stand up to criticism better than that theory does, thus leading to its revolutionary overthrow.

The growth of knowledge is thus a revisionary process of conjecture and criticism. An important kind of criticism is empirical, that is, the discovery of points at which a conjecture clashes with reality as we experience it. Thus an empirical statement is one that is falsifiable. A conjecture incapable of such an empirical clash is deemed metaphysical. However, what makes a conjecture scientific is not merely that it is susceptible to empirical criticism, but that it generates *novel* falsifiable predictions that survive testing. A conjecture may generate such predictions either directly or indirectly; and that enables some conjectures, which are metaphysical in that they are not falsifiable, to qualify as scientific because they generate novel falsifiable predictions indirectly and some of those predictions survive attempts to falsify them.

The process of conjecture and criticism leads to progress only when criticisms are not evaded in pseudo-scientific ways. What distinguishes science is not just that its theories generate, directly or indirectly, novel falsifiable predictions that survive testing, but also that its procedures forbid ad hoc manoeuvres. That requires that an amendment to a theory that removes an inconsistency identified by criticism is acceptable only if it solves some problem in addition to the problem of removing the inconsistency. Thus, falsifiability, novelty and success enable us to distinguish metaphysical, empirical and scientific *statements*; but the avoidance of ad hoc manoeuvres distinguishes scientific from pseudo-scientific *practices*. Popper often ran those two points together, for instance, saying of Marxism that it was falsified and that it was unfalsifiable (1957a, p. 37), when what he meant was that the Marxist *theory* was falsified (and thus falsifiable) but Marxist *practitioners* avoided admitting that the theory was falsified by rescuing it from falsification using ad hoc means. In the following I distinguish clearly theory and practice (statics and dynamics).

In section 2, I deal with Popper's demarcation of different types of statement. The terms 'empirical,' 'falsifiable,' and 'scientific' seem to be used interchangeably by Popper and by those who have been influenced by him; but there are three different types of statement that those terms can appropriately be used to distinguish, and each of those types has an important role to play in Popper's epistemology. Similarly, metaphysical statements are often contrasted with scientific statements, especially in Popper's earlier work; but Popper recognises, especially in his later work, two types of metaphysical statement, one of which is an integral part of science. In section 3, I turn to Popper's demarcation of different types of epistemic procedure into rational or irrational or, less broadly, scientific or pseudo-scientific. Popper sometimes calls statements that are defended by means of pseudo-scientific procedures 'metaphysical' (1959, section 9) or 'non-empirical' (1959, section 20). However, empirical and scientific statements can be defended in pseudo-scientific ways; though, as a consequence, they *may* suffer amendments which turn them into non-empirical or non-scientific statements. Pseudo-scientific *procedures* should not be confused with metaphysical or non-empirical *statements*. I ignore Popper's theory of verisimilitude because it seems to me to be indefensible. In section 4, I conclude. All citations in parentheses in the following sections are references to works by Popper.

2. Theories (Statics)

One of Popper's concerns is to demarcate empirical statements from those which belong to metaphysics, logic or mathematics (1959, sections 4 and 5). He offers the following criterion:

(E)   an *empirical statement* is one that is falsifiable (1959, sections 6, 15 and 21).

The term 'falsifiable' is defined using the term 'observation statement.' The latter is explained as follows:

(O1)   an *observation statement* is one such that

     (a) it has the form 'There is a ϕ in the spatio-temporal region k,' where 'k' represents a term that denotes a delimited spatio-temporal region, perhaps by means of co-ordinates,

     (b) it describes something that we could conceivably observe, given our actual powers of observation, so 'ϕ' represents a term which connotes an observable property (1959, section 28);

(O2)   an *accepted observation statement* is one which is agreed by observers to describe an observed situation which is reproducible (1959, sections 8, 22, 28 and 29).

A reproducible situation is one that either occurs regularly in nature or which we can bring about regularly ourselves, for instance, by means of experiments. Where the spatio-temporal region denoted by the term represented by 'k' is within our current field of observation, an observation statement may be expressed more colloquially by using an indexical, as in 'This is a swan,' 'That is black,' 'Here is a glass of water,' 'Over there is a red swan.'

The notions of falsifiability are explained as follows:

(F1)   a statement is *falsifiable* if and only if it is inconsistent with an observation statement (1959, sections 6 and 21);

(F2)   a statement is *falsified* if and only if it is inconsistent with an *accepted* observation statement (1959, sections 6, 21 and 22).

An example of a falsifiable statement is 'All swans are white.' It is also an example of a falsified statement, given that statements of the form 'This is a black swan' have been accepted recurrently in the light of observations.

Here is the explanation of a metaphysical statement:

(M)   a *metaphysical statement* is one which is not a part of logic or mathematics and which is not falsifiable (1959, section 15).

Popper often equates scientific statements with falsifiable ones, yet he also recognises that:

- some scientific statements are not directly falsifiable (1959, section 18);
- some metaphysical statements play a role in the growth of scientific knowledge (1959, section 4; 1982, sections 20 and 27);
- scientific statements teach us something new, that is, we would expect them to be falsified in the light of some of our background knowledge (1963a, p. 220).

For example, if we take Newton's theory as being the three laws of motion and the law of gravity, then Newton's theory is not falsifiable. Any motion that we could conceivably observe is compatible with Newton's theory because the motion could, in principle, be explained in terms of Newton's theory by assuming the existence of an appropriate set of forces. The theory is therefore metaphysical, according to (M). However, when we combine Newton's theory with our background knowledge concerning the bodies and forces actually involved in a situation, we can derive falsifiable predictions. A prediction is an observation statement. Its derivation from a universal statement requires at least one accepted observation statement to be conjoined to the universal statement. Thus, from a universal statement, perhaps in conjunction with some accepted background knowledge, we may be able to derive a statement of the form 'If p, then q,' where 'p' and 'q' represent observation statements. If the observation statement represented by 'p' is accepted, we can derive as a *prediction* the observation statement represented by 'q' (1959, section 12). A prediction is *novel* if and only if what it predicts is unexpected in the light of our background knowledge (1963a, p. 220).

Newton's theory, then, is indirectly falsifiable; that is, it is a conjunct in a falsifiable conjunction of statements. That conjunction will typically include general background knowledge and more particular statements describing 'initial conditions' (1959, section 12), that is, some features of the situation to which the theory is being applied. The indirectly falsifiable theory will count as scientific only if some of the falsifiable predictions generated are novel and some of those novel falsifiable predictions survive attempts to falsify them (1959, sections 18-20). One attempts to *falsify* a prediction if and only if one seeks to find or bring about a situation in which an observation statement which contradicts the prediction is accepted.

There is a further condition that an indirectly falsifiable statement must satisfy in order to count as scientific, namely, it must be logically required for the deduction of the falsifiable predictions. Suppose that Newton's theory conjoined with some background knowledge, including a statement of initial conditions, entails a novel falsifiable prediction. Then the statement 'God exists' conjoined with Newton's theory and the same background knowledge will entail the same prediction. Deductive logic is monotonic: if P implies Q, then P-and-R implies Q, for any R. Thus, 'God exists' is indirectly falsifiable: it is a conjunct in a falsifiable conjunction of statements. However, unlike Newton's theory, 'God exists' in this example is not a scientific statement because it is not needed for the derivation of the falsifiable prediction; it is redundant (1957b, pp. 132-34).

The notion of a scientific statement is therefore explained thus (1963a, pp. 240-45):

(S)   a statement is *scientific* if and only if
- it entails novel falsifiable predictions that survive attempts to falsify them, *or*
- it is one conjunct of a conjunction that entails novel falsifiable predictions which survive attempts to falsify them, *and* those novel falsifiable predictions could not have been deduced from the conjunction without it.

So, the statement

(1)   all swans are white

is an empirical statement because it is falsifiable. But it is a scientific statement only if, when it was first uttered, our background knowledge did not imply that all swans are the same colour and, for some time afterward, the search for non-white swans found only swans that were white. A statement once classified as scientific remains scientific even if it is later falsified, as (1) was falsified after the acceptance of some observation statements of the types 'That is a swan' and 'That is not white,' where the two occurrences of the word 'that' denoted, in context, the same thing (a black swan).

Newton's theory is a scientific statement because, in the eighteenth century, in conjunction with

- some accepted general background knowledge concerning the properties of familiar phenomena, including light and the working of telescopes,
- some accepted observation statements about the (reproducible) positions and motions of objects and a statement to the effect that there are no other forces acting in the situation apart from those we know about (statements describing the 'initial conditions'),

it entailed *novel* falsifiable predictions, about the positions of the planets and the motions of terrestrial bodies, which survived attempts to falsify them, and those predictions could not have been derived from the accepted background knowledge and statements describing the initial conditions without Newton's theory being conjoined with them.

From (F1), bold theories like Newton's are not falsifiable: they must be conjoined with a bulk of background knowledge and statements describing initial conditions before we get a falsifiable statement. Thus, by (E), they are not empirical statements. So, major scientific theories are often not empirical statements. They are also plainly not axioms or theorems of logic or mathematics (although they generally *employ* a good deal of logic and mathematics, that is, they include such statements as implicit parts of themselves). Consequently, from (M), major scientific theories are typically metaphysical statements (1959, section 4; 1982, sections 20 and 27). We can nevertheless distinguish such statements from *purely* metaphysical statements as follows:

(PM) a *purely metaphysical statement* is one which is not falsifiable and the conjunction of which with accepted background knowledge and statements of initial conditions entails no novel falsifiable predictions, except those, if any, which are implied by the rest of the conjunction without it (1959, section 85).

An example of a purely metaphysical statement is the theory of atomism in the time of the ancients (1959, section 4; 1982, section 20; 1983, pp. 191-92). That theory stated that the world consisted of atoms and the void and that all changes were to be explained in those terms. It maintained that the atoms were too small to be detected and that the void was unobservable, so from (O1) it was not an observation statement. It was also not falsifiable, since no observation statements were inconsistent with it, so from (E) it was not an empirical statement. Further, in conjunction with accepted background knowledge and statements of initial conditions it entailed no novel falsifiable predictions (except those, if any, which were implied by the rest of the conjunction without it). Therefore, from (S), it was not a scientific statement.

However, with the progress of our knowledge and the development of the atomic theory to include many hypothetical assumptions about the nature of atoms, the theory came non-redundantly to imply novel falsifiable predictions which survived attempts to falsify them (as with the kinetic theory of heat), so the theory became scientific (1959, section 85). Further, with the development of microscopes which made atoms observable, some statements of the theory became falsifiable, and thus empirical, because they were then inconsistent with some observation statements (1983, p. 191). Thus, what is a purely metaphysical theory at one time may become a scientific theory at a later time, depending on the progress of our hypotheses and their testing (1958, pp. 186-88; 1959, section 4; 1982, section 20; 1983, pp. 191-92). Further, what is not an observation statement at one time may become an observation statement at a later time if the invention of new devices, such as telescopes and microscopes, enhance our powers of observation.

Observation statements are 'theory-laden,' that is, the observable terms employed in them have implications that transcend the particular situation of observation. For example, 'This is a tree' is an observation statement to which observers may agree in a particular situation of observation. But if the thing thus described suddenly shed its leaves and retracted its branches, or if it waddled off, or if it screamed when carvings were made on its bark, the previously accepted observation statement, 'This is a tree,' would be falsified by the acceptance of the observation statements describing the unexpected behaviour. Thus, accepted observation statements are falsifiable and they may later be rejected on the basis of observations (1959, section 29 and appendix *x, (1) - (5)).

Parenthetically, there is a difference between the falsifiability of observation statements and that of universal statements. For a universal statement, falsifiability is normally a matter of *formal* inconsistency with an observation statement. For example, a universal statement of the form, 'every x is such that, if x is F then x is G' is formally inconsistent with an observation statement of the form 'this F is not G.' For observation statements, in contrast, falsifiability is normally a matter of *informal* inconsistency with another observation statement. For example, 'this is a tree' cannot be true if 'this (referring to the same thing) is walking around the garden.' But those two propositions are *formally consistent*, being of the forms 'Fa' and 'Ga.' The inconsistency arises because the *meaning* of the term 'tree' excludes the possibility of a tree walking around the garden. That is an *informal inconsistency*.

We have no available indicators for whether an observation statement is true or false. Such a statement is accepted by the agreement of observers in light of what they take themselves to have observed; but future observations may lead to its rejection. Even if all accepted observation statements were true, a falsifiable but severely tested and unfalsified universal statement may still be false, since the next accepted observation statement might falsify it. Similarly, the failure to falsify any of the novel falsifiable predictions entailed by the conjunction of a scientific statement with accepted background knowledge and statements of initial conditions cannot preclude that the next accepted observation statement will falsify one of those predictions (1959, sections 1, 3 and 82). A severely tested but unfalsified theory may be false. Further, since observation statements may be false, a falsified theory may be true. Thus, we have no available indicators for whether a self-consistent empirical or scientific theory is true or false. By (PM), there is no way of falsifying a purely metaphysical theory. Provided it is consistent it may be true; but it might also be false. We have no available indicators for whether a self-consistent purely metaphysical theory is true or false. With the possible exception of logical and pure mathematical statements, then, we have no available indicators, for any statement, for whether it is true or false. This point is developed in more detail in Chapter 3.

3. Practice (Dynamics)

Another of Popper's concerns is to demarcate rational from irrational epistemic procedures and, as part of this, to demarcate scientific from pseudo-scientific procedures. We just noted that, with the possible exception of logical and mathematical truths, and self-contradictions, we can have no way of telling whether a statement is true or false. Popper thus proposes that the aim of our search for knowledge is to obtain better explanations (1957b, pp. 132-34). He then proposes a number of procedures that should help us to succeed in our aim if anything can (1959, sections 11 and 20). Thus, the procedures are proposed as being instrumentally rational. In contrast, epistemic procedures which prevent or undermine our success in achieving our epistemic aim are instrumentally irrational.

Since our epistemic aim is to achieve better explanations, we need to agree on ways in which an explanation may be better than a rival explanation. Here are some ways:

- it offers solutions to genuine problems rather than spurious ones (1958, pp. 190-92, 199-200);
- it is consistent rather than self-contradictory (1959, sections 23-24);
- the solutions offered by it actually solve the problems rather than leaving them unsolved, and they better withstand criticism than the solutions provided by rival explanations (1982, sections 27 and 30; 1983, p. 20);
- it solves not only the problems it was proposed to solve, but also other problems besides (1957b, pp. 132-34; 1959, section 20; 1982, section 27);
- it generates, directly or indirectly, more novel falsifiable predictions than its rivals and those predictions survive testing (1957b, pp. 132-34; 1959, section 20; 1963a, pp. 217, 219-20, 241-42);
- it generates new and interesting problems to solve (1963a, p. 222);
- it is simpler than its rivals (1957b, p. 139; 1963a, p. 241; 1982, section 27);
- it provides a uniform solution to problems that rival explanations have to treat differently (1957b, pp. 197-202; 1963a, p. 241);
- it corrects its previously successful rivals (1957b pp. 139-45);
- it is either falsifiable or scientific, rather than purely metaphysical, and has survived attempts to falsify it (1959, sections 5 and 20; 1982, section 27).

Popper proposes the following procedures to help us to achieve our aim:

(i)   we should study, and try to criticise, existing explanations, subjecting them to experimental tests if they are falsifiable or scientific, and we should attempt to propose explanations which offer better solutions to the problems for which the existing explanations provide solutions (1959, section 27, including footnote *1; 1982, section 27; 1976, pp. 40-43);

(ii)   we should try to identify new problems posed by our study and criticism of existing explanations and try to propose explanations which solve them (1958, pp. 184, 190);

(iii)   we should state our problems and proposed explanations as clearly and simply as we can (1983, p. 8);

(iv)   we should subject our proposed explanations to critical scrutiny and seek out and invite criticisms of them, including experimental tests in the cases of falsifiable and scientific explanations (1959, section 9);

(v)   where a criticism is telling, we may defend a proposed explanation by modifying it or by combining it with additional hypotheses so that the criticism is rebutted, but only if these manoeuvres allow the explanation to solve additional problems (Popper 1959, sections 6, 19 and 20);

(vi)   in the case of a falsifiable or a scientific explanation, we may seek to overturn a falsification of it by modifying the explanation or by combining it with additional hypotheses so that the falsification is explained away, but only if these manoeuvres give us a revised explanation which generates novel falsifiable predictions that survive attempts to falsify them or which solves a problem that the explanation had previously not solved (1959, sections 6, 19 and 20);

(vii)   we should accept (at least until it is falsified, or until it is rebutted in accordance with (vi)) any observation statement describing a reproducible situation that is agreed by observers to describe an observed situation;

(viii)   we should abandon a proposed explanation if the problems it is intended to solve are shown to be not genuine problems (1958, pp. 190-92, 199-200);

(ix)   we should never attempt to justify a proposed explanation but should rather be keen to improve it or to replace it with something better (Popper 1959, sections 1, 8, 11, 85; 1976, section xvi).

Any proposed epistemic procedures which conflict with (i)-(ix) are irrational, given our epistemic aim; and they are pseudo-scientific in connection with scientific statements (1959, section 11). Violations of (i) and (ii) are incompatible with the search for knowledge, since they eschew the attempt to find better explanations. Any violation of (iii) is obscurantist. That damns most 'Continental philosophy.' Violation of (iv) or (ix) is incompatible with the search for better explanations. Thus, contemporary epistemology is irrational. Violations of (v) or (vi) are ad hoc. They are thus irrational in a way similar to violations of (iv) and (ix) because they are attempts to buttress a defective existing explanation rather than to seek a better one. Violation of (vii) ignores our empirical contact with the world and is thus irrational and pseudo-scientific, given our epistemic aim. Violations of (viii) are scholastic, producing statements which are irrelevant, obscure, confused or trivial. A good deal of contemporary 'analytic philosophy' seems to be of that kind.

4. Conclusion

Popper's critical rationalist epistemology is a great advance over traditional and contemporary epistemology. It emphasises criticism rather than dogmatism, imaginative problem-solving rather than pedestrian fact-collecting or scholastic nitpicking, continual progress rather than stagnation, and insight into the development of scientific and metaphysical theories and the progress of our understanding of the world.

However, Popper's lax use of language obscures his message and generates misinterpretations of his views and much misplaced criticism of them. In an attempt to remedy that I have proposed that Popper's technical terms be subject to regimentation; and I have used that regimentation to essay a clear and concise exposition of the main points of Popper's epistemology. I propose that this regimentation should become standard until it is improved upon.

2 FALSIFIABILITY AND THE DUHEM PROBLEM(S)

Abstract. It is a common complaint against Karl Popper's account of science that it falters on the Duhem problems which undermine the utility of the notion of falsifiability. I explain how Popper addressed and solved the Duhem problems in his first major published work.

Keywords. Pierre Duhem; falsifiability; independent test; novel prediction; observation; Karl Popper; theory-laden.

1. Introduction

Pierre Duhem pointed out that observation statements are theory-laden, so a negative test result need not show a theory to be false. He also explained that scientific theories can often be tested only if they are conjoined with some other theories, so a negative test result does not point unambiguously at a specific theory. To that extent, scientific theories are not falsifiable.

These problems were raised and resolved by Karl Popper in his *The Logic of Scientific Discovery* (1959), as explained in Chapter 1. Nevertheless, the Duhem problems are standardly raised as objections to Popper's account of science. It may therefore be worth addressing them explicitly.

2. Falsifiability

An observation statement describes something we could conceivably observe, given our actual powers of observation, such as a black swan, a white swan or a blue swan. An accepted observation statement is one that we agree describes some observable and reproducible state of affairs

(Popper 1959, sections 8, 22, 28-29). A statement is falsifiable if and only if it is inconsistent with an observation statement. A statement is falsified if and only if it is inconsistent with an *accepted* observation statement (Popper 1959, sections 6, 21-22). 'All swans are white' is falsifiable because it is inconsistent with 'This is a blue swan,' which is an observation statement; it is falsified because it is inconsistent with 'This is a black swan,' which is an accepted observation statement.

3. The Duhem Problems

Pierre Duhem (1954, pp. 180-90) pointed out that our theories make contact with observations only through the mediation of other theories. When a theory clashes with an observation statement, the theory may be true if some theory presupposed in the observation statement is false. For example, perhaps those things we took to be black swans look like swans but are actually members of a different species; or perhaps they are swans but are not naturally black (some weirdo painted them). Even if we assume that the observation statement is true, in the case of scientific theories the clash with an observation statement often depends upon the acceptance of other theories. For instance, Newton's first law, 'Every body stays at rest or moves in uniform motion in a straight line unless acted on by a net force,' is not inconsistent with any observation statement, because we cannot observe forces, only their effects; so it is not falsifiable. The *conjunction* of Newton's first law with other statements from Newton's theory and statements describing the state of the world is falsifiable; but the falsification of the conjunction is not a falsification of Newton's first law since it could be one (or more) of the other statements in the conjunction that is causing the trouble.

4. Observation Statements

The fact that all observation statements are theory-laden entails that falsification does not imply falsity. When we agree to accept an observation statement it is because it reports what we seem to observe; but what we seem to observe may not be the case, so the observation statement may, for all we know, be false. That means that, at least in empirical matters, certainty is not available to us and that any accepted observation statement may be rejected at a later time. However, in serious theoretical enquiry, rejection of a previously accepted observation statement must be constrained so that it happens only when it facilitates, rather than frustrates, the creation of ever better theories. That can be illustrated with an example from the history of science.

In the late-seventeenth century, Isaac Newton proposed a new theory which seemed to solve the problems of *both* terrestrial *and* celestial motion; it treated what had been thought to be different things in the same way. The theory contradicted the theories of both Galileo and Kepler, but its predictions for the motions of bodies, both terrestrial and celestial, were very similar to the predictions of Galileo's and Kepler's theories, respectively. So, if Newton's theory were true, it would explain why the theories of Galileo and Kepler *seemed* true. Unfortunately, the observational records of the Astronomer Royal contained statements of the positions of the moon that were inconsistent with the predictions derived from Newton's theory (in conjunction with background knowledge). Newton's response was to propose that all these observation statements be rejected. What made that a scientific, rather than an ad hoc, response was the way that Newton did it.

When the Astronomer Royal recorded his observations of the moon, he presupposed a theory about atmospheric refraction. That was inevitable: either the earth's atmosphere refracts light or it does not; and if it does, there is a an infinity of ways in which it might do so. So any observation statement that says where the moon is at a particular time presupposes one of the alternative theories of atmospheric refraction. What Newton did was to replace the theory presupposed by the Astronomer Royal with a different one, which required each of the previously accepted observation statements about the moon's positions to be replaced with new observation statements which were consistent with Newton's theory (Lakatos 1978a, p. 216). Newton thereby explained why the moon was where his theory said it was but *appeared* to be where the Astronomer Royal thought he saw it. That was acceptable only because Newton's new theory of refraction was independently testable. It applied not only to light reflected from the moon but to light in general that travels through the earth's atmosphere; so it made novel predictions concerning the observable positions of other objects and those predictions survived testing.

5. Conjunctions

The fact that it is normally a conjunction of propositions, rather than a simple proposition, that is falsified by an accepted observation statement means that, if we do not reject the accepted observation statement, then we have a choice concerning which element of the conjunction to reject. However, in serious theoretical enquiry, the choice concerning which element of the conjunction to reject must be constrained so that it facilitates, rather than frustrates, the creation of ever better theories. That can be illustrated with an example from the history of science.

In the mid-nineteenth century, accepted observation statements describing the motions of Uranus were inconsistent with some of the predictions entailed by the conjunction of Newton's theory with accepted statements about the solar system. Rather than rejecting Newton's theory, Urbain Leverrier chose to revise the assumption that there were seven planets. He introduced the new hypothesis that there was an eighth planet with a size and an orbit that would generate a gravitational pull on Uranus sufficient, according to Newton's theory, to account for the observed motions of Uranus. What made that a scientific, rather than an ad hoc, response was that the new hypothesis implied novel predictions concerning when and where, on a clear night, the hypothesised planet would be seen, if a telescope were pointed in the right direction. Those novel predictions were *falsifiable* and they survived testing: when telescopes were pointed as directed, the new planet was discovered; it was named 'Neptune' (Kuhn 1957, pp. 261-62).

6. Conclusion

A statement is scientific if, in conjunction with a statement of initial conditions, and perhaps also some more general accepted background knowledge, it entails a novel falsifiable prediction that is not entailed by the conjunction without it and the prediction survives attempts to falsify it. When an accepted observation statement is inconsistent with a conjunction of statements, the conjunction is falsified. To restore consistency, at least one of the statements involved must be replaced, either the observation statement or one of the statements that forms part of the conjunction. Any of the statements may be replaced. But any replacement will be scientific, rather than pseudo-scientific, only if it generates an additional contribution to our knowledge, such as novel falsifiable predictions that survive testing (Popper 1959, sections 18-20). A falsifiable prediction is *novel* if its truth is unexpected in the light of our background knowledge (Popper 1963a, p. 220).

What the Duhem problems show is that a falsification is never definitive: a theory may be saved from falsification by rejecting the observation statement or, in the case of a theory that is falsifiable only when conjoined with some others, by rejecting one or more of the other theories in the conjunction. However, rescuing a theory from falsification in such a way is scientific, rather than pseudo-scientific, only if the rejection is a consequence of an amendment to theory that generates new falsifiable predictions that survive testing (as in the two historical examples given above) or that resolves some problem *in addition* to the problem of rescuing the theory from falsification. The Duhem problems, then, do not undermine the utility of the notion of falsifiability; but they do show that the notion has utility only in the context of methodological rules that make acceptable rescues from falsification conditional upon discernible improvements in the state of our knowledge (Popper 1959, sections 19-20).

3 TRUTH CANNOT SENSIBLY BE OUR EPISTEMIC AIM

Abstract. I show how Karl Popper reconciled scepticism with epistemology and how he retrogressed when he identified truth as our epistemic aim. I criticise David Miller's defence of Popper's mistake and I consider and rebut objections to a purely sceptical epistemology.

Keywords. Conjecture; epistemic aim; David Miller; Karl Popper; refutation; scepticism; test; truth.

1. Introduction

Karl Popper showed how we could make epistemic progress even in the face of far-reaching sceptical doubts. Yet he backtracked when he deemed truth, or getting closer to the truth, our epistemic aim. David Miller has defended Popper's epistemology, including the unsceptical adherence to the aim of truth. I criticise Popper and Miller and I defend instead a fully sceptical epistemology.

In section 2, I outline the sceptical arguments and Popper's revolutionary sceptical epistemology. In section 3, I criticise Popper's importation of the aim of truth into the theory and Miller's defence of it. In section 4, I consider and rebut objections to the fully sceptical epistemology. In section 5, I conclude. In sections 2-4 I consider logically contingent theories only; but in section 5 I make a brief comment on self-contradictions and logical truths.

2. Scepticism and Epistemology

David Hume famously pointed out that particular experiences tell us only about themselves: they give us no information about other experiences. So the fact that every thing of type *T1* that we have experienced has also been of type *T2* does not imply that things of type *T1* that we have *not* experienced will also be of type *T2*. The fact does not even imply that it is *probable* that things of type *T1* that we have not experienced will be of type *T2*, because we can have no idea whether our experience of things so far has been *representative* of how things are in general. Consequently, we can have no justification for thinking that our general theories are either true or even probably true. Of course, we may find our general theories plausible, or 'subjectively probable,' given our particular experiences or inclinations; but we can have no grounds for linking plausibility or subjective probability to truth or to objective probability (Hume 1739, part III, section vi, pp. 86-94 and section xii, p. 139; part IV, section ii, p. 218; 1748, section IV, part II, pp. 32-39; section V, part I, pp. 40-47).

Philosophers tend either to ignore Hume's problem or to try to show that Hume was mistaken. Some of them attempt to show that some of our general theories can be justified on *a priori* grounds. However, such attempts fall foul of the traditional sceptical arguments: any attempt to justify a theory leads either to an infinite regress or to a vicious circle or to dogmatism or fideism (Sextus Empiricus 2000, book I, chapter xv). Further, Russell's Paradox showed that "from premises which all logicians of no matter what school had accepted ever since the time of Aristotle, contradictions could be deduced" (Russell 1959, p. 58), so apparent self-evidence is not security against self-contradiction; and Gödel's second incompleteness theorem showed that any theory that assumes arithmetic, as virtually all theories of any interest do, can be proved to be consistent *only* by presupposing a stronger theory for which the question of consistency arises with greater force. Other philosophers have tried to show that our general theories are justified in a weak sense, that they are 'supported' or 'prima-facie justified.' However, since those philosophers admit that such weakly justified theories may turn out to be false, they provide no solution to Hume's problem: it remains the case that we are not justified in thinking that our general theories are true, or even probably true in an objective sense of 'probability.' Indeed, even if it could be shown that supported or prima-facie justified theories were, objectively, probably true, we would not be justified in thinking them to be true, since even highly probable things may fail to be the case.

Popper (1959) showed the way out of this quagmire. The fact that we cannot obtain general theories that are justified is not a calamity because we can proceed well enough with general theories that are *conjectures* that we *test* against statements describing particular events that we experience. All such observation statements are theory-laden; but we can usually reach agreement on such observation statements because we can usually find a way of describing what we observe that is neutral between whatever theories are currently in contention (Frederick 2016a, p. 641). An observation statement is a description of an observable state of affairs that we agree to accept in the light of our observation, though we can have no idea whether it is true (it may be a misinterpretation of what we observe). If a general theory contradicts such an observation statement, we reject that general theory, otherwise we retain it for additional testing. Further, since any of our conjectures may end up being rejected after testing, we should strive to come up with *better* conjectures than the ones we already have, either by modifying existing conjectures or by propounding novel ones, and we should look for ways to test those conjectures. We can agree that, where we have rival conjectures each of which is consistent with all currently accepted observation statements, one of those conjectures is *better* than another if it explains more, or explains more simply, and if it implies more novel falsifiable predictions that survive testing. What we should not do is waste time trying to justify any existing conjectures, not only because it cannot be done, but also because it is an attempt to block progress, to stand still instead of moving forward. Contemporary epistemology, being preoccupied with justification, is thus epistemically perverse: it stands opposed to the growth of knowledge.

Philosophical objections to Popper's response to Hume's problem tend to focus on issues concerning refutation and truth. It is frequently objected that scientific theories are usually so general that they can clash with no observation statements: it is only a conjunction of such theories plus statements describing particular situations that is inconsistent with observation statements. However, all that means is that, when such an inconsistency appears, we have a choice of which theory or statement in the conjunction to revise. Popper proposes that any revision is acceptable if, but only if, it implies novel falsifiable predictions that survive testing or it solves a problem in addition to removing the inconsistency. Thus, acceptable revisions are those that constitute progress in the growth of knowledge (Popper 1959, chapter 4, sections 19-20; 1974b, p. 982).

It is often objected that observation statements, being theory-laden, may be false; so a theory that is refuted by such a statement might be true. However, observation statements may be tested also, so a previously accepted observation statement may be rejected later. Admittedly, we can never be sure that an observation statement is true or, correlatively, that a refuted theory is false; but we can adopt procedures that allow previously accepted observation statements to be rejected in favour of a general theory only as a consequence of a revision to theory that contributes to the growth of knowledge (Popper 1959, chapter 4, sections 19 and 20; chapter 5; appendix *x).[1]

On this Popperian or *critical rationalist* view, our epistemic aim is ever more satisfactory explanations (Popper 1957b, pp. 131-35). The procedures just described are designed to help us achieve that aim. We can assess our progress in achieving that aim if we have some sufficiently clear indicators of when one explanation is superior to a rival explanation. One obvious *negative* indicator is inconsistency with observation statements; *positive* indicators concern how much a theory explains, how illuminatingly and simply it explains, and the range of surprising new testable predictions it generates that are successful. All of these indicators are matters of more or less, yet it seems unlikely that any of them is measurable quantitatively (Miller 2006d). Further, there can be trade-offs between the indicators. Our reliance on qualitative assessments and trade-offs means that there may often be disputes about which of a pair of rival theories is currently best; yet there may also often be cases in which it is clear which of a set of rival theories is currently best in its domain.

On this view, then, our epistemic aim is neither justification nor truth; and nor is it avoiding falsity. We seek *better theories*; ideally, theories that contradict no observation statements and that give illuminating, deep and simple explanations of a wide range of phenomena, resolving many problems, and generating surprising predictions that survive empirical testing. If we manage to get any such explanations, we try to replace them with even better ones. This is in some ways a parsimonious view. It is realist, in that it acknowledges that our theories are either true or false, depending on how things stand in the real world; but there is no pretension that explanations that score better than others according to our indicators are either true or probably true or approximately true or even nearer the truth than their worse-scoring rivals; and there is no pretension that rejected theories are false. We can never know whether a theory is true or false.

This parsimonious view is derived from the writings of Popper and it may, at some time, have been Popper's own view. However, most of the time, it seems, Popper himself preferred a more prodigal view.

3. Popper, Miller and Truth

> Truth – absolute truth – remains our aim; and it remains the implicit standard of our criticism: almost all criticism is an attempt to refute the theory criticised; that is to say, to show

---

[1] The first five paragraphs of section 2, above, reprise material in my Forthcoming, section 2.

that it is not true... Thus we are always searching for *a true theory*... even though we can never give reasons (positive reasons) to show that we have actually found the true theory we have been searching for. At the same time we may have good reasons – that is, good *critical reasons* – for thinking that... we have progressed toward the truth. For first, we may have learnt that a particular theory is not true according to the present state of the critical discussion; and secondly, we may have found some tentative reasons to believe... that a new theory comes nearer to the truth than its predecessors (Popper 1983, p. 25).

That view seems to be untenable. It seems silly to say that truth is our aim when we can have no indication that we have got the truth or even that we are approaching it (Watkins 1984, p. 125). On Popper's own view the strongest empirical criticism of a theory is that it is inconsistent with a observation statement and thus refuted; but Popper himself insists that observation statements may be false. So, contrary to the above, refuting a theory does *not* show that it is not true. Even if it did, the fact that a theory is currently unrefuted would give no indication that the theory is true, since an unrefuted theory might be refuted the next time we test it. Further, that a theory has greater explanatory merits than a rival, or its predecessors, does not imply that the theory is true. The theories of Kepler and Galileo were successful explanatory theories; but they were replaced with Newton's theory which explained more and gave more accurate predictions. Newton's theory was in turn replaced by Einstein's theory, which similarly explained more and gave more accurate predictions. If having greater explanatory merits than its earlier rivals were a mark of truth, then both Newton's and Einstein's theory would be true; yet they contradict each other.

It may be claimed that a theory that has greater explanatory merits than another theory is *closer to the truth* than that other theory. Closeness to truth, it may be said, is what *generates* relative explanatory success. That appears to be Popper's contention when he says, for instance, that relativity theory is closer to the truth than Newton's theory, which is closer to the truth than Ptolemy's theory (1972a, p. 59; 1983, p. 61; 1974b, p. 1192, footnote 165b). But that claim seems to be refuted. According to Aristotelian-Ptolemaic theory we inhabit a closed world; according to Newtonian theory, we inhabit an infinite universe; according to relativity theory, we inhabit a closed world.[2] If Newton's theory got us closer to the truth than its predecessor, its successor seems to have taken us farther from the truth than Newton's theory. As the theories in the progression give radically

---

[2] Thomas Kuhn makes this point somewhere.

different pictures of the world, they give no indication of how the world will be described in the theory that will constitute the next theoretical advance. Wherever the truth is, the progress of our explanations does not seem to be moving us steadily in one direction.

Popper's view that our epistemic aim is truth is defended vigorously by David Miller.

> What matters is whether the hypotheses in question are true. This is what science investigates (Miller 2006c, p. 165).

> We want true theories. Testing is important because it is only by subjecting our theories to tests that we have any opportunity of eliminating those that are false (Miller 1994, p. 120).

> In science a hypothesis is criticized by showing that it fails to meet the standard of truth; in short, that it is false (Miller 1994, p. 80).

> The central idea of falsificationism is that the purpose of empirical investigation is to classify hypotheses as false, not to assist... in classifying them as true (Miller 1994, p. 6).

All of that sounds like what has been called "dogmatic falsificationism" (Lakatos 1970, pp. 95-97), that is, the contention that observation statements may be known with certainty to be true. Consider also what Miller says elsewhere:

> failure [of a test] does imply that the hypothesis is false (1994, p. 31);

> The falsity of a scientific theory, if false, and the inconsistency of a mathematical theory, if inconsistent, may both be established finitistically... in the first case the proof is material, an empirical falsification (1994, p. 99).

But, in his more considered position, neither Popper nor Miller is a dogmatic falsificationist, each being, rather, a methodological falsificationist who recognises that all observation statements are theory-laden and thus that the truth of an observation statement is never certain (Popper 1959, chapter 5; Miller 1994, p. 11). A slide between dogmatic and methodological falsificationism appears evident in the following passage.

A theory T_1 that is refuted is definitely false (given the truth of the test statements involved), while an unrefuted theory T_2 may be true. That is what leads Popper to say that, since we prefer truth to falsehood, we prefer the unrefuted T_2 to the refuted T_1. But this preference is not a logical consequence of the empirical record, since it goes beyond a summary of the state of the discussion... All that may be derived from the empirical report that T_1 is refuted and T_2 is not refuted (together with a statement of our preference for truth over falsehood) is not that T_2 *should be preferred to* T_1 but that T_1 *should not be preferred to* T_2... Anyone who denies it exposes himself at once to deadly criticism (Miller 2006b, p. 127).

There is a crucial ambiguity in the phrase "given the truth of the test statements involved." It could mean *assuming for the time being that the observation statements are true* or it could mean *it is a given (that is, a certainty) that the observation statements are true*. A methodological falsificationist would choose the former meaning; yet Miller's use of the term 'definitely false' suggests the latter, dogmatic-falsificationist, meaning. Further, what he says later in the passage makes sense only on the dogmatic-falsificationist reading. For a methodological falsificationist, a preference for truth over falsity, together with the empirical report that T_1 is refuted and T_2 is not refuted, says *nothing* about which theory should be preferred (because the relevant observation statement may be false). It would follow from the empirical report and a preference for truth over falsity that T_1 should not be preferred to T_2 only if the empirical report contained an affirmation entailing that *the refuting observation statement is true*. A methodological falsificationist may without embarrassment deny that T_1 *should not be preferred to T_2*; and he could rebut the supposedly "deadly" criticism that T_1 is inconsistent with the observation statement by explaining why he thought that the observation statement is, or may be, false.

A perhaps surprising consequence of this analysis is that, when we are testing a theory empirically, what we are actually testing is whether the theory is inconsistent with any observation statements. When we test a thing, we are always, if we are sensible, testing for its possession of a specific property. We can test a proposition for its inconsistency with observation statements. We can also test it for its explanatory power by considering the problems it solves and how well it solves them. We can similarly test it for its successful novel predictions. But we cannot test it for truth or falsity because we can have no way of doing that.

4. Objections

It might be objected that, since the proposition that p and the proposition that it is true that p are logically equivalent, then, when we are testing whether p, we are testing whether it is true that p. So, any test of a theory is a test of whether that theory is true.

The apparent force of that objection derives from sloppy formulation. When we test a theory, A, empirically, we test whether A is inconsistent with observation statements. If A survives the tests, we conclude that A has not, so far, been shown to be inconsistent with any observation statements. The same applies to the theory that A is true: we tested it when we tested A (because the two theories are logically equivalent), and we conclude that 'A is true' has not, so far, been shown to be inconsistent with any observation statements. So we concede that when we tested whether A we *ipso facto* tested whether A is true; but in the former case what we tested is whether A is inconsistent with observation statements; so, in the latter case we tested whether 'A is true' is inconsistent with observation statements. We did not test either A or 'A is true' for truth. When we test A for its *explanatory merits* we are similarly testing the claim 'A is true' for its *explanatory merits*; but we are not testing either A or 'A is true' for *truth*.

Thus, we must distinguish (at least) two kinds of acceptance. The claim that theory A is true may be *accepted as the currently best hypothesis*, along with the logically equivalent theory, A; but neither should ever be *accepted as true*. All that the evidence can show is that A (and, thus, that A is true) has not been refuted and that A (and, thus, that A is true) is better than its rivals in terms of explanatory power and such like. But that does not bear on whether it is true that A (and, thus, it does not bear on whether it is true that A is true). Consequently, when we accept A, or 'A is true,' *as currently best*, because it is consistent with all accepted observation statements and explains more, or more simply, or successfully predicts more novel facts, than its rivals, we do not thereby accept A, or 'A is true,' *as true*. When we accept-as-currently-best that A is true we do not accept-as-true that A is true.

It might be thought that I am conflating the impossibility of assessing whether a theory is true with the impossibility of justifying such an assessment. Thus, Miller (1994, pp. 117-18) objects to John Watkins,

> it seems quite clearly wrong to say that 'there is no possibility of assessing the truth or falsity of' the claim that one theory is true, another false, unless by 'assess' one means 'justifiably assess'.

It should be clear from what has been said above that Miller is mistaken there. No assessment can be either justified or justifiable: justification is always impossible. We can no more justifiably assess a theory as so far unrefuted than we can justifiably assess it as true or false. But we can do things to assess, fallibly, that a theory is currently refuted or unrefuted, or that it has greater explanatory merit than its current rivals. In contrast, there is nothing we can do to assess whether a theory is true or false, because all of the properties of the theory that we *can* assess are, both singly and in combination, *logically independent* of the property of truth. It is not inconsistent to affirm that a theory that exemplifies all the properties of a good explanation, and exemplifies them more fully than any available rival, is false. And it is not inconsistent to affirm that such a theory is true. The question of justification is irrelevant to the point that our performance indicators for theories identify properties that are logically independent of the theories' truth-values.

One who is sympathetic to Miller might continue to press the objection. It might be said that, once it is admitted that all our assessments are fallible, it is no objection, to an assessment as true or false, that it is fallible. Our assessment of a theory as true may be mistaken; but our assessment of a theory as consistent with current evidence, or as a better explanation than a rival theory, may also be mistaken. If we are willing to accept fallible judgments about whether a theory is currently best, why should we be reluctant to accept fallible judgments about whether a theory is true?

The trouble is that a judgment that a theory is true, or that it is false, is not merely fallible; it is entirely arbitrary. A judgment concerning whether a theory is inconsistent with accepted observation statements will be agreed after success or failure in deriving a contradiction from the conjunction of the theory with accepted observation statements. The judgment may be mistaken: the derivation of the contradiction may be fallacious or the failure to derive a contradiction may be remedied in future. But the judgment is sensitive to those logical results. Although it is fallible, it is not entirely arbitrary. Similarly, a judgment concerning whether a theory provides a better explanation than a rival will be agreed (if it is agreed) after a comparison of the two theories with regard to properties that make for better explanations. The judgment is sensitive to that comparison: it is fallible but not entirely arbitrary. That is analogous to the way in which acceptance of an observation statement is sensitive to the experiences had by trained observers: such acceptance is fallible but not entirely arbitrary. But any judgment that a theory is true, or that it is false, *is* entirely arbitrary because there is nothing in the state of the discussion that has any logical bearing on the theory's truth or falsity.

It might be queried, given that none of our theories can be justified, whether there is anything wrong in holding an arbitrary opinion. Perhaps there is not; but such an opinion cannot be taken seriously as knowledge unless it has stood up to criticism and done so better than its rivals, in which case it is no longer arbitrary.

It might be objected that the property of feeling ill is logically independent of the property of being ill, since one may feel ill whether or not one is ill, and one may be ill whether or not one feels ill, yet we *do* use feeling ill as a fallible indicator of being ill. So the fact that the properties that we use to rate a theory as better or worse are logically independent of the theory's truth does not seem to exclude using those properties as fallible indicators of truth or closeness to truth.

There is, however, a crucial contrast between the two cases. We have discovered empirically the (somewhat loose) connection between feeling ill and being ill: we have various theories that have survived testing that explain how illnesses of various types give rise to feelings of illness of various types. So in any new case we may sensibly use feeling ill as a fallible indicator for being ill. In contrast, the theory that there is a factual connection between truth and the combination of properties we take to make a good explanation (consistency with observation statements, explanatory scope, prediction of novel facts and such-like) is refuted every time that the currently best theory is superseded by a better one. A superseding theory typically contradicts the theory it supersedes, as Copernicus's theory contradicts Ptolemy's, and Kepler's contradicts both Ptolemy's and Copernicus's, and Newton's contradicts Ptolemy's, Copernicus's and Kepler's, and relativity theory contradicts all of the former. Since at most one of a set of mutually inconsistent propositions can be true, many (perhaps all) of the theories that have had the status of being currently best are false (though we cannot know *which* ones are false). So, the combination of properties that we take to make a good explanation does not have a factual connection with truth. Further, as noted in section 3, the supposed factual connection between being a better explanation and being *closer* to the truth has been refuted by the serpentine progress of the descriptions of the world offered by successive theories in the progress of science.

Popper considers an objection to his own position that might be turned against mine.

> A justificationist… may point out that even if he were to admit that these 'reasons why we believe that one theory is better than another' are perhaps not of the same character as would be reasons for believing that, say, the first of these theories is *true*, he could still claim that they are 'positive reasons': that they are reasons for believing in the truth of *some* theory – that is, of the theory (the meta-theory as it may be called) that the first theory is better than the second. In this

way the justificationist might conclude that I have not really replaced the problem of justification by a different one (1983, p. 23).

Popper offers a twofold response to the objection, the second part of which says that he makes no attempt to establish or justify that a preference for one theory over another is the true one: the meta-theory is itself conjectural. Popper's response here mirrors my response to Miller's objection to Watkins, recently discussed. However, that response cannot rebut the following objection to my position that is a counterpart to the justificationist objection that Popper considered.

It might be objected that, while our performance indicators for theories tell us nothing about the truth of the theories being assessed, they will do their intended job only if we accept that it is *true* that a theory satisfies the indicators, and thus only if we can test the *truth* of statements of the forms 'theory A is unrefuted,' 'theory A is a better explanation than theory B,' 'theory A has successfully predicted novel facts,' and such like. The fact that statements of the quoted forms are conjectural does not rebut the objection because the objection is that our process of assessment depends upon us having, not *justified* statements of performance, but statements of performance that *we accept as true*. But if our acceptance of such statements as true is not entirely arbitrary, then we must have indicators of the *truth* of statements of theory performance. Yet the claim of my theory of assessment is that there are no indicators of the truth of statements. Thus, my theory of theory assessment appears to be inconsistent.

It seems to me that this objection is mistaken. We have no way of telling whether any statement is true or false: we have no indicators of truth or falsity. Consequently, if we are sensible, we will accept no statement as true; which means that we will not accept any *assessment statement* of the performance of any theory as true. Just as we accept a scientific theory, not as true, but as the best currently available, so we accept an assessment statement that a specific scientific theory is the best currently available, not as true, but as the best currently available. The indicators according to which we make the first type of decision concern being consistent with observation statements, having greater explanatory merit than its rivals, and so on. The indicator according to which we make the second type of decision is that the assessment statement *is a logical consequence of the comparative propositions agreed through the critical discussion*. The property of being a logical consequence of the comparative propositions agreed through the critical discussion is logically independent of the property of truth.

It might be thought that this position involves an infinite regress. For, it might be said, we accept scientific theory A because we accept the assessment statement (a1) *A* is superior to all its rivals on our performance indicators for theories;

and we accept (a1) because we accept

(a2) (a1) is a logical consequence of the comparative propositions agreed through the critical discussion;

and we accept (a2) because we accept

(a3) (a2) seems to be true;

and we accept (a3) because we accept

(a4) (a3) seems to be true;

and so on *ad infinitum*. However, the objection fails because, normally, there is no need to progress to consideration of (a3). We might stop when we reach agreement on an assessment statement, (a1), without considering explicitly what the reasons for the agreement are. If someone queries (a1) and we resolve the query, we then accept (a2); but we do not need to move on to (a3) – unless someone queries our acceptance of (a2). That works because there is no claim of justification here, there is no claim that (a1) is justified. This is similar to the acceptance of observation statements: we can never discover whether they are true or false, but we accept those which, we agree, describe what we observe. Thus, observation statements can never justify and we avoid infinite regress because we do not call upon them to justify.

5. Conclusion

Traditional epistemologies are undermined by scepticism, whether of the ancient, the Humean or the metamathematical varieties. Popper showed how we can still have realistic epistemic aims and adopt suitable procedures that can help us to achieve them, if anything can. We cannot sensibly aim for certainty or justification; but we *can* sensibly aim to improve our explanations of the world. We proceed by:

- accepting (as currently best) those observation statements that we can agree upon as descriptions of our observations;
- proposing bold explanatory theories which we develop into a form

which we can test against accepted observation statements;

- comparing rival explanations according to their explanatory merits and their avoidance of inconsistency with observation statements;
- accepting (as currently best) those statements of comparative explanatory merit on which we can agree;
- accepting *as currently best* any hypothesis that our accepted statements of comparative explanatory merit imply is currently best;
- proposing new explanatory theories to rival those which are accepted as currently best.

Popper, and Miller following him, mistakenly imported into this sparse scheme of epistemic progress the ideas that epistemic progress is, ideally, a progress toward truth; that, accordingly, our epistemic aim should be truth or getting closer to the truth; and that refutations can help us to identify theories which are false. I have shown that those ideas do not belong in any realistic epistemology because:

(a)   the types of assessments of theories that are available to us can test only for properties that are *logically independent* of truth and falsity;

(b)   claims of a *factual dependence* of those properties on either truth or closeness to truth have been refuted time and again.

As indicated in section 1, I have been speaking of logically contingent theories. The situation may seem different when we turn our attention to logically true and logically false propositions. For a logical truth may be proven to be true and a logical falsehood may be shown to imply a contradiction. Of course, any such assessment is *fallible*, since our derivation might involve an error. But if a theory has the *property* of being self-contradictory, then it is *false*, so there is, in such a case, a logical connection between falsity and a property that we can assess. Similarly, if a theory has the *property* of being a logical truth, then it is *true*, so there is, in such a case, a logical connection between truth and a property that we can assess.

However, I doubt whether there really are such connections. How do we know that a contradiction is false? It may *seem* false to us, if we are imbued with classical logic. But some people reject classical logic; and some of those people accept that at least some contradictions are true. Similar things may be said about logical truths. However, that is a topic requiring a separate paper, which is why I did not raise it in the body of this one. Suffice it to say here that, above, I assumed that we accept classical logic because it is the only one to which we can obtain fairly general agreement; and thus we reject contradictions because they are false in classical logic (though we remain agnostic as to whether they are false in reality); and we accept so-called logical truths because they are true in classical logic (though we remain agnostic as to whether they are true in reality).

4 WHAT IS WRONG WITH CETERIS-PARIBUS LAW-STATEMENTS?

Abstract. It is often contended that the special sciences, and even fundamental physics, make use of ceteris-paribus law-statements. Yet there are general concerns that such law-statements are vacuous or untestable or unscientific. I consider two main kinds of ceteris-paribus law-statement. I argue that neither kind is vacuous, that one of the kinds is untestable, that both kinds may count as scientific to the extent that they form parts of conjunctions that imply novel falsifiable statements which survive testing, but that one kind has an affinity with ad hoc manoeuvres that are unsatisfactory from a scientific point of view. I show that the contemporary debate about ceteris-paribus law-statements is afflicted with error and confusion because of a general failure to disentangle the notions: non-vacuous, testable, scientific, verifiable, falsifiable, and ad hoc.

Keywords. Ad hoc; ceteris paribus; falsifiability; law-statement; scientific; vacuous.

1. Introduction

Recent debate about ceteris-paribus law-statements reveals disagreements about what such statements are, whether they are vacuous, whether they are empirically testable, whether law-statements of fundamental physics, or even of the special sciences, are ceteris-paribus, and why ceteris-paribus law-statements are problematic. I argue that ceteris-paribus law-statements are not vacuous, are often empirically testable, and even when not empirically testable may belong to fundamental physics and other sciences;

yet there is sometimes reason to be wary of them. I show that the contemporary debate is marred by errors due to confusions between non-vacuous, empirically testable, and scientific statements, and between scientific statements and scientific procedures. In what follows 'testable' always abbreviates 'empirically testable,' as I am not here concerned with non-empirical forms of testability.

John Earman, John Roberts and Sheldon Smith (Earman and Roberts 1999; Earman, Roberts and Smith 2002; Smith 2002) have done a great deal to expose errors and confusions in the ceteris-paribus debate. I will not repeat what they say. Instead I try to dispel some errors and confusions that remain, even in the writings of those authors. My aim is not to provide a comprehensive understanding of ceteris-paribus law-statements, but to disentangle some notions that are commonly conflated in discussions of ceteris-paribus law-statements and to exhibit the errors to which those confusions lead. In prosecuting that task, I make use of three ideas of Karl Popper, namely, falsifiability, novel predictions and ad hoc manoeuvres. I make no attempt to expound or defend Popper's philosophy of science in general; but I explain in section 5 that those three ideas should be incorporated into any reasonable theory of science.

In section 2, I distinguish ceteris-paribus law-statements into two general types and I explain that neither is vacuous. In section 3, I show that some ceteris-paribus law-statements are testable. In section 4, I show that even ceteris-paribus law-statements that are not testable may be scientific insofar as they form a non-redundant part of a conjunction that entails novel falsifiable statements that survive testing. I show that some law-statements of fundamental physics fall into that category, using Newton's Laws in a clear, step-by-step illustration that should be comprehensible to people who are neither physicists nor mathematicians. In section 5, I distinguish testable and scientific *statements* from ad hoc *procedures* and I suggest that what is wrong with one kind of ceteris-paribus law-statements is their affinity for the latter. In section 6, I conclude.

2. Ceteris Paribus and Vacuity

A law of nature is a necessary relationship between natural phenomena. It is what makes a *statement* of a law of nature – a 'law-statement,' for short – true (if it is true). Simplifying a little (see footnotes 1, 2 and 3, to section 4, below), a law of nature may be expressed by a universal material-conditional preceded by a necessity operator (Carroll 1994; Kneale 1949, chapter 2; Popper 1959, appendix *x), as follows:

(L0)   necessarily, everything, x, is such that, if x is G, then x is H.

The necessity-operator implies that a law-statement has counterfactual instances of the form: 'if this had been G, it would have been H.' We need not here take a view on what kind of necessity is involved or what specific account should be given of the semantics of counterfactuals.

The term 'ceteris paribus' may be rendered in English as 'other things are equal.' A ceteris-paribus law-statement is one that is qualified by a ceteris-paribus clause. For example:

- necessarily, everything, x, is such that, if x is G and other things are equal, then x is H;
- necessarily, other things being equal, everything, x, is such that, if x is G, then x is H;
- necessarily, everything, x, is such that, if x is G, then x is H, other things being equal.

In each of those statement-forms, 'necessarily' should be read as having wide scope. I assume that the three are equivalent.

A persistent complaint about ceteris-paribus law-statements is that they are vacuous. There is some difficulty in saying what a vacuous statement is. A vacuous statement is not one that says nothing at all; otherwise it would not be a statement. It must therefore be a statement that says something minimal. Different proposals may be made for what such minimal statement consists in. At one time it would have been said that a vacuous statement is one that is 'analytic' or 'true in virtue of meaning,' but nowadays it is highly contentious whether those terms have any serious use. A better proposal would be to say that a statement is vacuous if and only if it has, or can with little distortion be given, the form of a logical truth, or if it is such a statement prefixed with a necessity or a possibility operator. The following two statements are then vacuous:

(V1)   we are where we are;
(V2)   either the square root of 9 is 3 or it is not.

Each of those statements says something, as can be seen from the fact that each says something different to the other: (V1) talks about people and places; (V2) talks about numbers and their square roots. However, neither says anything of substance and each is a logical truth: (V1) can be viewed as an instance of the form 'every x is such that, if Fx, then Fx,' where 'x' ranges over places and 'we are in' replaces 'F,' while (V2) is an instance of the form 'p or not p.' Consequently, prefixing either with a necessity operator results in a vacuous statement. Notoriously, logicians disagree over which statements are logical truths (Priest and Thomason 2007, 96-98); but that does not affect our discussion. It simply means that there are some disagreements about which statements are vacuous, which is unsurprising.

Marc Lange (1993, p. 235) attributes to Carl Hempel the claim that, because they do not identify a finite list of specific types of other things that must be equal, ceteris-paribus law-statements of the kind illustrated above are vacuous, saying only that

(V3)   necessarily, everything which is G is H, except when it is not.

That is vacuous because what follows the necessity operator is an instance of the form 'everything, x, is such that, if Gx, then Hx or not Hx.'

It seems clear, though, that when researchers propound a ceteris-paribus law-statement, they intend to say something substantive, so an interpretation of their claim that renders it a logical truth is a misinterpretation. The formulation of a ceteris-paribus law-statement should therefore exclude a vacuous interpretation by fiat, as in:

(L1)   necessarily, everything, x, is such that, if x is G, then x is H, if there is no material reason why not.

A different formulation that is often encountered is:

(L2)   necessarily, everything, x, is such that, if x is G, and there is no interfering F, then x is H

where 'F' stands in for a description of a specific type of thing, as opposed to standing in for a term connoting a non-specific property that may apply to everything, such as 'thing' or 'factor.' A statement of the form (L2) says more than the corresponding statement of the form (L1) because, in replacing the ceteris-paribus clause of (L1), 'there is no material reason why not,' with the ceteris-paribus clause, 'there is no interfering F,' it says which sort of material reason (namely, an interfering F-type thing) must be present if a thing which is G is not H.

Some true statements of the forms (L0), (L1) and (L2) do not express laws of nature (see, for example, Earman and Roberts 1999, pp. 453-54; Earman, Roberts and Smith 2002, p. 294); but we need not attempt here to articulate the features which differentiate law-statements from all other statements of those forms. There is a variety of forms of ceteris-paribus law-statements where 'ceteris paribus' may be taken to mean *under normal conditions*, or *under ideal conditions*, or *in abstraction from other aspects of the situation* or some other qualifying condition. I do not consider law-statements of such forms explicitly, but I expect that most, if not all, of them can be represented by, or assimilated to, a law-statement of one of the general forms (L1) or (L2), so that what I say will be applicable to them either directly or mutatis mutandis.

3. Testability

A statement is *falsifiable* if and only if it is inconsistent with an observation statement. An *observation statement* is a singular statement, with demonstrative singular term(s), that describes something we could conceivably observe, given our actual powers of observation. Example observation statements are: 'this swan is not white,' 'that raven is not smaller than this dog,' 'the needle there is moving,' 'here is a pink elephant.' A statement is *falsified* if and only if it is inconsistent with an *accepted observation statement*, that is, an observation statement describing a reproducible type of event that has been agreed by observers to describe an actual situation. A *reproducible type of event* is one that occurs regularly in nature or that we can bring about regularly (Popper 1959, sections 6, 8, 15, 21, 22, 29).

A statement is testable if and only if it is falsifiable. It is easy to see that falsifiability is *sufficient* for testability. If a statement, S, is inconsistent with a statement that we would accept as reporting a reproducible circumstance of type C, and it is conceivable that we observe such a circumstance with our current powers of observation, then we can test S by trying to bring about our observation of a circumstance of type C. If we succeed, then S is falsified. If we fail, then S has survived an attempt to falsify it: it has passed a test. Falsifiability is also *necessary* for testability. If a statement is not falsifiable, then there is no observation statement with which it is inconsistent; in which case the statement is compatible with every conceivable observation we could actually make. We therefore have no way of testing it.

As our central concern is the testability, that is, *falsifiability*, of law-statements, I will use 'this G is not H' as the standard form of an observation statement. A finite conjunction of mutually consistent observation statements is also an observation statement. Any of the demonstrative singular terms that occurs in the conjunction can be viewed as the logical subject of the statement, with the rest of the conjunctive sentence being viewed as the complex predicate. Let us say that a statement is empirically verifiable or, for short, *verifiable*, if and only if it is implied by an observation statement; and it is empirically verified or, for short, *verified*, if and only if it is implied by an *accepted* observation statement. The statement

(T1)   all swans are white

is not verifiable: even if every swan we have observed is white, it is conceivable that a non-white swan will be observed in future. However, it is falsifiable, and thus testable, because it is inconsistent with the observation statement 'this swan is not white.' In contrast,

(U1)   every event has a cause

as well as being not verifiable, because of the universal quantifier, is also not falsifiable, and is thus untestable, because of the embedded existential quantifier: our failure to find a cause for a particular event does not exclude there being a cause which we have not yet discovered (Watkins 1958, pp. 318-19). That is, 'this event has no cause' is not an observation statement. However, despite being untestable, (U1) is not vacuous. It is a substantive issue relevant, for example, to the debate about free will and the interpretation of quantum mechanics, whether every event has a cause or some events do not. Neither (U1) nor its negation, 'some events are uncaused,' has the form of a logical truth.

The fact that our actual powers of observation change over time means that what is untestable at one time may be testable at another. For instance, prior to the invention of telescopes, the statement

(*)   all stars are visible to the naked eye

was unfalsifiable, because

(†)   this star is not visible to the naked eye

was not an observation statement, since it did not describe something we could conceivably observe, given our actual powers of observation at the time. Since the invention of powerful telescopes, (*) has been falsifiable, and it has indeed been falsified, since (†) describes a reproducible type of event that has been agreed by observers to be exemplified in actual situations. The reason that the observers agree that what they are seeing is a star is that they have accepted theories about how the telescopes work and what stars look like when viewed by means of them. Of course, it is possible that future scientific discoveries will lead to some of those accepted theories about telescopes being rejected, in which case some previously accepted observation statements may need to be rejected too. But all observation statements are theory-laden and open to possible rejection in the light of future discoveries: how we describe what we observe depends upon our background theories, which give us our interpretative framework (Popper 1959, appendix *x). As a consequence, it can happen that a false observation statement is accepted and a true law-statement is falsified, though the reproducibility requirement on accepted observation statements reduces that risk.

We can therefore conclude that a law-statement of the form (L0) is testable if and only if each of the terms corresponding to 'G' and to 'not H' connotes an observable property. That condition is not, however, sufficient for the testability of a statement of the form (L1). An observation statement of the form, 'this G is not H,' is consistent with (L1), because there might be some material reason why this particular G is not H. A statement of the form, 'this G is not H, and there is no material reason why it is not,' is inconsistent with (L1); but such a statement is not an observation statement, because things which are material reasons need not be observable. Thus, statements of the form (L1), though not vacuous, are untestable.

A statement of the form (L2), on the other hand, may be testable, but only if both of two conditions hold: first, each of the terms corresponding to 'not F,' 'G' and 'not H' connotes an observable property; second, the term 'F' imposes a spatio-temporal restriction on the existential quantifier within the ceteris-paribus clause. For illustration, consider the following instance of (L2):

(T2)   necessarily, everything, x, is such that, if x is a swan, and there is no interfering elephant in the room, then x is white.

That statement is obtained from (L2) by supplanting 'F,' 'G' and 'H' with 'elephant in the room,' 'swan' and 'white,' respectively. It is testable because it is inconsistent with the observation statement 'this swan is not white and there is no elephant in the room' (since, if there is no elephant, there is no interfering elephant). That last-quoted statement is an observation statement because it is conceivable that there should be a room containing a non-white swan and no elephant and that, with our current powers of observation, we should observe the swan, its non-whiteness and the absence of an elephant in the room. The observation statement is a singular statement with 'this swan' as logical subject and 'not white and there is no elephant in the room' as complex predicate. The ceteris-paribus clause of (T2), 'there is no interfering elephant in the room,' although a negative existential statement (and thus equivalent to a universal statement) is spatio-temporally restricted because its predicate contains a spatial restriction ('in the room'). So the clause is equivalent to a finite conjunction of observation statements of the form 'this space in the room contains no elephant.' The oft-supposed fact that there can be an elephant in the room even though no one who is present notices it, just reminds us that people can be mistaken when they agree that an observation statement describes a situation they are observing.

4. Scientific Law-Statements

We have seen that some statements of the forms (L0) and (L2) are testable. Typically, however, scientific law-statements of those forms are untestable because some or all of the terms that correspond to 'not F,' 'G' and 'not H' do not connote observable properties or the ceteris-paribus clause is not spatio-temporally restricted. An untestable law-statement may yet qualify as scientific if

(a)   its conjunction with some background knowledge and statements describing a particular situation (the initial conditions) entails some novel falsifiable statements that are not entailed by the conjunction without it,

(b)   some of those novel falsifiable statements survive serious attempts to falsify them,

where a falsifiable statement is *novel* if it is unexpected in the light of our background knowledge (Popper 1959, sections 18-20; 1963a, sections iv, xviii-xx).

Let 'p' represent any law-statement. The conjunction of 'p' with 'if p, then Nelson's Column is in Trafalgar Square' entails the falsifiable statement 'Nelson's Column is in Trafalgar Square.' However, 'p' is not thus rendered scientific because 'Nelson's Column is in Trafalgar Square' is not unexpected in the light of our background knowledge. Hence the requirement of novelty. Let 'c' represent any conjunction that entails some novel falsifiable statements. Then 'p and c' also entails those novel falsifiable statements. However, 'p' is not thus rendered scientific because 'c' by itself entails the novel falsifiable statements. Hence the requirement of non-redundancy. The conjunction of 'p' with the hypothesis 'if p, then Nelson's Column is not in Trafalgar Square' entails the novel falsifiable statement 'Nelson's Column is not in Trafalgar Square,' which is not entailed by 'if p, then Nelson's Column is not in Trafalgar Square' alone. However, 'p' is not thus rendered scientific because that novel falsifiable statement has been falsified. Hence the requirement of surviving serious attempts at falsification.

An example of a scientific law-statement is Newton's Law of Universal Gravitation. It may be stated as follows:

(NG)   necessarily, everything, x and everything, y, is such that, if x is a body and y is a body and it is not the case that $x = y$, then x exerts on y a gravitational force which is equal to the gravitational constant multiplied by the product of the masses of x and y, divided by the square of the distance between x and y.

That is a law-statement of the form (L0).[3] It is untestable because there is no observation statement that is inconsistent with it. A statement of the following kind is inconsistent with (NG): 'the Earth and that apple are different bodies, but the Earth does not exert on the apple a gravitational force which is equal to the gravitational constant multiplied by the product of their masses divided by the square of their distance.' However, statements of that kind are not observation statements: the clause following 'but' does not describe something we could conceivably observe given our actual powers of observation.

We come closer to a testable statement if we conjoin (NG) with four quantitative statements attributing values to the gravitational constant, the masses of the Earth and the apple, and the distance between them. Those statements may be either hypotheses or accepted observation statements or elements of background knowledge. The resulting conjunction will imply a statement ascribing a value, which we can designate '$V1$,' to the gravitational force exerted by the Earth on the apple. Thus, the conjunction will be inconsistent with:

(Q1)   the Earth and that apple are different bodies, but the Earth does not exert on the apple a gravitational force of value $V1$.

However, (Q1) is still not an observation statement because its second conjunct does not describe something that our actual powers of observation would enable us to observe: we cannot perceive the magnitudes of gravitational forces.

We need to add to our conjunction another law-statement. Here is a statement of Newton's Second Law:

(N2)   necessarily, everything, x, is such that, if x is a body of mass, m, and x is subject to a force of magnitude, f, in a direction, d, and there is no interfering force, then x moves in d with an acceleration of f/m.

That is a law-statement of the form (L2).[4] It links magnitudes of force with

---

[3] Strictly speaking, it is not (NG) that exemplifies the form (L0), but an instantiation of (NG), in which the universal quantifier 'everything, y,' is deleted and each of the further occurrences of 'y' is replaced by the same singular term for a particular body. We can ignore that nicety here.

[4] Again, strictly speaking, it is not (N2) that exemplifies the form (L2), but an instantiation of (N2), in which the expression of generality, 'a force,' is replaced by a singular term for a particular a force, the dummy names 'm' and 'f' are replaced with singular terms for magnitudes of mass and force, respectively, and the

magnitudes of acceleration, and thus with motions, which are observable. When Newton proposed his Second Law it was a hypothesis, but it later became a part of background knowledge. *If* the conjunction of (NG), the four quantitative statements and (N2) implies a specific value other than zero for the acceleration of the apple toward the Earth, then the conjunction is testable because the following is an observation statement:

(O1)   the Earth and that apple are different bodies, but the apple is not accelerating toward the earth (it is still in the tree).

However, our conjunction implies no specific value for the acceleration of the apple toward the Earth because of the ceteris-paribus clause in (N2). We get a testable conjunction, one which implies a falsifiable statement, only when we conjoin the ceteris-paribus *proviso*

(P1)   there is no interfering force

to (NG), the four quantitative statements and (N2). That proviso may be a new assumption or it might be part of background knowledge.

We can therefore draw three conclusions. First, since the falsifiable statement ascribing a specific acceleration to the apple was not expected in the light of existing background knowledge, then (NG) and (N2) are untestable law-statements that are non-redundant conjuncts of a conjunction that entails a novel falsifiable statement. Second, historically, (NG) and (N2) formed non-redundant conjuncts of conjunctions which implied many novel falsifiable statements that survived serious attempts to falsify them, so (NG) and (N2) are scientific law-statements. Third, even in fundamental physics, some scientific law-statements, like (N2), are ceteris-paribus law-statements exemplifying the form (L2).

It may be objected that (N2) is a poor statement of Newton's Second Law and that a better statement of it eliminates the ceteris-paribus clause, thus:

(N2*) necessarily, everything, x, is such that, if x is a body of mass, m, and x is subject to a net force of magnitude, f, in a direction, d, then x moves in d with an acceleration of f/m.

That statement exemplifies the form (L0) rather than the form (L2).[5]

---

expression of generality, 'a direction, d,' and the occurrence of its bound variable, 'd,' is each replaced by the same singular term for a specific direction.

[5] Once again, strictly speaking, it is not (N2*) that exemplifies the form (L0), but an instantiation of (N2*), in which the expression of generality, 'a net force,' is

However, it leaves us where we were before (Hempel 1988, pp. 23-30). We cannot calculate an acceleration for the apple, given the conjunction of (NG), the four quantitative statements and (N2*) unless we also conjoin the proviso:

(P2)   the gravitational force is the net force acting on the apple.

But that is equivalent to the proviso (P1). It seems that (N2*) is a disguised ceteris-paribus law-statement, with its ceteris-paribus clause hidden behind the phrase 'net force.'

It should be obvious that I have presented a simplified discussion to focus on the points I want to clarify. There is never just one force acting in any situation. For example, the force of gravity between the Earth and an apple is always present with gravitational forces from innumerable other bodies, as well as nuclear and electro-magnetic forces and others besides. Some of the forces acting in a situation may cancel each other out, and some may make a negligible difference in the situation. Thus, even where there is only one force that is worth taking into account, (N2*) is superior to (N2) as a formulation of Newton's Second Law. Where account must be taken of conflicting forces (N2*) is clearly preferable to (N2). In that case, the calculation of the net force requires the theory of vector composition, which says that the net force acting on a body is the vector-sum of all the forces acting on the body (where the vector-sum of any two forces acting on a body is calculated by the parallelogram rule or other equivalent method); and it also requires the ceteris-paribus proviso that there is no force interfering, apart from those of which we have taken account.

Earman and Roberts describe a ceteris-paribus law-statement as one "qualified by a proviso to the effect that nothing else interferes, where what would count as an interference cannot be stated explicitly" (1999, p. 439), that is, a statement of the form (L1), so long as it is not simply an abbreviation of a statement of the form (L2) (1999, p. 461). Thus, they do not count law-statements of the form (L2) as being ceteris-paribus, although they recognise that such law-statements are called 'ceteris-paribus' in the philosophical literature (1999, p. 461). They admit that some scientific law-statements have the form of (L2) (1999, p. 461) and, although they deny that (N2) is a formulation of Newton's Second Law, preferring the formulation (N2*), they acknowledge that (N2*) is testable only as part of a conjunction which includes a proviso like (P1) (1999, pp. 443-46). They

---

replaced by a singular term for a net force, the dummy names 'm' and 'f' are replaced with singular terms for magnitudes of mass and force, respectively, and the expression of generality, 'a direction, d,' and the occurrence of its bound variable, 'd,' is each replaced by the same singular term for a specific direction.

say that statements of the form (L1) suffer an "apparent lack of determinate content" because "the all-things-equal clause stands for we-know-not-what," which renders the statements unfit to "play a legitimate role in scientific testing and explanation" (1999, p. 452; also pp. 465-66).

We saw in section 3 that law-statements of forms (L0) and (L2) may be testable; and we have seen in this section that even when they are not testable they may be scientific. We noted in section 3 that no law-statement of the form (L1) is testable; but it should be fairly obvious that such a statement may be fit to "play a legitimate role in scientific testing and explanation." Provided that the terms corresponding to 'G' and 'not H' are observational, its conjunction with the proviso 'there is no material reason why this G is not H' will entail a falsifiable statement of the form 'this G is H,' and the latter statement might be novel and might even survive testing. Even for a statement of the form (L1) in which the terms corresponding to 'G' and 'not H' are not observational, there may be a suitable conjunction including the statement 'there is no material reason why this G is not H' which implies a novel falsifiable statement that survives testing. We get such a conjunction by using the preceding example of (NG) and (N2), but with 'there is no material reason why x does not move in d with an acceleration of f/m' substituted for the ceteris-paribus clause, 'there is no interfering force,' in (N2), and with 'there is no material reason why the apple does not move in d with an acceleration of f/m' substituted for the proviso (P1). Thus, contrary to the claim of Earman and Roberts, law-statements of the form (L1) are on a par with some scientific law-statements with regard to testability.

Earman, Roberts and Smith refine their claim when they add that it is not enough simply to assert "other things are equal" or, in our terms, 'there is no material reason why not:' it is also necessary that "we be able to *tell* when" (Earman & Roberts 1999, p. 467) or "to check whether" (Earman, Roberts and Smith 2002, p. 293) there is no material reason why not. That strongly suggests that an untestable law-statement which forms a non-redundant conjunct of a testable conjunction including a ceteris-paribus proviso is scientific only if the proviso is *verifiable*. As we recently noted, however, a proviso of the form 'there is no interfering F' is equivalent to a universal statement which, when the term represented by 'F' does not introduce a spatio-temporal restriction, is unverifiable. So this additional requirement suggested by Earman, Roberts and Smith would disqualify Newton's Law of Gravity and Newton's Second Law from being scientific, since, as we have seen, and as Earman and Roberts themselves argue (1999, pp. 443-46), each of those law-statements is untestable but forms part of a testable conjunction which contains a non-spatio-temporally restricted proviso of the form 'there is no interfering F.' It seems likely, however, either that they do not intend the suggestion of verifiability or that they are confusing verifiability with falsifiability, for it seems clear from the following passage that their contention is that a scientifically legitimate proviso should itself be *testable*:

> What if the [testable conjunction does]…include the claim that other things are equal? Then either this auxiliary can be stated in a form that allows us to check whether it is true, or it can't. If it can, then the original CP law [i.e., law-statement of form (L1)] can be turned into a strict law [i.e., law-statement of form (L2)] by substituting the testable auxiliary for the CP clause. If it can't, then the [testable] prediction relies on an auxiliary hypothesis that cannot be tested itself. But it is generally, and rightly, presumed that auxiliary hypotheses must be testable in principle if they are to be used in an honest test (Earman, Roberts and Smith 2002, p. 293).

They cite no references for that general presumption. Unfortunately, it may be doubted whether the proviso that Earman, Roberts and Smith agree is required to render Newton's Laws testable, namely, (P1), is itself testable. If we were to look for a possible interfering force, we might try to find a magnet or another planet, for example. But while 'here is a magnet' and 'there is another planet' are observation statements, neither is inconsistent with (P1) because, for all we can observe, those objects might not be generating forces at the time, or the forces they are generating might not be interfering. It might be replied that, just as scientists accept 'there is a planet' as an observation statement when they see an odd-looking spot of light by means of a telescope, because they accept a set of background theories about telescopes, so scientists could accept 'there is an interfering force' as an observation statement when they see a magnet or a planet, because they accept a set of background theories about magnets, planets and forces. Whether or not a particular statement should be counted as an observation statement is, to a significant extent, a pragmatic matter, so let us concede the reply, give Earman, Roberts and Smith the benefit of the doubt, and thus accept that (P1) is testable.

So we grant Earman, Roberts and Smith their point that, while some provisos of the form 'there is no interfering F' are testable, the proviso 'there is no material reason why not' is not testable. Still, that point falls short of showing that, *every* proviso of the form 'there is no interfering F' is testable if it forms part of a testable conjunction which includes conjuncts which are untestable scientific law-statements. Indeed it seems doubtful that it should be so, given that there are testable conjunctions *none* of the conjuncts of which is testable but some of which are scientific law-statements. Consider the example (adapted from Watkins 1984, pp. 188-91) of William Gilbert's magnetic theory, according to which every source of magnetic force transmits incorporeal and invisible rays of magnetic force in all directions. Part of the theory can be set forth in the following law-statement, two spatial hypotheses, a hypothesis about iron, and one about loadstones:

(G1)   necessarily, if two sources of magnetic force are placed close together with like poles facing each other, they will repel each other;

(G2)   if one source of magnetic force has a north-south direction which matches that of a second, and a third has a north-south direction which matches that of the second, then the first and the third have matching north-south direction;

(G3)   if two sources of magnetic force are placed side-by-side above a third and all three have matching north-south direction, the two above will have like poles facing each other;

(G4)   a piece of iron which gets close to a source of magnetic force becomes itself a source of magnetic force with matching north-south direction;

(G5)   every loadstone is a source of magnetic force.

None of (G1) - (G5) is testable because there is no observation statement that is inconsistent with any of them individually, since 'magnetic force' connotes a property which is incorporeal and invisible, so neither it nor its absence is observable.[6] Yet the conjunction implies the falsifiable statement, unexpected in the light of background knowledge at the time, that two iron needles suspended by silk threads close together, side-by-side, and almost touching a loadstone, will repel each other (see Appendix for derivation); and that statement survived serious attempts to falsify it. Gilbert's theory thus became the first scientific theory of magnetism and (G1) qualified as a scientific law-statement.

So why should it be, as Earman, Roberts and Smith contend, that in the case of a testable conjunction containing a proviso matching the ceteris-paribus clauses of (L1) or (L2), any untestable law-statements in the conjunction are scientific only if the proviso is testable? Until Earman, Roberts and Smith provide a satisfactory answer, their contention seems to be an ad hoc way of saving their claim that law-statements of the form (L1) are not scientific; and ad hocness is not admirable from the viewpoint of scientific procedure.

---

[6] At least, that was so in 1600 when Gilbert published his theory: nowadays, given our accepted theories about magnetic force, we may treat some statements about the presence or absence of magnetic force as observation-statements.

5. Scientific Procedure

If we are to improve our understanding of the world, we need ways of testing our theories against our experience of the world and ways of rating rival explanations as better or worse. That rather simple thought suggests a couple of procedural maxims:

(M1) we should prefer a theory that is falsifiable to a rival theory that is not, provided it is no worse with regard to other epistemic merits, and we should try, where we can, to produce falsifiable theories;

(M2) we should prefer a theory that explains more to a rival theory that explains less, provided it is no worse with regard to other epistemic merits, and we should try, where we can, to amend our existing theories so that they explain more.

From (M1) and (M2) we can derive something like:

(M3) we should prefer a theory that entails novel falsifiable statements to a rival theory that does not, provided it is no worse with regard to other epistemic merits, and we should try, where we can, to produce theories with novel falsifiable consequences.

A falsification is an inconsistency between an accepted observation statement and a falsifiable statement, where the latter may be a conjunction which has some unfalsifiable conjuncts. An inconsistency, I assume, cannot be true (even dialetheists concede that to be usually the case), so if we want to improve our understanding of the world, we should remove the inconsistency by amending or replacing at least one of the statements involved in the inconsistency. There is an indefinite number of ways of going about that task; but some ways are better than others.

For instance, in the mid-nineteenth century, a conjunction including the law-statements expressing Newton's Laws, statements concerning the numbers, positions and masses of the planets and the ceteris-paribus proviso (P1) was inconsistent with accepted observation statements describing the motions of Uranus. One way of removing the inconsistency would have been to amend the law-statements expressing Newton's Laws so that they made an exception of Uranus. That would have explained everything that the falsified conjunction explained, but it would have explained nothing new. It would have been ad hoc (Popper 1959, sections 19-20). An alternative way of removing the inconsistency, proposed by Urbain Leverrier, involved modifying the ceteris-paribus proviso, (P1), by adding to the testable conjunction a statement positing an interfering gravitational force from a previously unknown planet with just the mass and orbit necessary to account for Uranus's anomalous motions in terms of Newton's Laws.[7] That additional statement, in conjunction with background knowledge, implied the novel falsifiable statement that the new planet would be observable in a specific region of the sky at a particular time, which was inconsistent with observation statements of the form 'this region of the sky contains no observable planet at this time.' But people did not accept observation statements of that form when they tested the novel falsifiable statement; instead, Neptune was discovered. Leverrier's amendment predicted, and thus explained, something new, as well as explaining all that was explained by the falsified conjunction and by the amendment to Newton's theory that would have made an exception of Uranus. Thus, by (M1), (M2) and (M3), Leverrier's amendment was preferable.

An amendment to theory that removes the inconsistency generated by a falsification but explains nothing new need not be ad hoc if it exemplifies a different way in which one theory may be better than another, for example, by being simpler. However, an amendment to theory is ad hoc if the only way in which it is better than the prior explanation is in avoiding the inconsistency that the falsification engendered.

If, as few would deny, science is intended to improve our understanding of the world, then falsifiability, novel predictions, and a preference for changes to theory that are not ad hoc are important parts of good scientific practice. Of course, theories which are testable, or which form non-redundant parts of conjunctions which entail novel falsifiable statements that survive testing, are often difficult to achieve, as are non-ad-hoc changes to theory which enable escape from a falsification without generating a new one. So it should not be surprising that even good scientists sometimes settle for less; but, if they are good scientists, they should regard such compromises as temporary.

We saw in section 4 that a law-statement of the form (L1) is comparable to law-statements of the form (L2) and is eligible to be a scientific law-statement because it may form a non-redundant part of a conjunction, including the proviso 'there is no material reason why this G is not H' and perhaps some other statements, which entails a novel falsifiable statement that survives testing. In another respect, however, it is different to law-statements of the form (L2). For example, the law-statement (N2), of the form (L2), has a clause and accompanying proviso, 'there is no interfering force,' which prompts us to look for possible additional forces *both* before affirming the proviso *and* in amending theory in response to a falsification;

---

[7] The *sentence* expressing the proviso (P1) is indexical: it expresses a different proviso when conjoined with different sets of sentences. It says that there are no further forces apart from those already mentioned.

and our accepted theories about forces give plenty of clues as to what to look for. But with a law-statement of the form (L1), the affirmation of the proviso, 'there is no material reason why this *G* is not *H*,' will be largely or entirely arbitrary, because we lack a theory about which sorts of reason are material with respect to the law-statement. So, if we add the proviso to a conjunction containing the law-statement so that we can derive a falsifiable statement, that falsifiable statement will almost inevitably be falsified; and, when it is falsified, our lack of a theory about which sorts of reason are material means that we will have little idea of how to amend the testable conjunction *in a non-ad-hoc way*. So the problem with law-statements of the form (L1) is not one of testability, with respect to which they are logically on a par with scientific law-statements of the form (L2), but one of affinity with sub-standard procedure. When we use them, we are at particular risk of being seduced into ad hoc manoeuvres which do not fulfil maxim (M2).

Earman and Roberts (1999, pp. 450-51) come close to making this point themselves, but they do not state it clearly because they do not distinguish ad hoc manoeuvres from issues of vacuity and testability.

> Could not the scientific community as a whole capriciously and tacitly change what counts as an "interfering factor" in order to accommodate the new data as they come in (as the psychoanalytic community does, according to some critics of psychoanalysis)? This danger can be ruled out if we can say, in advance of testing, what the content of a law is, without recourse to vague escape clauses. Otherwise, we confess that we don't see how to rule the danger out…And if the danger cannot somehow be ruled out, then a proviso-ridden law-statement still threatens to become either false or trivial.

The first sentence expresses a concern to avoid ad hoc manoeuvres. It should be plain that avoiding such bad practice requires norms, such as (M1) - (M3), to which adherence is generally secured by means of traditions and institutional structures that encourage and reward compliance and discourage and penalise non-compliance; in short, it requires the recognition and maintenance of scientific *procedures*. The second and third sentences say that ad hoc manoeuvres can be avoided if and only if we prohibit law-statements that have 'vague escape clauses' which talk of 'interfering factors.' But such tampering with the meaning of law-statements is neither necessary nor sufficient. First, prohibiting 'vague escape clauses' is not necessary to avoid ad hoc manoeuvres. As we saw in section 4, Newton's Laws, which played a huge part in scientific advance, entail no falsifiable statements unless conjoined with a bundle of other statements, including the 'vague escape clause' that there are no interfering forces. That escape clause could have been used in an ad hoc way by positing a force from an invisible planet; but it was used by Leverrier to make an amendment to theory that was not ad hoc, but rather a startling scientific success. Second, prohibiting 'vague escape clauses' is not sufficient to avoid ad hoc manoeuvres. Any statement, S_0, which must be conjoined with some other statements, S_1 - S_n, before it is inconsistent with an observation statement, can be made immune to rejection by adopting the *policy* that, if S_0 in conjunction with S_1 - S_n is inconsistent with an accepted observation statement, then one or more of S_1 - S_n is to be rejected. That remains true if each of the component statements S_0 - S_n is not vague. Earman's and Roberts' fourth sentence says that, if we cannot rule out ad hoc manoeuvres, then a ceteris-paribus law-statement threatens to become either false or trivial. But whether a statement is false or trivial depends upon its meaning; and a resort to ad hoc manoeuvres does not affect the *meaning* of our law-statements. Could it be that Earman and Roberts are led into this muddle by a lingering positivism or operationalism that links the *meaning* of a statement to the *procedures* employed in its 'verification'?

The trouble with law-statements of the form (L1) is not that, in response to a falsification, they can be protected from rejection by rejecting instead the ceteris-paribus proviso or some other statement that forms part of the testable conjunction. The problem is twofold. First, unless such manoeuvres yield an amendment to theory which explains more than its predecessor or is better in some other recognised way, such as being simpler or more unified, they will be ad hoc and fail to improve our understanding of the world. Second, ad hoc manoeuvres seem more likely in connection with law-statements of the form (L1) because the testable conjunctions of which they form part will be easily falsified, and because when falsified the ceteris-paribus clause and the corresponding proviso give little, if any, guidance about how amendments to theory can be made in a non-ad-hoc way.

Paul Pietroski and Georges Rey (1995, section 2.1) equate a vacuous statement with a tautology. They propose a curious sufficient condition for a ceteris-paribus law-statement of the form (L1) to be non-vacuous.[8] Informally, the condition is that the law-statement be interpreted as saying that everything that is G is H except where there is an independently testable explanation for a G not being H; and an explanation is independently testable if it explains not only the failure of the G to be H but also something new.

We noted in section 2, above, that a ceteris-paribus law-statement must, at a minimum, amount to a statement of the form (L1), which says that, if

---

[8] They give a different logical form for ceteris-paribus law-statements, but the difference does not matter for our purpose here.

there is a *G* which is not *H*, then there is a material reason for it. That corresponds to the part of Pietroski and Rey's condition that refers to an explanation for a *G* not being *H*. However, that is sufficient to secure non-vacuity. So why do Pietroski and Rey add that the explanation must be independently testable?

Perhaps they have confused vacuity with untestability and are concerned to render law-statements of the form (L1) *testable*. However, the claim that *there is* an independently testable explanation is an unrestricted existential claim, and such claims are unfalsifiable: even if we have been unable to find such an explanation, it could always be the case that there is such an explanation awaiting discovery. The hypothesis 'If ever a *G* is not an *H*, there is an independently testable explanation why not' is consistent with every possible observation statement and is thus untestable. So, if Pietroski and Rey are trying to show how ceteris-paribus law-statements are testable, they have signally failed.

Their demand that the posited explanation be independently testable suggests that, like Earman and Roberts, they are confusing the vacuity or untestability of a *statement* with a practice of saving that statement from a negative test result by ad hoc *manoeuvres* (which presupposes that the statement is testable or forms part of a testable conjunction). As they say: "Our requirement that factors be 'independent' is intended to exclude factors whose only explanatory role is to save a proposed cp law" (1995, p. 90). Considering a proposed law-statement of the form, 'in the absence of ectoplasmic interference, if medium X predicts *p*, then *p*' they say:

> If the only possible evidence that is recognized for this interference is the failure of…[the contained regularity, revealed in] experiments, then the appeal to ectoplasmic interference would seem to be a thinly disguised way of tautologizing the law[-statement] (1995, p. 90)…Citing the further phenomena that is also explained by appeals to ectoplasm would amount to citing the "independent evidence" that is frequently felt to be needed to save an appeal from being *ad hoc*' (1995 p. 91).

Their first sentence is false: 'in the absence of ectoplasmic interference, if medium X predicts *p*, then *p*' is not a logical truth; and it does not become a logical truth simply because it is unfalsifiable (see section 3, above). Having thus mixed up untestability with vacuity, they go on in the second sentence to mix up both with the employment of ad hoc manoeuvres.

6. Conclusion

We have taken (L0) as our standard form of a strict (non-ceteris-paribus) law-statement: 'necessarily, everything which is G is H.' A ceteris-paribus law-statement is of the same form except that it is qualified by a ceteris-paribus clause. There is a variety of types of ceteris-paribus clause. We have considered two general kinds: 'there is no material reason why not,' which gives us a ceteris-paribus law-statement of the form (L1); and 'there is no interfering F,' which gives us a ceteris-paribus law-statement of the form (L2).

If a vacuous statement is one that has the form of a logical truth, or such a statement prefixed with a necessity or possibility operator, then neither type of ceteris-paribus law-statement is vacuous. However, many statements which are not vacuous are not testable. Ceteris-paribus law-statements of the form (L1) are not testable, but those of the form (L2) are testable if each of the terms corresponding to 'not F,' 'G' and 'not H' connotes an observable property *and* the ceteris-paribus clause is spatio-temporally restricted.

Newton's Law of Gravitation is not a ceteris-paribus law-statement, but Newton's Second Law can be expressed in a ceteris-paribus law-statement of the form (L2), or in a law-statement with a disguised ceteris-paribus clause, such as (N2*). None of these law-statements is testable. However, each may be conjoined with a ceteris-paribus proviso affirming that there is no interfering force, descriptions of the properties of specific physical bodies, other law-statements and the theory of vector composition to form a conjunction that entails novel falsifiable statements that survive testing. A ceteris-paribus law-statement of the form (L1) is untestable directly but indirectly testable in a similar way; it is thus similar to some law-statements that are uncontroversially scientific.

What does distinguish ceteris-paribus law-statements of the form (L1) from law-statements of the other two forms is that the lack of specification in the ceteris-paribus clause, and thus in the associated proviso, means that:

(i)   barring exceptional luck, when a testable conjunction containing such a law-statement and its associated proviso is subjected to tests, the test result will be negative;

(ii)   there is little guidance as to how the law-statement or other statements in the conjunction could be amended in a way which not only rectifies the falsification but also explains something new.

As a consequence, advocates of law-statements of the form (L1) are at great risk of adopting ad hoc manoeuvres, which are less than satisfactory from a scientific point of view. So long as scientists are alert to ad hoc manoeuvres (their own as well as those of other scientists), this danger of law-statements of the form (L1) can be avoided; but insofar as it is avoided in a particular case, amendments to a law-statement of form (L1) are liable to turn it into a law-statement of form (L2) or of form (L0).

The contemporary debate about ceteris-paribus law-statements suffers from confusion and error due to failures, even by leading authors, to distinguish between vacuous, untestable, unverifiable, and unscientific statements, and between unscientific statements ad hoc procedures.

Appendix: Testability of Gilbert's Theory

The portion of Gilbert's theory, (G1) - (G5), set forth in section 4, can be formalised as follows:

(1) necessarily, (x) (y) (if $(Sx$ & Sy & Cxy & $LFxy)$ then Rxy))
(2) (x) (y) (z) (if $(Mxy$ & $Mzy)$ then Mxz)
(3) (x) (y) (z) (if $(SSAxyz$ & Mxy & Myz & $Mxz)$ then $LFxy$)
(4) (x) (y) (if $(Ix$ & Sy & $Cxy)$ then $(Sx$ & Mxy))
(5) (x) (if Lx then Sx).

Key:

'Sx' = x is a source of magnetic force;
'Cxy' = x and y are close together;
'$LFxy$' = the pole of the magnetic force of x is facing the like pole of the magnetic force of y;
'Rxy' = x and y repel each other;
'Ix' = x is a piece of iron;
'$SSAxyz$' = x and y are close together, side-by-side, above z;
'Mxy' = the magnetic forces of x and y have matching north-south direction; 'Lx' = x is a loadstone.

The observation statement 'these two iron needles are suspended by silk threads close together, side-by-side, and they are almost touching a loadstone, but they do not repel each other' can then be formalised thus:

(6) Ia & Ib & Lc & Cab & Cac & Cbc & $SSAabc$ & $\sim Rab$.

The following derivation (which, to save on space, does not fully spell out every step) shows that (6) is inconsistent with (1) - (5):

(7) (x) (y) (if $(Sx$ & Sy & Cxy & $LFxy)$ then $Rxy))$ [(1), 'necessarily p' entails 'p']

(8) Sc [(5), (6)]

(9) Ia & Sc & Cac [(6), (8)]

(10) Sa & Mac [(4), (9)]

(11) Ib & Sc & Cbc [(6), (8)]

(12) Sb & Mbc [(4), (11)]

(13) Mbc & Mac [(10), (12)]

(14) Mab [(2), (13)]

(15) $SSAabc$ & Mab & Mbc & Mac [(6), (13), (14)]

(16) $LFab$ [(3), (15)]

(17) Sa & Sb & Cab & $LFab$ [(6), (10), (12), (16)]

(18) Rab [(7), (17)]

(19) Rab & $\sim Rab$ [(6), (18)].

II REASON, REASONS AND REASONING

58

5 THEORETICAL AND PRACTICAL REASON

Abstract If the task of theoretical reason is to discover truth, or reasons for belief, then theoretical reason is impossible. Attempts to circumvent that by appeal to probabilities are self-defeating. If the task of practical reason is to discover what we ought to do or what actions are desirable or valuable, then practical reason is impossible. Appeals to the subjective ought or to subjective probabilities are self-defeating. Adapting Karl Popper, I argue that the task of theoretical reason is to obtain theories that we can agree to instate given that they appear to have greater explanatory merit than their rivals. I then argue that the task of practical reason is to decide which ought-propositions to act on. As a consequence theoretical reason is seen as a branch of practical reason. This approach makes both theoretical and practical reason practicable and free of the defects of the usual accounts.

Keywords. Expected utility; explanatory merit; instate; ought-proposition; practical reason; Karl Popper; scepticism; subjective ought; subjective probability; theoretical reason.

1. Introduction

In this paper 'ought' will always mean *ought, all things considered*. R. Jay Wallace (2014, section 1) suggests that the concern of practical reason is to discover what we ought to do, while the concern of theoretical reason is to discover what we ought to believe.

> Practical reason…typically asks, of a set of alternatives for action none of which has yet been performed, what one ought to do, or what it would be best to do. It is thus

> concerned…with matters of value, of what it would be desirable to do. In practical reasoning agents attempt to assess and weigh their reasons for action, the considerations that speak for and against alternative courses of action that are open to them…
>
> …theoretical reflection…is concerned with…the question of what one ought to believe. It attempts to answer this normative question by assessing and weighing reasons for belief…
>
> Theoretical reason… addresses the considerations that recommend accepting particular claims as to what is or is not the case. That is, it involves reflection with an eye to the truth of propositions, and the reasons for belief in which it deals are considerations that speak in favor of such propositions' being true, or worthy of acceptance.

Although they dispute details of each other's accounts, very many philosophers agree with Wallace that theoretical reason is concerned with what is true and is relevant to our beliefs while practical reason is concerned with the value or desirability of actions and is relevant to what we ought to do or intend (for example, Bratman 1987, Broome 2002, Grice 2001, Harman 1986, Korsgaard 1986, Raz 2010).

I argue that this standard approach cannot be correct. For simplicity, I argue explicitly against Wallace's formulation; but my arguments can be modified easily to tell against the variants. In section 2, I explain why theoretical reason cannot be concerned to ascertain what is true or what we ought to believe. In section 3, I present an alternative account of theoretical reason which is drawn, with some modifications, from Karl Popper. In section 4, I explain why practical reason cannot be concerned to discover what we ought to do, or what it is best, desirable or valuable to do. In section 5, I offer and defend an alternative account of practical reason which is a counterpart of the account of theoretical reason given in section 3. In section 6, I conclude the discussion and offer some general reflections on theoretical and practical reason. My main aim is to propound a sceptical account of theoretical and practical reason, which I do in sections 3, 5 and 6, so sections 2 and 4 present a summary of sceptical arguments rather than a detailed exposition and defence of them.

2. Critique of Theoretical Reason

The contention that theoretical reason is concerned to discover what is true or evidence for truth, and thereby what to believe, makes theoretical reason impossible. The arguments for this have been set out in detail by others. Here is an incomplete but sufficient summary.

First, any finite set of mutually consistent observation statements is consistent with an infinite number of mutually inconsistent general theories each of which explains all the observation statements in the set. So, even if we knew all the observation statements in the set to be true, a general theory that explained them all might still be false, and the observation statements would not be evidence for the truth of that theory as opposed to any of its rivals (Popper 1959, sections 1, 2, 3, 82 and passim). As a trivial illustration (adapted from Goodman 1954, pp. 73-81), suppose that we have a large number of true observation statements reporting the greenness of particular emeralds and no true observation statement reporting an emerald of any other colour. The general theory that all emeralds are green may still be false because it may be that all emeralds are green until 1 January 2150 but not thereafter, or that all emeralds are green until 2 January 2150 but not thereafter, and so on.

Second, when we test a theory, we normally need to conjoin it with a large number of other theories in order to derive a testable prediction, in which case a failure of the prediction may be due to one of those other theories rather than to the theory under test. So, even if we knew our observation statements to be true, the fact that the theory under test conflicts with some of them would not tell us that the theory is false (Duhem 1954, pp. 180-90).

Third, observation statements inevitably involve theoretical interpretations which may be false. Even so simple an observation statement as 'Here is a glass of water' implies that the receptacle will exhibit the law-like behaviour of glass and that its contents will behave in the law-like way that water does; and these implications may be inconsistent with other observation statements (Popper 1959, section 25). Indeed, even if all scientists agreed to accept the observation statement 'Here is a glass of water' because the liquid in the glass has passed all the scientific tests for being water, they may still be mistaken. Urey's discovery of heavy hydrogen in 1931 showed that what scientists had previously taken to be water was in fact a mixture of two physically different substances (Popper 1961, pp. 374-75): some of the theories about water presupposed by the previously accepted observation statement, 'Here is a glass of water,' were rejected. Thus we can never know of any observation statement that it is true.

Fourth, as a consequence, we can never know of any self-consistent explanatory theory (or self-consistent conjunction of such theories) that it is false, since if it is inconsistent with an observation statement, it may be the latter that is false. Fifth, and consequently, since observation statements are themselves theoretical, we can never tell whether an observation statement is false.

A standard response to such considerations is to retreat from truth to probable truth. However, a statement of the objective probability of an empirical statement is itself an empirical statement which could be known to be true only via our knowledge of the truth of observation statements; and since we cannot know whether any observation statement is true or false, we cannot know whether any statement assigning an objective probability to an empirical statement is true or false. A retreat to *seeming* probable truth (subjective probability) is self-defeating, for what only *seems* probably true may be false: in breaking the connection with truth, it abandons the conception of theoretical reason that is supposedly being defended. Indeed, the same applies to the retreat to objective probability, since a proposition that is *objectively* highly probable may turn out to be false. So, if we ought to believe what is true, it is in general not the case that we ought to believe what is or seems most probable. Further, given that the history of science shows one seemingly most probable theory after another being replaced by something better (Popper 1983, pp. 75, 131-49), the claim that we ought to believe, rather than try to replace, the seemingly most probable of a set of rival propositions could frustrate further progress.

The preceding considerations are drawn from the study of scientific theories. However, scientific theories are an outgrowth of our common-sense theories, and examination of them brings into relief the epistemic problems with general statements and observation statements that also afflict our common-sense theories (Popper 1959, Preface to the 1959 edition), as the example of the emeralds shows. In all empirical matters, then, we can never ascertain what is true or false or have any evidence for truth or falsity; and nor can we have reasons for belief, or any indications about what we ought to believe, if we ought to believe what is true.

It is often claimed that some knowledge of truth, particularly logic and mathematics, is *a priori*. But that cannot be so. There are, broadly, two ways of conceiving supposed *a priori* knowledge. First, it may be conceived as quasi-empirical, in that axiomatic systems are regarded as explanatory theories from which consequences are derived using sound rules of inference, those consequences being tested against simple propositions (traditional 'theorems') which are declared *a priori* evident on the basis of intuition (Lakatos 1962, 1967; Russell 1924, pp. 325-26; Whitehead & Russell 1927, pp. 59-60). Second, and more usually, it is the axioms of the systems that are held to be either self-evident or in some sense 'true in virtue of meaning,' so that truth flows into the theorems of the system by means of sound rules of inference. Unfortunately, it is not *a priori* evident which rules of inference are sound: every significant rule of inference has been impugned by some serious and expert logicians trying to resolve logical problems, for example, double negation in intuitionist logic, modus ponens in some fuzzy logics, and conjunction elimination in connexive logic (Priest & Thomason 2007, pp. 96-98). Further, neither the theorems, on the quasi-empirical view, nor the axioms, on the alternative view, can be known to be true *a priori*. Propositions that were once universally, or almost universally, thought to be true self-evidently or 'in virtue of meaning,' such as the absoluteness of simultaneity, have since been either jettisoned or impugned. And Russell's Paradox showed that even the logicians' supposed self-evident truth that every property defines a set was a latent self-contradiction (Russell 1959, pp. 58-59; Whitehead & Russell 1927, pp. 37-65). There is no *a priori* criterion of falsehood either: dialetheic logicians argue that even some self-contradictions are true (Priest 2004). In supposedly *a priori* matters we can never ascertain what is true (or false) or have any evidence for truth (or falsity); and nor can we have reasons for belief, or any indications about what we ought to believe, if we ought to believe what is true.

Therefore, if theoretical reason had to ascertain what is true or to unearth evidence for truth, it would have an impossible task; and if we ought to believe what it true, it is impossible for theoretical reason to discover what we ought to believe.

3. Practicable Theoretical Reason

It may seem that our apparent inability to discover truth, or evidence for truth, leaves theoretical reason with no worthwhile task. But that is not so. For, we can resolve to make the best of the thoroughly fallible epistemic situation in which we are placed (Popper 1983, pp. 18-22). We thus adopt a realistic aim for theoretical reason and devise procedures that, it seems, should enable us to achieve that aim, if anything can, even in the face of universal doubt. That may be done in a number of ways. I outline an emended version of Popper's 'critical rationalist' approach (1945, vol. 2, pp. 212-58; 1957a; 1959; 1963a; 1976; 1983). This is inevitably a simplified summary; and I say nothing about Popper's theory of verisimilitude, which seems inconsistent with his earlier view and is otherwise problematic. I use 'theory,' 'proposition' and 'statement' interchangeably, but these must not be confused with beliefs: whether or not anyone believes the propositions in question is a matter of his personal psychology.

The approach involves the notion of *instating* a proposition.[9] I cannot define that notion, but I offer an informal explanation here and I provide additional clues, below, in the way the notion is used when I describe our aim and our procedures. This is, in fact, the sort of way in which the

---

[9] I think that the notion of instating a theory is equivalent to the notion of accepting a theory as currently best that is employed in Chapter 3.

meaning of new terms is generally explained (Feyerabend 1960; Findlay 1962; Kuhn 1974). An instated proposition is the best substitute for knowledge that we can obtain. We find that we can attain pretty general agreement to instate some propositions of particular kinds under particular circumstances, in view of how things appear to us, either experientially or intellectually, provided we co-operate with each other in seeking such agreement. We recognise that things may not be as they appear, so the agreement to instate a proposition involves no commitment to the truth of that proposition.

Thus, consider that, while people often disagree over observation statements, it is generally possible to find a formulation on which agreement can be reached. For example, an Aristotelian, a Galilean, a Newtonian and an Einsteinian may, respectively, describe the same observed event in the following mutually inconsistent observation statements:

- that apple moved to the ground in search of its natural place;
- that apple fell to Earth;
- that apple was pulled to the ground by the Earth's gravity;
- that apple took the easiest course through curved space-time.

However, there is a neutral observation statement that all four can agree upon; perhaps,

- that apple moved to the ground in approximately a straight line.

An observation statement which is neutral with respect to the preceding four theories will not be neutral with respect to some others. For example, a fifth person may say: 'that was not an apple.' In that case, a neutral observation statement may be:

(p)   that approximately-spherical object moved to the ground in approximately a straight line.

A sixth person may have some startling new theory of motion which requires formulating a neutral observation statement in a way which we cannot anticipate. There is no observation statement describing the event which is neutral with respect to all theories. Still, we expect that the alternative interpretations in contention can be stripped away, not to reveal a statement that is free of interpretation, but to enable us, with effort, to find an interpretation on which we can agree. So far, I guess, we have not often been disappointed in that expectation, at least where the participants are co-operating with each other. Even someone like the quantum physicist Erwin Schrödinger (1960), who denies the existence of the physical world, who therefore thinks that (p) is false, may agree, without inconsistency, to *instate* (p) in view of how things appear to him (Frederick 2016a).

It is also usually possible to obtain agreement to instate some propositions concerning what follows from what in classical logic. Even a deviant logician who denies that modus ponens is sound may agree to instate the proposition that modus ponens is sound *in classical logic*. Even a sceptic about our powers of discerning inferential connections, who doubts even whether modus ponens is sound in classical logic, may agree, in view of how things *seem* to him, to *instate* the proposition that modus ponens is sound in classical logic. With regard to inferences in which people disagree whether the conclusion follows in classical logic, agreement to instate an inference can usually be reached by employing one of the algorithms available in the propositional or predicate calculi.

We must decide:

(i)   what our aim is;
(ii)   where to begin;
(iii)   how to evaluate whether we are making progress;
(iv)   how else to proceed.

Popper proposed that our aim should be to discover better explanatory theories. However, that would be a sensible aim only if we could discover that it is *true* that one theory is a better explanation than another; but we saw in section 2 that we have no way of discovering what is true. We therefore decide that our aim is to generate new theories that we can agree to instate in view of a critical discussion which appears to show that they have greater explanatory merit than their rivals. Our aim is recursive: once we instate a new theory, we try to generate other new theories to oust it. An *ousted* theory is one which was previously, but is not currently, instated. An ousted theory may later be reinstated. A *decision to* instate a theory in view of a critical discussion which appears to show its explanatory superiority over its rivals is not a *decision that* the theory is a better explanation than its rivals. Instatement involves no statement; in particular, it does not commit us to *affirming* that (it is true that) the instated theory is a better explanation than its rivals, or even that (it is true that) it appears that the instated theory is a better explanation than its rivals.

We decide to *start from where we are*, that is, from the theories that we already have, as that seems the most practical starting point. Indeed, starting *largely* from where we are seems unavoidable, since

- even if we begin by proposing a new theory, we will normally need other theories to be able to derive testable consequences from it and to supply the premises of potential criticisms of it,
- we are not even conscious of most of our presuppositions.

So, we decide to instate our inherited theories, which provide our starting frame of reference, to be modified in the course of enquiry. We decide to count classical logic as part of that inheritance.

We decide to evaluate whether we are making progress in our aim by agreeing to a set of desirable features in a good explanation and *we compare rival theories in terms of these explanatory merits*. We decide to count the following as explanatory merits of a theory: self-consistency, employment of universal principles (laws or rules), extensive scope, simplicity, precision, falsifiability, and yielding surprising predictions which survive testing. Some of these merits may be traded off against others: even an inconsistent theory may have compensating merits, as the history of the calculus shows (Popper 1983, pp. 266-71). Agreement to a set of explanatory merits makes it easier, though not often easy, to reach agreement on whether to instate a new theory.

We must adopt further procedures to try to move us in the direction of our aim, though we recognise that no procedures can guarantee success, because success depends upon our ingenuity and perseverance as well as on nature, or our sensory experience, not being too complex or chaotic. We instate observation statements concerning repeatable events or states to which all or nearly all observers agree (unanimity, even amongst scientific researchers, is not always to be expected). To discourage humbug we decide that no new theory can be instated unless the claim is instated that, either on its own or in conjunction with some other instated theories, the new theory entails a novel *falsifiable* prediction; and no instated proposition can be ousted unless it is instated that the ousting is not *ad hoc*. Those two technical terms need explanation.

A theory is scientific if and only if, either on its own or in conjunction with instated theories, it entails a statement which is *falsifiable* and which is not entailed by the conjunction minus the theory. A statement is falsifiable if and only if it is inconsistent with an observation statement, that is, *a statement that describes something we could conceivably observe, given our actual powers of observation*. A theory is *falsified* if and only if, either on its own or in conjunction with instated theories, it is inconsistent with an *instated* observation statement (Popper 1959, sections 18, 21-23 and 27-28). A falsified theory may be true if the instated observation statement with which it is inconsistent is false or if some of the instated theories used in the derivation of the inconsistency are false. So, one can try to rescue a theory from falsification by replacing one or more of those instated propositions with an alternative (either its negation or a contrary). However, such a manoeuvre will be *ad hoc* unless the conjunction of

- the falsified theory,
- the replacement statements,
- the rest of the instated theories that were used in the falsification (excluding those that have been replaced),

is consistent and implies surprising new falsifiable predictions which survive testing (Popper 1959, sections 19-20) or, at a minimum, provides a new solution to some problem in addition to the problem of rescuing the falsified theory.

Since progress requires creativity and criticism, we permit anyone to:

- propose a new explanatory theory to solve a problem;
- criticise any theory (instated or other) or propose possible experimental tests of it which anyone may try to carry out;
- propose a rival theory to any instated theory and try to develop it into a form which has greater explanatory merits, for example, by improving its testability by spelling it out, making it quantitative or adding auxiliary hypotheses;
- defend any theory by thinking up applications of it to new problems or by developing it to improve its explanatory merits, for example, by enabling it to be tested in new experiments, or by criticising criticisms of it.

To assess our progress we decide to compare rival theories, periodically, as better or worse in the light of all the criticism and testing to date and the agreed explanatory merits, with a view to instating one of the rivals. As a result we may oust one theory and instate, or reinstate, another. Then we continue according to the same procedures indefinitely.

Parenthetically, we can note three points. *First*, since none of the reasons for instating a proposition bear upon its truth, they are not reasons for belief, if we ought to believe what is true. *Second*, instating a proposition does not amount to accepting it as true or adopting it: one is at liberty to try to oust a proposition one has just instated, by trying to develop a rival that may eventually have greater explanatory merit. *Third*, the employment of theoretical reason is essentially a social enterprise dependent upon inter-subjective agreement and co-operation, but I have said nothing about the framework of this enterprise (producers, consumers, institutions, funding, traditions) or *which* people (or how many of them) need to agree before instating a proposition. That is a large topic that I cannot pursue here.

Popper argued that his procedures were followed instinctively by good scientists and that this explained scientific progress (1949b, p. 356; 1959, section 11; 1975, pp. 15, 18-19; 1983, p. xxxi); though he also realised that the behaviour of scientists sometimes deviates from the procedures (1975, pp. 14-17; 1976, p. 57). Of course, he did not think that scientists got together collectively to agree on such procedures. But, insofar as the procedures, and deviations from them, are recognised in scientific practice, they can be regarded as evolved conventions produced by an 'invisible hand' process, the unintended consequences of intentional actions within a social network. The following three examples from the history of science provide illustrations of action in accord with the procedures.

Galileo acknowledged that the observed variations in brightness of the planets as revealed to the naked eye was inconsistent with the variations in their distance from the earth as predicted by Copernican astronomy; but he set out to *oust the instated observation statements* by developing a telescope, which revealed variations in brightness consistent with the Copernican theory. The completion of his task required the ousting of instated optical theories by better theories that could explain why the telescopic observations were to be preferred; but Galileo left that as a task for others (Feyerabend 1975, pp. 141-43, 160).

In the mid-nineteenth century, the observed motions of Uranus falsified Newton's theory. However, Newton's theory was not ousted, because it was instated that the theory still had greater overall explanatory merits than any available alternative. But the falsification posed a challenge for defenders of the theory: to remove the contradiction between the theory and instated observation statements they had to amend *either* the theory, *or* other instated theories used in deriving the falsified predictions, *or* the instated rules of inference used in that derivation, *or* some instated observation statements. Each type of amendment could have been done in an ad hoc way. For example, Newton's theory could have been replaced with a weaker version that made an exception for Uranus; or some other instated theories could have been amended by supposing that the perturbations of Uranus were explained by a previously unknown force the existence of which could not be tested independently; or the derivation of the falsified prediction could have been declared an exception to the standard rules of inference; or the repeated observations of Uranus' anomalous motions could have been dismissed as hallucinations. But such manoeuvres would have been ad hoc, introducing complications of theory (the exception to Newton or to rules of inference, the mysterious force, the hallucinations affecting only observations of Uranus) that did not generate any novel falsifiable predictions to be tested. In contrast, Leverrier set out to *oust* the instated theory concerning the number of planets. He hypothesised the existence of a previously unknown planet with just the properties necessary to account, in terms of Newton's theory, for Uranus' anomalous motions. That hypothesis had a novel falsifiable prediction, that the new planet would be seen in a particular portion of the sky at a particular time; and that prediction survived testing when Neptune was discovered (Kuhn 1957, pp. 261-62). That explanatory merit meant that Leverrier's hypothesis was instated in place of the previously instated theory about the number of planets that it contradicted, and the falsification of Newton's theory was overturned.

Finally, in the late seventeenth century Newton *ousted the instated explanatory theories* of Kepler and Galileo by proposing a theory which contradicted them and which, it appeared, explained what they explained as well as other things besides, such as the motions of the tides (Popper 1983, pp. 139-45, 190-91).

Imre Lakatos (1962, 1967, 1976) extended Popper's approach to mathematics. He regarded axiomatic mathematical theories as quasi-empirical explanations that are tested against simple mathematical propositions (theorems) which are accepted in the light of *a priori* intuitions. Following Goodman (1954, pp. 63-64), we could regard logic in the same way, treating logical systems as general hypotheses about validity which are tested against simple arguments that we accept in the light of our intuitions concerning validity. We can also go a step farther and regard all supposed *a priori* propositions as being ultimately empirical, in the sense that they may, for all we know, eventually succumb to empirical refutation, perhaps in the way that the axiom of parallels and the absoluteness of simultaneity are inconsistent with relativity theory. Our supposed *a priori* intuitions are then viewed merely as expectations that reflect the theories we take for granted, principally, theories we have inherited biologically or culturally (or sub-culturally); and any, perhaps all, of these theories may be false, though we can review them critically and improve or replace them (Popper & Eccles 1977, pp. 43-46, 132-35). This conclusion is similar to that of W. V. Quine (1951), though our argument is based simply on our fallibility and does not assume verificationism, radical meaning scepticism, or holism. A further step extends the critical rationalist approach to moral and other normative theories, as we note in section 5.

4. Critique of Practical Reason

The contention that practical reason is concerned to discover what we ought to do, or what it is best, or desirable, or good, or valuable to do, makes practical reason impossible. For, whether an option for action has the characteristics that would make it worthy of performance depends not only on our aims and values but also on facts about the option, whether these are facts about its consequences or its constitution, or facts that make it an exemplification of a virtue or an exemplification of a specific moral or other rule. But we can never know which factual propositions are true. So even if we had perfect knowledge about our aims and values, we could still never know which action we ought to perform. The problem is therefore compounded once we acknowledge that our command of the appropriate aims and values is fallible too (Schueler 2009 and Frederick 2013a, pp. 66-70).

This problem has long been recognised by philosophers, at least so far as the limitations of our factual knowledge is concerned, and the standard response is to distinguish the subjective from the objective ought. The *objective ought* is entailed by propositions stating the objective facts and the right aims and values, but the *subjective ought* is the ought-proposition which is entailed by the factual and normative propositions that we believe or accept. For example, if the man next to me has fainted and can be revived by my shouting, then I objectively-ought to shout, if I am able to shout and if my shouting has no adverse consequences. But if my shouting will make no difference, or will make things worse, then it is not the case that I objectively-ought to shout. It is nevertheless the case that I subjectively-ought to shout if I *think* that shouting will revive him and will not be untoward in any way. The problem of our ignorance of the objective ought is then sidestepped by claiming that it is the subjective ought that tells us what we ought to do (see, for example, Prichard 1932).

There are two substantial objections to the subjective ought. The first concerns cases where the propositions that an agent accepts imply that she ought to *a*, where '*a*' stands in for a description of a specific action-type, such as 'shout.' The propositions in question will include some about *how things stand*, including her aims and values, and some about the *options for change* available and their possible consequences. However, the irremovable possibility of error means that it is always open to the agent, rationally, to question those propositions and her inferences from them. In many cases she might not have the time or other resources needed to try to think up and test alternative propositions about how things stand, or to think up alternative, perhaps entirely novel, options and criticise them in view of their possible consequences. But there is always time to doubt her currently accepted propositions. And it is always open to her to try to falsify the conjunction of those propositions by attempting to achieve her aim in a way that the conjunction rules out: she can try to falsify the conjunction by acting against it. This is so even if the propositions include currently instated theories. For example, Galileo succeeded, through trial and error, in constructing a telescope through which to view the heavens despite the fact that the most advanced optical theory ruled it impossible (Feyerabend 1975, pp. 104-5, including footnotes). Thomas Edison's production of his electric light falsified the unanimous scientific opinion that such a light was impossible (Kuhn 1959, p. 238). But not only are agents sometimes successful in falsifying accepted views by their actions, they also often meet with disaster when acting in accord with accepted propositions. For example, there have been mass ergot poisonings of people who acted on the generally accepted view that bread nourishes, and many people in totalitarian societies were betrayed by their best and most-trusted friends (Popper 1983, p. 63). Many drivers a little while ago came to grief when they acted on the then uncontroversial proposition that Toyota cars are safe; and a number of people have died from variant Creutzfeldt-Jakob disease because they acted on the commonly held view that it is safe to eat beef bought from the supermarket. As Popper put it (1957, p. 56):

> it is perfectly reasonable to *act* on the assumption that [the future] will, in many respects, be like the past, and that well-tested laws will continue to hold (since we can have no better assumption to act upon); but it is also reasonable to believe that such a course of action will lead us at times into severe trouble, since some of the laws on which we now heavily rely may easily prove unreliable.

The fact of the matter is that whenever we act we are making a guess. Since the agent is rationally entitled to try to falsify the propositions she accepts, including instated ones, by acting against them, it is arbitrary to insist that she ought to act in accord with the subjective ought (Frederick 2013a, pp. 66-70).

The second objection to the subjective ought concerns situations in which the propositions we accept leave significant and relevant gaps in our picture of how things stand. We can borrow an example from Kolodny and MacFarlane (2010). We accept the following. Ten miners are trapped either in shaft A or in shaft B, but we do not know which. Flood waters threaten to flood the shafts. We have enough sandbags to block one shaft, but not both. If we block one shaft, all the water will go into the other shaft, killing any miners inside it. If we block neither shaft, both shafts will fill halfway with water, and just one miner, the lowest in the shaft, will be killed. The only missing relevant fact concerns which shaft the miners are in. Our aim is to save as many of the miners as possible and none of our values inhibit us from blocking the shafts with sandbags to save the miners. From these accepted propositions we may derive, validly, the following:

(1)   if the miners are in shaft A, we ought to block shaft A;
(2)   if the miners are in shaft B, we ought to block shaft B;
(3)   either the miners are in shaft A or they are in shaft B;

therefore,

(4)   either we ought to block shaft A or we ought to block shaft B.

That conclusion, (4), is a disjunction of ought-propositions rather than a specific ought-proposition; but it follows from our accepted views, so it is a step towards, and a constraint upon, our subjective ought. It does not, however, tell us what we ought to do: we are left to guess whether we ought to block shaft A or shaft B.

In such cases, advocates of the subjective ought try to fill the gap. The most common recourse is to combine subjective probabilities with expected utility theory, according to which we ought to perform the action that maximises expected utility. Thus, given the fact that our accepted views render it equally plausible that the miners are in shaft A as that they are in shaft B, it is affirmed that there is a 0.5 subjective probability that the miners are in shaft A and a 0.5 subjective probability that they are in shaft B. If we block shaft A, there are two possible outcomes: we save ten or we save five. Each outcome has a 0.5 probability. So, identifying utility with lives saved, the expected utility of blocking shaft A is (0.5 x 10) + (0.5 x 0) = 5. Similar calculations are done for the other options, as shown in the following table.

Action	**Expected Utility**		
	Miners in A	Miners in B	Total
Block shaft A	0.5 x 10 = 5	0.5 x 0 = 0	5
Block shaft B	0.5 x 0 = 0	0.5 x 10 = 5	5
Block neither shaft	0.5 x 9 = 4.5	0.5 x 9 = 4.5	9

Since we maximise expected utility if and only if we block neither shaft, it is concluded that we ought to block neither shaft. However, that contradicts (4), with which the subjective ought must be consistent.[10]

Therefore, if practical reason had to ascertain what we ought to do, it would have an impossible task. We cannot discover what we objectively-ought to do, or what is best, or valuable or desirable. The attempt to circumvent this problem of our fallibility by substituting the subjective for the objective ought is self-defeating, because our fallibility means that we are rationally entitled to question the subjective ought and even to try to falsify it by acting against it; so it cannot be the case that practical rationality requires us to do what we subjectively-ought to do. Further, in decision-making situations in which there is a significant and relevant gap in our

---

[10] See Frederick 2020, chapter 3, section 3.4 for detailed criticism of the perverse treatment of the miners case in Kolodny and MacFarlane (2010) and also of the subjective ought, expected utility and maximin.

information, the subjective ought is too indefinite to identify what we ought to do; and the attempt of subjectivists to fill the gap using expected utility theory leads to self-contradiction.

5. Practicable Practical Reason

Many of our actions are joint-actions, that is, things that we do with others; and many are things that we do by ourselves. In what follows, my talk of what we should do should be understood as covering both types of case; in the latter case, it means what each of us individually should do. Indeed, both types of action involve *individual* practical reason: even when we are deciding that *we* shall do something together, each of us is deciding that *he* shall do something with the others.

Practical reason is concerned with deciding how to act. For the most part we act according to habit, that is, we act in familiar ways in familiar situations. When we face the problem of deciding how to act, it is either because we face an unfamiliar situation or because we want to re-evaluate one of our familiar ways of behaving. What we *ought* to do is to act on the ought-proposition that is true; but since we cannot know which ought-proposition is true, we cannot know what we ought to do. Our concern must therefore be to decide what we *shall* do, that is, to decide which ought-proposition to act on (Frederick 2020, chapter 3, section 3.4). I suggest that we proceed as follows.

We need a description of

- the situation we are in,
- our aims and values,
- our options for action and their consequences.

In so far as we can, we assemble the relevant factual propositions from those that have been instated by means of our exercise of theoretical reason. We may need further exercises of theoretical reason in order to acquire new instated factual propositions. We then describe the aims and values that we think we currently have and that we think are relevant to our decision. Those aims and values will largely be inherited from the culture and subculture in which we were brought up. We instate the propositions describing those aims and values. From the assembled instated propositions, we try to derive a statement about what specific action we ought to perform. If we succeed, then we instate that ought-proposition. We then decide, more or less arbitrarily, whether to act on that ought-proposition or whether to try to falsify it by acting against it. However, it may be that our previously instated propositions do not entail a statement, concerning a specific action, that we ought to perform it. Very often, they will entail the negations of some ought-propositions while leaving us to choose between several other ought-propositions by some arbitrary means, such as flipping a coin or rolling a die. That was so in the miners example in section 4, where our accepted propositions entailed the negation of the proposition that we ought to block neither shaft, leaving us to choose between the proposition that we ought to block shaft A and the proposition that we ought to block shaft B. But we could, of course, have decided to try to falsify the conjunction of our instated propositions by acting on the proposition that we ought to block neither shaft. Which decision we make will be influenced by our gambling temperament, which differs from person to person (see Frederick 2020, chapter 3, section 3.4 for detail).

Our current aims and values can be roughly divided into those that are moral and those that are personal. All of them should be subject to review through our exercise of theoretical reason. The process of 'reflective equilibrium,' beloved of contemporary philosophers, can help to remove inconsistencies from our instated moral theories and to improve their coherence; but it will not lead to the revolutionary overthrow of our theories and their replacement with novel theories that are substantially better (Frederick 2016b). We can gain that advantage by evaluating our moral theories according to the opportunities for good outcomes that they provide, which is partly an empirical matter (Frederick 2020, chapter 5, sections 5.2 and 5.5). Similarly, we can subject our personal aims and values to the same processes of theoretical reason if we test them empirically by living in accord with them and then evaluating whether we are fulfilled by living in that way (Frederick 2014, pp. 124-26; 2016c; 2020, chapter 4, sections 4.3 and 4.4).

Instating an ought-proposition and then trying to falsify it by not acting on it does not involve inconsistency, any more than a scientist is inconsistent when he tries to falsify an instated theory. Suppose that in our exercise of practical reason concerning what we shall do in a particular situation, we assemble from among our instated propositions those that we think relevant to our decision, and we deduce from those assembled propositions the following:

(a)   we ought to a

where 'a' stands in for a description of a specific type of act. Since we deem (a) to follow logically from our instated propositions, we will instate it, so long as it is consistent with itself and with other instated propositions. We then decide that, rather than acting on (a), we will try to falsify it by evaluating the results of acting on a contrary ought-proposition:

(b)   we ought to *b*

where '*b*' stands in for a description of a specific type of act that is incompatible with *a* in our situation. However, while the conjunction of (a) and (b) is inconsistent, there is no inconsistency in *instating* (a) and *acting on* (b). Acting on (b) does not involve instating it.

6. Conclusion: The Primacy of Practical Reason

It is common for philosophers to distinguish practical from theoretical reason by attributing to the former a concern with the value of actions or what we ought to do, and to the latter a concern with truth or what we ought to believe. I have argued that on such characterisations practical and theoretical reason are impossible. It is impossible for us to discover what is true. There are always potential rivals to any explanatory theory, and no matter how good a particular explanatory theory may be, it is always possible that a different theory will be far better at some future time. Further, the observation statements against which theories are tested always involve interpretations which may be false; and all our supposedly *a priori* intuitions are fallible. A retreat to probability is self-defeating because even highly probable propositions may be false. Since the value of an action depends upon facts about it, and since we can never know which factual propositions are true, and since we can also be mistaken about our aims and values, we can never know which action we ought to perform. A retreat to the subjective ought accomplishes nothing, for our fallibility means that we are always rationally entitled to try to falsify the subjective ought by acting against it, no matter how painstaking and competent was the investigation that led to it. Further, in some cases of decision-making in which a vital piece of information is missing there is no definite subjective ought, and attempts to obtain one via subjective probabilities lead to self-contradiction.

In the face of universal doubt, a suitable and practicable task for theoretical reason is to generate new theories which we can agree to instate in view of a critical discussion which appears to show their explanatory superiority over their rivals. Popper has shown how that may be achieved by instating inherited theories and agreed observation statements, agreeing a set of explanatory merits, and encouraging open competition in which rival explanatory theories are proposed, developed, criticised, tested and defended. Periodically, the state of the critical discussion is reviewed and we agree to instate any explanatory theory which appears to us to be better than its rivals with regard to our agreed explanatory merits. A decision to instate a proposition does not conflict with the admission of universal doubt; in particular, it does not imply a statement that the proposition is better than its rivals in any respect. The experiences or evaluations which prompt the decision do not bear upon the truth of the proposition, so they are not reasons for believing the proposition, if we aim to believe what is true.

In the face of our fallibility, a suitable and practicable task for practical reason is to appraise rival ought-propositions, not with a view to discovering which is true, but with a view to deciding which ought-propositions to act on. We are rationally permitted to act on an ought-proposition which is contradicted by our instated propositions, if we are attempting to falsify those propositions. In such circumstances we avoid self-contradiction because a decision to act on an ought-proposition does not involve a decision to instate it.

It should be clear from our discussion that theoretical reason is a species of practical reason. We exercise our reason in attempts to solve problems, using arguments to evaluate rival solutions. The task of practical reason is to produce arguments that conclude in a *rating* of ought-propositions that helps us to decide which ought-proposition *to act on*, given our *aims* and *values*. The task of theoretical reason is more specific, namely, to produce arguments that conclude in a *rating* of theories that helps us to decide which theory to instate – effectively, which ought-proposition concerning instatement *to act on* – given the *aim* of generating new theories which we can agree to instate because it appears to us that they better exemplify the *values* articulated in our agreed explanatory merits.

And there is a further peculiarity of theoretical reason. In practical reason in general, even if our evaluation of rival ought-propositions identifies a specific ought-proposition as clearly better than all its rivals, we need not act on it: we are rationally entitled to try to falsify the conclusion of our evaluation by acting on one of the rivals. In contrast, in theoretical reason, if our critical discussion of rival theories appears to us to show that a particular theory has greater explanatory merit than its rivals, then, if we do not instate it, we are no longer engaged in theoretical reason, because theoretical reason, or the 'game of science' (Popper 1959, section 11), is *constituted* by a specific set of procedures, aims and values (for a discussion of the notion of constitutive rules see Searle 1969, pp. 33-42). Of course, in theoretical reason, once we instate a theory, we can then, if we wish, set out to falsify it or in some other way bring about a situation in which we oust it.

All reason is practical reason, since the exercise of reason is a goal-directed procedure, guided by values, in which we construct arguments to inform our decisions. Even pure deductive inference is a matter of deciding which proposition *to* infer from a set of premises (effectively, which ought-proposition concerning inference to act on). I offer an account of deductive reasoning elsewhere (Frederick 2020, chapter 3, section 3.2).

6 THE CONCEPTION OF REASONING AS ANALYSIS

Abstract. It is often claimed that in a valid deductive argument the conclusion is contained within the premises. That raises a question as to how valid arguments can be informative rather than question-begging; but the claim seems to be false in any case, since there appear to be many valid arguments in which the conclusion is not contained in the premises. I explain that the claim came to be accepted because it was a consequence of a widely held conception of inference as analysis that derived from early modern theories of the nature of mind, ideas and reasoning. I refute those theories and I reject the claim. I suggest an alternative account of inference as guessing logical relationships and then testing the guesses.

Keywords. Analysis; circular; deductive validity; guessing; inference; Immanuel Kant; Gottfried Leibniz; logic; *petitio principii*; question-begging; testing.

1. Introduction

It is often maintained that the conclusion of a valid deductive argument is contained in its premises. For instance, Michael Dummett says:

> For it [deductive inference] to be legitimate, the process of recognising the premisses as true must already have accomplished whatever is needed for the recognition of the truth of the conclusion (1973, p. 297; see also 1981 pp. 290-91).

David Miller avers:

> every deductively valid argument is question-begging in the
> sense that its conclusion is (implicitly or explicitly) included
> within its premises taken together (2005, p. 64).

Alan Musgrave agrees:

> the conclusion of a valid deductive argument is contained in
> its premises and says nothing new (2011, p. 2).

Such commonplace claims are puzzling in that, as Dummett recognises,

> If it [deductive inference] is to be displayed as fruitful, a sense
> must be acknowledged in which the conclusion represents
> new knowledge (1981, pp. 290-91; see also 1973, p. 297).

Further, as we will note shortly, there are cases of valid deductive
arguments for which the claim that the conclusion is contained within the
premises seems bizarre. In section 2, I report the views of some nineteenth-
century logicians on the matter. In section 3, I consider some valid
arguments the conclusions of which appear not to be contained in their
premises. In section 4, I offer an explanation for why philosophers and
logicians made the claim that the conclusion of a valid argument is
contained in its premises. In section 5, I refute the theories that underlie the
claim. In section 6, I conclude.

2. Some Nineteenth-Century Logicians

John Stuart Mill says:

> It is universally allowed that a syllogism is vicious if there be
> anything more in the conclusion than was assumed in the
> premises (1843, book 2 chapter 3, section 1, p. 197).

Augustus De Morgan, the man who gave us De Morgan's Laws, with which
every student of symbolic logic will be familiar, also says:

> That all premises [of a valid argument] do, when the argument
> is objectively considered, contain their conclusion, is beyond a
> doubt (1847, p. 257).

An argument is circular or question-begging or a *petitio principii* if its conclusion is assumed by its premises. Such an argument, though valid, is thought to be defective because 'it assumes what is to be proved.' A valid argument that is not defective is thus not question-begging. Yet, if the conclusion is assumed in the premises of *every* valid argument, then there are no non-defective valid arguments. Mill seems to accept that result:

> nothing ever was, or can be, proved by syllogism, which was not known, or assumed to be known, before (1843, book 2 chapter 3, section 1, p. 197).

He considers the following familiar argument:

(A)   All men are mortal
         Socrates is a man
         Therefore,
         Socrates is mortal.

He says that the premise, 'All men are mortal,' assumes the truth of the conclusion, 'Socrates is mortal.' Anyone who doubted or denied the conclusion, that Socrates is mortal, would also doubt or deny the premise, that all men are mortal (1843, book 2 chapter 3, section 1, pp. 197-98).

De Morgan objects that what Mill says is not quite right, because someone may be ignorant that Socrates is a man (1847, pp. 257-59). For example, suppose that, on a foggy day, Socrates is pointed out to me. I see a shape in the distance and I now know it to be Socrates but, for all I know, Socrates may be a man, a bear, a statue or something else. So, even if I know that all men are mortal, I cannot validly derive the conclusion that Socrates is mortal until I know that Socrates is a man. However, even with its second premise, says De Morgan, the syllogism (A) is not a gross *petitio*, and thus not a fallacy, not defective, because a person may have the premises in mind without having the conclusion in mind:

> Every collective set of premises contains all its valid conclusions; and we may fairly say that, speaking objectively of the premises, the assumption of them is the assumption of the conclusion; though, ideally speaking, the presence of the premises in the mind is not necessarily the presence of the conclusion (1847, p. 254).

Richard Whately spells out the point:

> the object of all reasoning…is merely to expand and unfold

> the assertions wrapt up, as it were, and implied in those with which we set out, and to bring a person to perceive and acknowledge the full force of that which he has admitted;—to contemplate it in various points of view;—to admit in one shape what he has already admitted in another (1853, p. 258).

That, says Whately, means that, while every valid deduction is circular, only those which are blatantly circular involve the fallacy of begging the question:

> *petitio principii* takes place when a premiss, whether true or false, is either plainly equivalent to the conclusion, or depends on it for its own reception. It is to be observed, however, that in all correct reasoning the premises must, virtually, imply the conclusion; so that it is not possible to mark precisely the distinction between the Fallacy in question [*petitio principii*] and fair argument (1853, p. 184).

3. Conclusions Not Contained in the Premises

The claim that in a valid argument the conclusion is contained, at least implicitly, in the premises, seems plausible for many arguments. It seems so for the valid syllogism (A), above, and also for the following slightly more complicated valid argument:

(B)   All wealthy people play chess
   If John is a phenomenologist, then John is wealthy
   John is a phenomenologist
   Therefore,
   John plays chess

However, there are other cases of valid argument for which it does not seem so plausible to maintain that the conclusion is contained in the premises. Consider:

(C)   It is not the case that John plays chess
   Therefore,
   It is not the case that: John is a phenomenologist, and if John is a phenomenologist then John is wealthy, and all wealthy people play chess.

That argument is valid. But none of the following assertions, taken from the logicians cited above, seems plausible:

- its complex conclusion is contained, or wrapt up, in its simple premise;
- there is nothing more in the conclusion than is assumed in the premise;
- anyone who admits the premise thereby admits the conclusion.

Imagine that I introduce my friend John to a person who has never studied philosophy and that I say 'It is not the case that John plays chess.' That person may understand the proposition I assert, but could he, by studying that proposition, arrive at the conclusion 'it is not the case that: John is a phenomenologist, and if John is a phenomenologist then John is wealthy, and all wealthy people play chess'? It seems doubtful. For one thing, the person concerned has no idea what a phenomenologist is; and no amount or quality of inspection of the simple premise, 'It is not the case that John plays chess,' will ever provide him with such an idea. No propositions about phenomenologists are, in any intuitive sense, contained in that premise: no one can discover any such propositions by examining or reflecting upon the proposition expressed in the premise.

John Watkins offers a recipe for constructing somewhat similar examples:

> Take some powerful new scientific theory which has recently led to a striking new prediction. Formulate all the premises used in the derivation of this prediction. Among these there will almost certainly be a truism known long before the new theory was invented. Call this a, call the theory together with all the other premises b, and call the prediction c. Then an impressive implication of the truism a is: if b then c (1973, pp. 8-9).

But if we go back to a time before the powerful new scientific theory had been invented, anyone announcing the deductively valid conclusion, if-b-then-c, from the premise, a, would surely have been saying something new, something that was not contained in the premise.

It might be objected that, still, the following assertion of De Morgan is true,

- the conclusion of (C) is *objectively* contained in its premise;

so the claim made by the nineteenth-century logicians should be understood as saying that the conclusion of a valid argument is objectively contained in its premises. Unfortunately, before that claim can be understood we need an account of the notion of 'objective containment.' It will plainly not help the esteemed logicians to stipulate that a proposition is objectively contained in another when the former is a logical consequence of the latter. That would render their claim empty: it would say only that the conclusion of a valid argument is a logical consequence of its premises. Any informative thesis about containment will have gone by the wayside.

4. Explanation of the Claim

Why was the curious claim that every valid argument is circular, because its conclusion is implicit, if not explicit, in its premises, so popular with nineteenth-century logicians? The answer, I think, lies in three interrelated components of the early-modern conception of logic, namely:

(i)   a building-block picture of concepts and propositions;
(ii)   a decompositional conception of analysis;
(iii)   a connection between necessary truth and analysis.

I explain those in turn.

The early modern philosophers, René Descartes, Pierre Gassendi, Antoine Arnauld, John Locke and their successors had a building-block conception of concepts and propositions. A concept, which was taken to be an *idea*, a mental item, was either simple or complex. A complex idea was composed out of other ideas which were its components; and a proposition, also conceived as mental, was composed out of ideas. Here are some passages from the *Port-Royal Logic*, by Arnauld and Nicole, which was the most influential logic book of the time, and which remained influential for two hundred years:

> The comprehension of an idea is the constituent parts which make up the idea, none of which can be removed without destroying the idea. For example, the idea of a triangle is made up of the idea of having three sides, the idea of having three angles, and the idea of having angles whose sum is equal to two right-angles, and so on (1662, p. 51).

> ...every proposition is necessarily composed of three elements – the subject-idea, the attribute and the joining of these two ideas (1662, p. 109).

Some later thinkers regarded concepts and propositions as abstract objects which are apprehended by the mind, but they retained the building-block conception. Bolzano says:

> That there are parts of ideas which are ideas themselves has always been accepted and so requires no further justification…It is self-evident that every part of an idea must be connected with every other part, if not directly, at least indirectly. For they are both parts of one and the same whole, namely the one idea in which they occur (1837, section 58).

> …every proposition is a composite and includes ideas as its parts. Scarcely anyone will dispute that. For even in the simplest proposition, even if its linguistic expression consists of a single word, we shall nevertheless on closer inspection become aware of many parts, which are nothing other than individual ideas (1837, section 123).

> The comment was made about ideas…that every one was capable of being a component of another. The same thing is true of propositions, that every one can be considered as a component of another proposition (1837, section 124).

Similar thoughts are found in the later logicians, Gottlob Frege (for example, 1914, p. 225) and Bertrand Russell (for instance, 1903, pp. 47-51).

The early moderns were familiar with analysis in the sense of physical dismantling, as in anatomy, in which the body is broken apart into its various components, and also from alchemy and early chemistry, in which the different constituents of a substance are separated. An analogous conception of analysis was familiar from geometry, where one tries to discover facts about a geometrical figure by bisecting it or splitting it into component figures (Koertge 1980, pp. 144-151). That is only *analogous*, because the geometrical figure is not literally broken up but is only imagined to be so. Similarly, in grammar, sentences and compound terms, the instances of which are spatial figures or temporal sounds, were, in imagination, split up into their component terms. Logic is concerned with concepts, propositions and arguments; but it deals with such abstract entities only insofar as they have linguistic expression. Logicians had followed grammarians in mentally decomposing sentences and compound terms into component expressions and, given the building-block conception of concepts and propositions, it was natural for them to assume that propositions and complex concepts could be dismantled into component concepts. However, use of the term 'analysis' in relation to concepts and propositions is even more metaphorical than its use in geometry and grammar, because concepts and propositions are not spatial or temporal. That point may have been hidden to the extent that concepts were taken to be ideas in the mind and the latter were thought, especially by empiricist philosophers, to be, or to be like, visual images. In short, it was thought that propositions and concepts are items which are open to inspection by the mind and that, if we examined them intently enough, we would be able to see the component concepts which constituted them.

Thus, in his *Logic*, which was part of his influential *Syntagma*, Gassendi says (1658, pp. 368-69) that, if we want to prove that man is a substance, we may proceed by resolving 'man' into his genus 'animal' and his differentia 'rational.' We then analyse 'animal' into 'living' (genus) and 'sentient' (differentia), and we similarly resolve 'living' into 'body' and 'animate.' Since a body is anything endowed with mass, and anything endowed with mass is a substance, we understand that the genus of 'body' is 'substance.' That passage from Gassendi shows the close connection between the idea of analysis and that of inference, which we can exhibit by converting the passage into a sequence of valid inferences in each of which a proposition appears to be drawn from another by means of analysis of a component concept:

(1)	Every man is rational and an animal	[true, by analysis of *man*]
(2)	Every man is living and sentient	[from (1), analysis of *animal*]
(3)	Every man is animate and body	[from (2), analysis of *living*]
(4)	Every man has mass	[from (3), analysis of *body*]
(5)	Every man is a substance	[from (4), analysis of *mass*].

Gottfried Leibniz (1679; 1686) and Immanuel Kant (1781/1787, Introduction, section iv) maintained that necessary truths are those that can be known by means of analysis of the concepts that they contain. There are two complications in their views that I will mention only to put on one side. First, Leibniz thought that *all* truths were knowable by analysis but that contingent truths required an infinite analysis which we were unable to carry out. Second, Kant thought that some necessary truths are knowable, not by analysis of the concepts they contain, but by analysis of the conditions of the possibility of experience. However, we can neglect those idiosyncrasies here. What became a standard doctrine in philosophy is that necessary truths are knowable by analysis of their content. When that is combined with the building-block conception of concepts and propositions, and with the decompositional conception of analysis, we end up with the false doctrine that the conclusion of a valid argument is contained in its premises, as I will now show.

Kant used the concepts of 'subject' and 'predicate' to explain the relevant notion of analysis. Thus, propositions like (1) are 'analytic' because the concept of being a man includes as parts the concepts of being rational and of being an animal. Such propositions are 'explicative.' They merely set forth more clearly what our concepts already contain, so they can be known by analysis. They are therefore necessary. In contrast, propositions like

All men are honest

are contingent because the concept of being honest is not a part of the concept of being a man. Such propositions are 'ampliative.' They go beyond analysis to say something new. We can know them only by appeal to experience. Leibniz's explanation (1765, p. 362) of necessary truths, which we can know by analysis, also talks of propositions in which the predicate is contained in the subject, such as

An equilateral rectangle is a rectangle

but in addition he includes conditional propositions in which the consequent proposition is contained in the antecedent proposition, such as:

If a figure with no obtuse angle can be a regular triangle, then a figure with no obtuse angle can be regular.

Every argument corresponds to a conditional proposition which takes the conjunction of the argument's premises as antecedent and the argument's conclusion as consequent. So, to syllogism (A) there corresponds the following conditional:

(a)   If all men are mortal and Socrates is a man, then Socrates is mortal.

If the argument (A) is valid, it is necessary that, if the conjunction of its premises is true, then its conclusion is true, which means that the argument's corresponding conditional, (a), is a necessary truth. Now, if all necessary truths are analytic, then the conditional corresponding to a valid argument is analytic, that is, on the Leibniz-Kant view, the proposition expressed in its consequent is contained in the proposition expressed in its antecedent. If that is so, then, on the building-block conception of propositions, and the taking-apart conception of analysis, we can discover the consequent by analysis of the antecedent. Therefore, on this view, the validity of an argument implies that its conclusion is contained in its premises and that we can find that conclusion in the premises if we mentally examine the premises intently enough. As Kant's contemporary, Moses Mendelssohn put it:

what else can the profoundest inferences do but analyze a concept and make distinct what was obscure? Such inferences cannot bring in what is not to be found in the concept, and it is easy to see that it is also not possible, by means of the principle of contradiction, to derive from the concept what is not to be found in it…The analysis of concepts is for the understanding nothing more than what the magnifying glass is for sight. It does not produce anything that was not to be found in the object. But it spreads out the parts of the object and makes it possible for our senses to distinguish much that they would otherwise not have noticed (1763, pp. 257-8, quoted in Beaney 2014).

The same thought seems to underlie the famous passage about deriving an 'ought' from an 'is' in Hume's *Treatise*: "a reason should be given, for what seems altogether inconceivable, how this new relation ['ought' or 'ought not'] can be a deduction from others ['is' or 'is not'], which are entirely different from it" (1740, p. 469).

Mill (1843, book 1, chapter 6, sections 1-4, pp. 147-51) and De Morgan (1847, p. 331) explicitly endorsed the three traditional dogmas (i) - (iii) about concepts, analysis and necessary truth. I guess that nineteenth-century logicians generally accepted them and that that is the explanation for why they held that in every valid argument the conclusion is contained in the premises.

5. Refutation of the Early Modern View

We have seen that there are valid arguments the conclusions of which do not appear to be contained in their premises, and the corresponding conditionals of those arguments, though necessary, are not analytic in the sense that the consequent can be derived by disclosing it within the antecedent. It follows that the conjunction of the three traditional dogmas, (i), (ii), (iii), is false. As it happens, I think that each of (i), (ii) and (iii) is false. I will briefly say why.

We have seen that there is such a thing as analysis, in the sense of dismantling, with regard to physical objects, as in anatomy, physics and chemistry, or, in an analogical sense, in geometry and grammar. However, there is no such thing as dismantling in the case of concepts or propositions because the building-block conception of such abstract entities is mistaken. The idea that propositions are built out of concepts, or out of any other elements, leads directly to the problem of the unity of the proposition. If a proposition can be analysed into a set of elements, then all we have is a collection of items, not a proposition that says something true or false. Russell (1903, pp. 49-50) struggled with that problem but despaired of a solution. Later he adopted Frege's solution (1892, pp. 54-55), which invokes the notion of the 'unsaturatedness' of concepts. However, Frege's solution is paradoxical and ad hoc, and it does not even solve the problem (Frederick 2017, section 4). It seems that the only way to solve the problem is to deny that propositions have components at all; though, of course, we must recognise that propositions are *related* to concepts (Frederick 2017, section 6.) For example, the proposition that all men are mortal is true if and only if everything that instantiates the concept *man* also instantiates the concept *mortal.* That fact does not require the concepts to be *parts* of the proposition.

The same applies to concepts. Concepts do not have other concepts as parts: being abstract, non-spatial and non-temporal, they are not the sort of entity that can have parts. Since no concept is compounded of other concepts, there can be no analysis which is a dismantling of concepts. However, concepts do have logical relations of involvement and exclusion with other concepts. Language is therefore misleading in that respect: the *term* 'rational animal' can be split into the two terms 'rational' and 'animal.' But when theorists say, for example, that the *concept* of a rational animal contains the concept of an animal, they are saying something which is literally false. The truth that lies behind their statement is that the concept *rational animal* logically involves the concept *animal.* That is to say that 'Socrates is a rational animal' entails 'Socrates is an animal' and similarly for other pairs of such subject-predicate propositions. Propositions about concept involvement are propositions about entailment relations between propositions. Similarly, to say that the concept *rational animal* excludes the concept *horse* is to say that 'Socrates is a rational animal' is incompatible with 'Socrates is a horse' and similarly for other pairs of such subject-predicate propositions.

Once we shift our attention from focusing on a particular concept to investigating its logical relations to other concepts, there seems to be no limit to the scope of our enquiry, since we can try to discover what relations our familiar concepts have to newly formulated concepts. Indeed, the formulation of new concepts *is* a matter of clarifying their relations to existing concepts. Philosophers who are proponents of 'conceptual analysis' have more or less come to recognise this. For some decades many of them, including A. J. Ayer (1946, pp. 31-33), Gilbert Ryle (1949, p. 9) and P. F. Strawson (1959, pp. 9-10; 1992, pp. 18-20), have preferred to view their enterprise as something like conceptual geography which traces the relations between different concepts, rather than breaking down a particular concept into its components. We can see that something similar applies to geometry too. For while, as I said in section 4, geometrical analysis often involves mentally breaking down a figure into components, it also often involves relating the figure to other figures. That is evident, for example, in the passage in Plato's *Meno* (1956, pp. 130-37) in which Socrates supposedly shows that the slave-boy has geometrical knowledge that he has never been taught but which is in some manner in abeyance. For, to show that the diagonal of a square is the side of a square which has twice the area of the original square, Socrates does not only divide the original square into two triangles, but also relates the original square to three other squares, and their components, which he draws. I said that Socrates only supposedly shows that the slave-boy had prior geometrical knowledge because Socrates is actually *teaching* the boy some geometry: he produces a demonstration and asks the boy questions the answers to which seem obvious given comparisons that Socrates has laid out.

But how does one go about discovering the logical relations between concepts? Is it a matter of mentally gazing at a collection of concepts in order to intuit their various relationships? Although some philosophers do write as if that is what is done (for example Huemer 2005, pp. 125-26), I suggest that there is no such activity. What philosophers actually do when they engage in so-called conceptual or logical analysis is guessing and testing. They develop theories about the logical relations between concepts, that is, they make conjectures about entailment or incompatibility relations between propositions, and they then test those conjectures by looking for counterexamples, or they develop the conjectures by means of tentative derivations which they may then test by looking for counterexamples (for a detailed exposition of that view of deductive inference see Frederick 2020, chapter 3, section 3.2). That, indeed, seems evident from the Socratic dialogues. The same applies in geometry: in the *Meno*, Socrates made a guess about the diagonal of a square and then tested it by drawing the other three squares and their diagonals and counting the four half-squares.

So, there is no such thing as conceptual or logical analysis, if such analysis is supposed to be something different to guessing and testing. We may, however, describe conceptual or logical analysis as *a particular kind* of guessing and testing, namely, guessing and testing a theory about logical relationships.

Having rejected the building-block conception of concepts and propositions, and the decompositional conception of their analysis, we must go on to reject the Leibniz-Kant explanation of necessary truth in terms of containment of one concept within another, or of one proposition within another. Indeed, once we replace talk of containment with talk of entailment relations between propositions, the Leibniz-Kant explanation of necessary truth begins to look circular, because it then explains necessary truth in terms of entailment; but it explained entailment in terms of necessary truth (recall section 4).

Finally, a further problem with the conception of inference as analysis is that the validity of some inferences is discoverable only empirically. For instance, if water is H_2O, then it is necessary that water is H_2O; and if Newton's Law of Gravity is a law of nature, then it is necessary that Newton's Law of Gravity obtains; yet both of these necessities (assuming, for the sake of argument, that both are true) were discovered empirically (Kripke 1980). So, from 'this is water' we may validly infer 'this is H_2O' (where 'this' in each sentence refers to the same thing), and from 'Socrates has mass' we may validly infer 'Socrates generates a gravitational force.' Those inferences are valid (in a 'model-centred' sense) because there can be no counterexample to them. Yet their validity was not discoverable *a priori* but only by empirical enquiry (they are invalid in a 'derivability-centred' sense).

6. Conclusion

A building-block picture of concepts and propositions that was widespread in the early-modern period gave rise to a theory of inference as grounded in analysis conceived as pulling apart. That in turn engendered the view that the conclusion of a deductively valid argument must be contained in its premises and thus that every deductively valid argument is circular. That was in conflict with the fact that, in many cases, the conclusions of deductively valid arguments are informative or surprising. Logicians negotiated that conflict by distinguishing implicit from explicit containment. However, the whole idea of concepts being contained within concepts or propositions, and of propositions being contained within other propositions, was misguided: non-spatial and non-temporal abstract entities, such as concepts and propositions, cannot be parts of each other or inside of each other. What makes a deductive argument valid is that it is necessary that if its premises are true, then its conclusion is true. We assess such necessities, fallibly, by producing derivations or by seeking counterexamples; but in contemplating counterexamples we sometimes have to take account of empirical discoveries.

The decompositional theory of conceptual or logical analysis has now largely been abandoned. Yet the claim is still often made that the conclusion of a valid argument is always contained in its premises. The claim seems to be an unfortunate hangover from an earlier but now discredited theory, akin to our contemporary talk of sunrise and sunset, except that the latter seems purely idiomatic, whereas the former can still lead theorists astray. The case of David Miller is considered in the next chapter.

7 ARGUMENT, KNOWLEDGE AND PERSUASION

Abstract. David Miller propounds a theory of objective knowledge from which he mistakenly derives some consequences about question-begging and persuasion that appear to be false. He makes a further claim about persuasion that also seems false. I argue that Miller's account of objective knowledge is explanatorily weak unless supplemented with an account of subjective knowledge and that the latter enables us to extricate Miller's theory from the falsehoods he associates with it.

Keywords: assertion; circular; growth of knowledge; logical content; David Miller; objective knowledge; persuasion; Karl Popper; question-begging; subjective knowledge; understanding.

1. Introduction

David Miller contends that every valid deductive argument "is *circular*... it *begs the question at issue*, or in more philosophical jargon commits the fallacy of *petitio principii*" (2006a, p. 70):

> Suppose that e is offered as a sufficient reason in favour of the proposition h. Then e will fail to establish or prove h unless e logically implies h. But if e logically implies h, h will not actually have been proved to be true, even though it may have been validly derived from e; for the derivation rests on an assumption, namely e, that itself asserts the truth of h (and perhaps more). As a proof of the truth of h the argument will be shamelessly circular. In an attempt to justify h the very question at issue will have been begged, and a rational person

91

> who recognizes the deductive connection between *e* and *h* and is not inclined to assent to *h* is not going to be inclined to assent to *e* either... (1994, p. 56).

> All valid arguments beg the question (1994, p. 58).

> Since... the conclusion... of every valid argument, is included entirely within its premises, the premises cannot lend any weight at all to the conclusion (2006a, p. 70).

Those contentions echo the claims of the nineteenth-century logicians considered in the previous chapter. Indeed, Miller cites John Stuart Mill with approval (1994, p. 58; 2005, pp. 63-64; 2006a, p. 70; 2006e, p. 265). The intellectual background to those claims was a philosophical doctrine that linked the inference of a conclusion in a deductively valid argument to an analysis of the content of the argument's premises. David Miller does not subscribe to that philosophical doctrine and he eschews its concern with subjective or psychological processes or items, such as ideas. However, he retains the doctrine that a proposition has a content with components and that a valid inference from the proposition will yield one of the components that is contained in that content. He connects that doctrine with five claims, four of which appear to be false.

In Section 2, I expound Miller's theory of objective knowledge and deductive validity as well as five claims that he makes in connection with it. I indicate some problems with four of the five claims. In Section 3, I introduce the notion of a person's understanding of a proposition and I use it to show that four of Miller's five claims are false. Miller's dismissal of the significance of subjective knowledge, and the associated notion of understanding, is what leads him to his mistaken claims; but without a theory of subjective knowledge Miller can give no coherent account of the growth of objective knowledge. Thus, Miller's theory is explanatorily weak. I conclude in section 4.

2. Miller's Theory

Miller's theory of objective knowledge derives from Karl Popper. For Popper, *objective knowledge* consists of abstract entities that have been expressed by humans in a physically realised code, particularly in articles, books and so on. It includes theories, problems, problem-situations, arguments, and states of a discussion. It is distinct from individuals' subjective knowledge, which is constituted by psychological states. When we create objective knowledge, by expressing our subjective knowledge in a code, we create at the same time all the logical consequences of the objective knowledge, whether or not we are aware (subjectively) of those consequences. For example, according to Popper, when we invented the natural numbers we also invented, without realising it, prime numbers, the distinction between odd and even numbers, and theorems and problems concerning those numbers. The latter were all parts of the objective knowledge that we created in inventing the natural numbers; but when we first created them they were not part of our subjective knowledge (Popper 1968a, pp. 106-7, 112, 115-18, 122, 138, 147; 1968b, pp. 155-56, 159-60; 1994c, lecture 2). As Miller puts it:

> objective knowledge consists of linguistically formulated hypotheses, theories, problems…; that is, of items that have discarded as much as possible of their psychological patrimony (2020, p. 6).

Miller, again following Popper, defines the *logical content* of a proposition as the class of its logical consequences (2020, p. 4). He calls what a proposition *says* or *asserts* its *assertoric content* (2020, p. 2) and he maintains that the assertoric content of a proposition is equal to its logical content (2020, pp. 2, 3). He thus affirms that a proposition says or asserts all of its logical consequences (2020, p. 2).

One difficulty of that view is the idea that abstract entities, such as propositions, are created by humans, rather than being eternal. However, I mention that difficulty only to put it on one side. The rest of the view seems to be little more than a set of definitions, and thus far unobjectionable, except that the terminology can be deemed to be misleading. Stripped of the misleading terminology, the theory can be stated as follows.

> MILLER'S THEORY. Objective knowledge consists of abstract entities, such as propositions, not psychological entities, such as beliefs. A proposition says something that may be true or false. Every proposition has a set of logical consequences, that is, other propositions such that, necessarily, if the proposition is true, then they are true too. Every proposition asserts each of its logical consequences, in the sense that, if what the proposition asserts is true, that guarantees that what each of its logical consequences asserts is also true.

The misleading terminology is that concerning content. Miller *defines* the 'logical content' of a proposition as the class of its logical consequences, so there is no commitment to the contention that a proposition *contains*, or is *constituted* by, its logical consequences, and thus no commitment to the view that a proposition *contains*, or is *constituted* by, its content. Yet the use of the word 'content' inevitably suggests the ideas of containment and constitution and strongly suggests the early-modern conception of a proposition as consisting of parts some of which may be other propositions. Indeed, the suggestion seems to be accepted by Miller himself:

> ...if the premises are already proved, then the conclusion, being a part of the premises... (2006a, p. 70).

However, Miller's theory does not need that false contention. I therefore strongly recommend that the term 'logical content' be repudiated. It is in any case unneeded since we can speak easily enough instead about the class of a proposition's logical consequences. We should also, for the same reasons, repudiate the term 'assertoric content,' which Miller makes equivalent to 'logical content.'

Miller draws four conclusions from his theory.

(1)   Since the conclusion of a valid argument is a logical consequence of its premises, the conclusion must be asserted by the conjunction of the premises (1994, p. 56; 2005, p. 65; 2006a, p. 70; 2020, p. 6).

(2)   Every valid argument is circular or question-begging (1994, p. 56; 2005, pp. 64, 65-66; 2006a, p. 70; also, though less explicitly, 2020, p. 2).

(3)   When valid deductive arguments are used to persuade, it is not the argument that does the persuading (2005, p. 66; 2006a, p. 68; 2020, p. 2).

(4)   Valid deductive arguments cannot be used to advance objective knowledge because all the logical consequences of a piece of objective knowledge are already asserted by that piece of objective knowledge (2006a, p. 69; 2020, pp. 2, 6-7).

He also affirms the following.

(5)   Valid deductive arguments *should not* be used to persuade (2005, p. 62; 2006a, p. 66; 2020, p. 2).

It seems clear that (1) does follow from Miller's theory and that it is unobjectionable given the way that the terms are defined. Every proposition asserts all its logical consequences in the sense that, if the proposition is true, then so are all of its logical consequences. However, there are some problems with (2), (3), (4) and (5).

Miller regards (2) as a straightforward consequence of (1). Yet (2) appears false in that philosophers and logicians customarily distinguish, *within* the class of valid deductive arguments, those that are circular or question-begging from those that are not. Standard examples of question-begging arguments are:

> God exists, therefore God exists;
> The Bible says that God exists and the Bible is the word of God, therefore God exists.

Such arguments are valid, so the conclusion is a logical consequence of the premises; and thus the premises assert the conclusion in the sense that, necessarily, if the premises are true, then the conclusion is true. However, what makes such arguments *question-begging* is that the premises assert the conclusion more or less *explicitly*; and thus anyone, or almost anyone, who understands the premises understands also that they assert the conclusion. That is not the case for all valid arguments. In a non-question-begging valid argument, the premises assert the conclusion in the sense that, necessarily, if the premises are true, then the conclusion is true, but one may understand the premises without realising that they assert the conclusion. A couple of examples of valid but non-question-begging arguments, involving Hobbes and Frege, are given in Section 3.

Conclusion (3) seems to be a straightforward consequence of (2), and thus also of (1) *if* (2) is a consequence of (1); for who could be persuaded by a question-begging argument, by an argument the premises of which more or less explicitly assert the conclusion? Yet there appear to be many examples of people being persuaded by valid arguments, which casts doubt on (2) as well as (3).

The fact that all of the logical consequences of a piece of objective knowledge are already asserted by that piece of objective knowledge does seem to imply that that deductive arguments cannot be used to advance objective knowledge *in a direct way*. However, if people can be persuaded by valid arguments and if such persuasion can *indirectly* contribute to the advancement of objective knowledge, then Miller's claim (4), and also his claim (5), will be false.

3. The Role of Understanding

We can detach the troublesome (2), (3), (4) and (5) from Miller's theory by distinguishing a proposition and a person's understanding of a proposition (compare Popper 1974a, pp. 19-20). The same, objective, proposition may be understood more fully by some persons than by others. For instance, a trained logician may see at a glance some logical consequences of a particular proposition that a non-logician might not see without help. The former understands the proposition to affirm those logical consequences; the latter does not. The former has a fuller understanding than the latter. The extent to which a person understands a given proposition may be different at different times. For example, once the non-logician has been shown how to derive some new consequences from the proposition, those consequences will (at least temporarily) become part of what that person understands by the proposition. A proposition asserts all of its logical consequences; but what a person understands it to assert will fall far short of that.

A valid argument is question-begging or circular for a particular person if the conclusion repeats part of what the person *understands* by the premises. Thus, an argument may be question-begging for one person but not for another, or for a particular person at one time but not at another; though many arguments, like the two mentioned in section 2, are question-begging for almost everyone. A valid argument which is not question-begging, not circular, for a particular person (at a particular time) is such that after, but not prior, to receiving the argument, the person's understanding of the conclusion was part of his understanding of the propositions that make up the premises. The argument therefore provides the recipient with new subjective knowledge that the conclusion follows from the premises (compare Cohen and Nagel 1934, pp.173-76). Therefore, Miller's (2) is false.

We saw that Miller maintains that every proposition asserts all of its logical consequences. That is true in the sense that, if the proposition is true, then so are all of its logical consequences. But there is a difference between what a *proposition* asserts and what a *person* understands himself to assert when stating the proposition. The person understands himself to assert what he understands by the proposition; he does not thereby understand himself to assert anything that he does not realise to be implied by it. For example, consider,

(6)   Karl Popper was born in 1902,
(7)   Karl Popper was born in 1902 or $E = mc^2$.

The *proposition* (6) *asserts* (7), because (6) logically implies (7), and thus the truth of (6) guarantees the truth of (7). However, a *person* who asserts (6) would not normally understand himself to be asserting (7), because (7) would not be part of what he understands by (6); he might even be mystified as to what (7) means.

The distinction between a proposition and a person's understanding of it allows us to explain how valid arguments may be used to persuade. Suppose that Alf asserts a proposition, *P*. Suppose that Freda does, but Alf does not, know that the proposition, P, logically implies the proposition, Q. Then Freda can sensibly attempt to persuade Alf of the truth of Q by showing him a derivation of Q from P. That is possible because, prior to the derivation, Alf's understanding of P leaves it open whether it is the case that if P then Q.

However, we need to consider in more detail Miller's claim, (3), that valid arguments cannot be used to persuade. First, Miller contends that, in rhetoric, there is a *misuse* of arguments to persuade:

> ...it would be foolish to deny that arguments are sometimes used to persuade others, and perhaps also oneself, of the truth, or of some doctrine asserted by some authority to be the truth. The field of activity known as rhetoric has as its task the investigation, classification, and evaluation of techniques of persuasion... Arguments can be used to persuade, and kitchen knives can be used to kill (2006a, pp. 67-68).

His contention seems to be that, in such cases, a person is persuaded not by appreciating logical implications but, rather, by some kind of manipulation. We can ignore such cases here.

Second, Miller claims that when arguments *appear* to persuade by rational means, that is, by appreciation of logical implications, it is not the *argument* that persuades but rather the *premises* of the argument:

> Persuasion fares no better as a goal of argumentation than does justification, for if anything persuades the listener of the truth of the conclusion it is the truth of the premises... The argument itself is no more than a way of presenting in a new light some or all of the content conveyed by the premises (2005, p. 66).

> ...it is never an argument acting alone that is persuasive (except perhaps to those people who are inordinately impressed by logical fireworks, and believe that cleverness is a sign of truth). What is normally needed for 'rational persuasion' is an argument accompanied by an assertion of the argument's premises... But then it is the premises that do almost all the work of conversion (2006a, p. 68).

> If a valid argument plays any part in persuading an agent that its conclusion is true, it is only by revealing that the agent is already persuaded that the premises are true. The argument itself has no persuasive power (2020, p. 2).

The following two examples illustrate the falsity of Miller's claim.

Thomas Hobbes was famously astonished by the proof of Pythagoras's theorem. He thought that Pythagoras's theorem was false but he became persuaded of its truth by seeing how it followed from propositions that seemed clearly true. Before the demonstration, Hobbes was persuaded of the premises but not of the conclusion because his understanding of the premises left it an open question as to whether the conclusion was true. After the demonstration Hobbes was persuaded of the premises *and* the conclusion. What persuaded Hobbes of the conclusion was the *argument*, the *derivation* of the conclusion from the accepted premises. That is *not* to say that Hobbes set out to persuade himself of, or even to discover the truth of, the theorem. At first, he was not persuaded of the truth of the theorem, even though he was persuaded of the truth of the premises; but after he saw the demonstration he was persuaded of the truth of the theorem.

Miller acknowledges such cases as Hobbes (2006a, p. 69) but he says that they show only that deductive argument may increase our *subjective knowledge* by revealing consequences we had previously not seen. It may not, he insists, increase our *objective knowledge* because surprising logical consequences are always a part of what is asserted by what we already know (2006a, p. 69; 2020, pp. 6-7). However, by increasing a person's subjective knowledge, by showing him consequences he had previously not seen, we may *persuade* him of the truth (or falsity) of something about which he was previously undecided or which he previously thought to be false (or true).

Gottlob Frege was famously shocked by Bertrand Russell's derivation of a contradiction from Frege's supposedly self-evident fifth axiom for arithmetic. Frege thereby discovered that his attempt to derive arithmetic from logic had failed. Frege had been convinced that his fifth axiom was true. When he read Russell's argument deriving a contradiction from that axiom, he was then persuaded that his fifth axiom was false. It was Russell's *argument*, the *derivation* of a contradiction from the axiom, that persuaded Frege that his axiom was false. Contra Miller, Russell did not persuade Frege of the falsity of his axiom by revealing to Frege that Frege was persuaded of the truth of his axiom. He did it by providing an *argument* that derived a contradiction from the axiom.

Incidentally, there is no claim here that Russell *intended* to persuade Frege of anything; by criticising Frege's axiom Russell *did* persuade Frege of its falsity, whether he intended that or not. It is also irrelevant that Frege tried to repair his system, that is, that he had not been persuaded that his enterprise should be abandoned. For he *was* persuaded that his faulty axiom needed changing after being persuaded by Russell's argument that the axiom is false.

Miller seems also to be mistaken when he says (see quotation above,

2006a, p. 68) that 'rational persuasion' normally requires an argument accompanied by an assertion of the argument's premises. One may be persuaded by an argument that proposition P implies proposition Q without affirming proposition P; indeed, if one is already persuaded that Q is false, the argument may persuade one that P is false.

Thus Miller is quite wrong when he says:

> Only those who are impressed by style rather than by substance could be convinced by an argument, rather than by what it is that the premises assert (2005, p. 66).

Therefore, Miller's claim (3) is false.

Miller affirms his claim (5), that valid deductive arguments *should not* be used to persuade because:

> persuasion reeks of authority, of the attitude of the person who wants to teach rather than to learn (2005, p. 62);

> it encourages dogmatism… [and] impedes the search for truth (2006a, p. 66)

> Even if arguments could be used to persuade… we should ask why they should be. A rational and open-minded person does not need to be persuaded (2020, p. 2).

In science, arguments are used to compare rival hypotheses and rate them as better or worse. The point is not necessarily, perhaps not usually, to persuade people to accept the (currently) best hypothesis; but, it seems, one point may be to persuade advocates of the weaker hypotheses that they have work to do to improve their theories. There is no attempt to justify anything: all may accept that the premises of the arguments are revisable and merely reflect the current state of the debate. Yet everyone may, more or less, agree to the premises, concerning

- the hypotheses under discussion
- the various problems they solve or fail to solve
- accepted observation-statements
- background knowledge
- the principles of evaluation of hypotheses

and they may accordingly be persuaded by an argument that a particular hypothesis is currently better than the others. Indeed some scientists may intend the critical argument to persuade at least some other scientists to abandon work on some of the hypotheses that are rated poorly and perhaps to join with them in developing further one of the more successful hypotheses. That is, persuasion can contribute to the growth of objective knowledge by recruiting scholars to more promising programmes. Since we aim to promote the growth of objective knowledge and since persuasion can help in that aim, Miller's (5) is false: it is not the case that valid deductive arguments *should not* be used to persuade.

It therefore follows that Miller's (4) is false. A valid deductive argument *can* be used to advance objective knowledge. For instance, if the argument shows a researcher, Betty, that the theory on which she has been working lacks the explanatory strengths of a rival theory, it may persuade her that the rival theory is more promising than the one she has previously favoured; and that may prompt her to switch from working on the latter to working on the former. If Betty is talented, or even just lucky, her contributions to research on the more promising theory may include new auxiliary hypotheses that generate novel falsifiable predictions that survive testing; in which case those auxiliary hypotheses will constitute an advance in objective knowledge. A valid argument, through persuasion that influences action, can thus be used to advance objective knowledge.

4. Conclusion

Miller's concern is with *objective knowledge*. A proposition asserts each of its logical consequences in the sense that, if the proposition is true, then so is each of its logical consequences. Valid arguments help to identify or clarify the logical consequences of a proposition; they do not make an addition to those consequences. So, valid arguments cannot be used *directly* to increase our objective knowledge. All of that seems true.

Miller acknowledges that subjective knowledge is a precondition of objective knowledge (2020, p. 6):

> The existence of the psychological states and processes that feature so largely in traditional, and contemporary, subjectivist epistemology is not denied by critical rationalism, and it is appreciated that without subjective knowledge there would be no objective knowledge. (Without shoemaking subjects there would be no shoes, but shoes are not subjective entities.)

Yet he is quite dismissive of subjective knowledge:

> they were part of the *objective scientific knowledge* of those earlier

times; that is, part of knowledge in the only sense that is of much significance to critical rationalism (2020, p. 6).

However, Miller's eschewal of subjective knowledge, and the associated notion of a person's understanding of a proposition, leaves much unexplained. What a person understands when she understands a proposition falls short of all of the proposition's logical consequences, so when she asserts the proposition, she does not understand herself to be asserting all of its logical consequences (she may, indeed, explicitly deny some of them). The fact that one proposition asserts a second does not tell us whether a particular *person* who asserts the first understands herself to assert the second. That depends upon how fully she understands the first proposition. A valid argument, by providing a derivation, can help a person to see some logical consequences that she had not seen before; it can thereby increase her subjective knowledge. Valid argument may also be used to persuade a person to accept a proposition by showing how it follows from another proposition already accepted, or to reject a proposition by showing that some of its consequences are unacceptable. These uses of valid argument to persuade can be successful only if the arguments are *not* circular, are *not* question-begging. That is, they can be successful only if the conclusion of the argument is not part of what the recipient *person* understands herself to be asserting when she asserts the conjunction of the premises. The reference to a person's understanding of a proposition allows us to distinguish question-begging arguments as a proper subset of valid arguments and to see how valid deductive arguments can be used to persuade, thereby increasing a person's subjective knowledge. Miller's false contentions, that all valid arguments are question-begging and that when a valid argument is used for rational persuasion it is the premises (rather than the derivation) that do the persuading, result from his refusal to take sufficient account of subjective knowledge and what persons understand. What is surprising, given Miller's dismissal of subjective knowledge, is that he talks about persuasion at all, since persuasion belongs to the phenomena of subjective knowledge.

Finally, it must be acknowledged that we cannot understand the growth of objective knowledge without taking account of subjective knowledge. It is people who contribute to the growth of knowledge and they do so by making use of their own limited understanding of the objective knowledge that exists. Valid arguments can help people to improve that understanding. If we are to understand and evaluate moves in the 'game of science,' we need to understand the problem situation facing an enquirer, which means that we need to understand how the enquirer understands the set of propositions that create the problem. We explain moves in the game of science by reference to the logic of the situation; but the situation includes the subjective knowledge of the actors in that situation. How a person acts depends upon *her understanding* of the propositions describing the situation, not on the full logical consequences of those propositions.

Popper contended that social-scientific explanations appeal to the logic of the situation *rather than* to idiosyncratic differences in subjective knowledge (Popper 1994a). He had in mind systematic sciences like economics where what a person would do is assumed to be what anyone would do in the same situation (Popper 1994a, p. 171). However, he also acknowledged that in historical explanations, that is, explanations of particular incidents involving particular individuals, the idiosyncratic understanding of the situation by key individuals can have a decisive effect on outcomes (Popper 1994a, pp. 172, 178-79). Ironically, when he considers Galileo's theory of the tides, he offers an explanation in terms of the state of objective knowledge (1968b, pp. 170-80), though toward the end of his discussion he acknowledges the importance of subjective knowledge when he says that we need to reconstruct the problem situation in a way that is adequate to the situation *as the agent saw it* as distinct from the situation as it was (Popper 1968b, p. 179). The point is developed by John Watkins (1970, 206-216) who shows how a puzzling naval disaster depended on the mistaken subjective knowledge of some of the agents involved. The growth of objective knowledge cannot be understood or explained without taking account of the subjective knowledge of its contributors, including their use of valid arguments to persuade. Since the use of valid arguments to persuade can assist in the growth of objective knowledge, it ought not to be deprecated.

8 ARE THERE ANY GOOD REASONS?

Abstract. David Miller argues that there are no good reasons, either sufficient or insufficient. I show that most of his arguments are invalid or unsound. Several of his arguments depend upon the false claim that every deductively valid argument is circular. I accept one of Miller's arguments for the conclusion that there are no good reasons which are less-than-sufficient. I accept one of his arguments to the conclusion that there are no probative sufficient reasons. But I explain how there are epistemic sufficient reasons which are relative to the game of science and how their existence is consistent with Miller's main contentions while avoiding Miller's apparently anarchic account of our knowledge.

Keywords. Epistemic reasons; insufficient reasons; game of science; good reasons; David Miller; Karl Popper; probative reasons; sufficient reasons.

1.Introduction

In chapter three of his *Critical Rationalism* (1994), David Miller contends that there are no good reasons. In sections 3.1 and 3.2 of his chapter Miller affirms the following (1994, pp. 52-55):

- there are subjective reasons (about which he says no more);
- a good reason is a sufficient, or partly sufficient, favourable or positive reason for accepting or rejecting a hypothesis or implementing a policy;
- there are no good reasons;
- we need no good reasons.

Miller offers further relevant considerations in his 2005 and 2006a.

A big problem with Miller's thesis is making sense of it. To help with that I make a distinction within good reasons between those that are epistemic and those that are not. An epistemic reason is one that concerns whether to accept a proposition as knowledge. It seems clear from Miller's discussion that his primary concern is with epistemic reasons. However, unlike Miller, within epistemic reasons I distinguish those that are probative from those that are not. A probative reason is a good reason for accepting a proposition as true. A probative *sufficient* reason is one that proves the proposition for which it is a reason. A probative *partly sufficient* reason is one that in some sense supports, or tends to prove, the truth of that proposition. An epistemic good reason that is not probative does nothing to prove or support the truth of the proposition for which it is a reason; but it does imply that the proposition has some other epistemic status. It may be a good reason for accepting a proposition as knowledge. To put it another way, an epistemic good reason is an indicator of epistemic status; a probative good reason is an indicator of truth; but being true is not the only valuable epistemic status. For instance, Newton's theory of motion and gravity is normally thought to have the status of knowledge and it is taught as such in schools and universities; but it is, in light of Einstein's theory of general relativity, thought to be false (because space and time are not absolute, there is no force of gravity, Newton's inverse-square formula is incorrect, and so on).

The only non-epistemic good reasons that Miller mentions are those that are reasons for or against a course of action; but he does not discuss those in chapter 3 of his 1994 and I will not discuss them directly here, though much of what I will say in section 5 is relevant, as is my Forthcoming.

I agree with Miller that there are no probative reasons but I criticise and reject some of his arguments. I disagree with Miller's claim that there are no epistemic good reasons. The following table may help. The headings '**Suff.**' and '**Insuff.**' are short for *sufficient* and *insufficient*, respectively.

<table>
<tr><th rowspan="3"></th><th colspan="2" rowspan="2">Non-Epistemic</th><th colspan="4">GOOD REASONS</th></tr>
<tr><th colspan="2">Epistemic
Probative</th><th colspan="2">*Non-Probative*</th></tr>
<tr><th>Suff.</th><th>Insuff.</th><th>Suff.</th><th>Insuff.</th><th>Suff.</th><th>Insuff.</th></tr>
<tr><td>Miller</td><td>?</td><td>No</td><td>No</td><td>No</td><td>No</td><td>No</td></tr>
<tr><td>Me</td><td>Yes</td><td>No</td><td>No</td><td>No</td><td>Yes</td><td>No</td></tr>
</table>

In section 2, I expound and discuss critically Miller's arguments against sufficient reasons. In section 3 and the appendix, I expound and discuss critically Miller's arguments against less-than-sufficient, or insufficient, reasons. In section 4, I present and criticise Miller's defence of his view that we can proceed in a rational way without reasons. In section 5, I give an account of epistemic sufficient reasons drawn from the writings of Karl Popper. I argue that this is the account that Miller should have given and I show how Miller's claims about the absence of good reasons can be made consistent with it. In short: epistemic good reasons exist but are relative; the good reasons that Miller rejects are absolute and do not exist. In section 6, I conclude.

2. Probative Sufficient Reasons

In section 3.3 of his chapter, Miller (1994, pp. 55-57) offers two arguments against *sufficient* good reasons, though his initial presentation does not distinguish the two. He begins:

> Suppose that e is offered as a sufficient reason in favour of the proposition h. Then e will fail to establish or prove h unless e logically implies h. But if e logically implies h, h will not actually have been proved to be true, even though it may have been validly derived from e; for the derivation rests on an assumption, namely e... (1994, p. 56).

I cut the passage short because it goes on to state one of the two arguments that Miller employs. We will consider those arguments shortly; but first we need to understand what Miller's purpose is. Of course, we know he is trying to show that there are no properly sufficient reasons; but that claim may be interpreted in different ways.

Suppose that e logically implies h. Then the truth of e is sufficient for the truth of h; or, more briefly, e is sufficient for h. We might well express that thought by saying that e is a sufficient reason for h, assuming that e is true. Let us say that, if e is true and e implies h, then e is an *ontological* sufficient reason for h. The existence of ontological sufficient reasons is a simple consequence of the fact of logical implication: every true proposition is an ontologically sufficient reason for each of its logical consequences. But Miller is not concerned with ontological sufficient reasons at all: his denial of the existence of sufficient reasons is not intended as a denial of ontological sufficient reasons. His concern is not with facts that necessitate other facts; it is rather with propositions that may be *employed by us* to try to *establish* another proposition, that is, to *prove a proposition to be true*. Miller's concern is with *probative* sufficient reasons; and, in his denial that there are any sufficient reasons at all, he seems entirely to have overlooked non-probative sufficient reasons.

The presentation of Miller's two arguments against the existence of probative sufficient reasons will be clearer if we reverse their order. Miller's second argument is one that derives from the ancient sceptics via Sextus Empiricus (2000, book I, chapter xv), which Miller expounds somewhat as follows (1994, pp. 56-57):

(i)   a probative sufficient reason for a proposition must logically imply that proposition;

(ii)   a probative sufficient reason for a proposition must not be open to doubt (otherwise it could not be used to prove its implications);

therefore,

(iii)   every probative sufficient reason needs a sufficient reason (to remove doubt about itself);

therefore,

(iv)   the concept of a probative sufficient reason involves a vicious infinite regress.

Although it could be spelt out in more detail, I think that this traditional sceptical argument is correct. The suppressed premise is that there can be no self-evident propositions (otherwise, (iii) does not follow). But that suppressed premise should be uncontroversial in light of Russell's Paradox, which showed that a proposition that seemed to be self-evident (Frege's fifth axiom for arithmetic) was actually inconsistent (Russell 1959, p. 58), thereby casting doubt upon every claim of self-evidence. So we can agree with Miller that *there are no probative sufficient reasons*.

But what exactly is it that a probative sufficient reason would be sufficient for, if there were such a thing? Miller talks of reasons for a proposition, or in favour of a proposition. But that language is appropriate to ontologically sufficient reasons. Probative sufficient reasons relate a proposition to *us*. They are concerned with *us* trying to *prove* a proposition to be true; they are sufficient reasons for us *to accept a proposition as true*. That is why they must be *certain* and why the ever present possibility of *doubt* rules out probative sufficient reasons (Miller 1994, pp. 56-57). So, a probative sufficient reason for a proposition h is a proposition e such that,

(a)   if we accept e as true, we must accept h as true, on pain of inconsistency;

(b)   we must accept e as true, on pain of inconsistency, because we are certain of its truth.

However, no propositions can meet the second condition. So, there can be no probative sufficient reason for *h*. Further, every proposition is such that there is some proposition such that, *if we accept the latter* then we must accept the former, on pain of inconsistency (because every proposition is implied by other propositions), so the first condition by itself cannot make *e* a sufficient reason of any kind.

Miller's first argument against probative sufficient reasons runs as follows (1994, pp. 55-56):

(i)   a probative sufficient reason for a proposition must logically imply that proposition;

(ii)   a probative sufficient reason for a proposition must not be open to doubt (otherwise it could not be used to prove its implications);

(v)   any proposition that logically implies another asserts that other;
therefore,

(vi)   any proposition that logically implies another is as much open to doubt as that other;
therefore,

(vii)   any proposition that logically implies another cannot be a sufficient reason for that other.

The argument is unsound because premise (vi) is false. Miller affirms (vi) because he maintains that every deductively valid argument begs the question. But that is false, as we saw in our previous chapter. Hobbes, recall, doubted Pythagoras's theorem but he did not doubt Euclid's axioms, which implied it. When he saw the derivation that showed that the axioms implied the theorem, it dispelled his doubt about the theorem rather than transmitting his doubt from theorem to axioms.

Thus, Miller presents two arguments for the impossibility of probative sufficient reasons. The second argument, which we considered first and which derives from the ancient sceptics, succeeds. The first argument, which we considered second, is unsound as it depends upon a false claim, namely, that any proposition that logically implies another is as much open to doubt as that other, which in turn depends upon Miller's mistaken contention that every deductively valid argument is a *petitio principii*.

3. Probative Insufficient Reasons

Miller next turns to consider good but insufficient reasons. He offers the following two arguments:

(viii)   the circularity of valid deductive argument means that uncertain premises that logically imply their conclusion cannot be good insufficient reasons for the conclusion (1994, p. 59);

(ix)   if a proposition *e* which does not logically imply another *h* is claimed (in some weaker way) to *support h*, it will fail to provide even an insufficient reason for *h* unless we have a reason for *e*; but that takes us back to the sceptical infinite regress (1994, pp. 59-62).

We cannot accept (viii) because it depends upon Miller's false contention that every deductively valid argument is circular. But (ix) seems to tell against probative insufficient reasons whether the insufficiency depends upon the doubtfulness of the reasons or their weaker-than-entailment relation to their conclusion.

In later work, however, Miller seems doubtful about (ix). He says that, since an invalid inference is supposed only to make its conclusion reasonable, it might not be necessary that its premises be proved, in which case it is not vulnerable to the traditional sceptical infinite-regress argument (2006a, pp. 70-71). Still, he adds, offering a third argument, an invalid inference is not a good one: a (probative) sufficient reason for a hypothesis, if there were such a thing, would tell us that the hypothesis is true; but nothing follows concerning the truth of the hypothesis if the reason is insufficient (2006a, p. 73). As he tersely put it in the earlier book: an insufficient reason for a hypothesis is not a sufficient reason for the hypothesis (1994, p. 64). Thus, insufficient reasons are not probative; that is to say, there are no probative insufficient reasons.

Miller offers a fourth argument against the notion of support (1994, pp. 62-63). The argument is invalid but it is somewhat technical, so I expound and criticise it in the appendix. The argument fails because:

- it depends upon the claim, which we saw in Chapter 7 to be false, that every valid deductive argument is circular or question-begging;

- even with regard to arguments that *are* circular because the premise is a conjunction and the conclusion is one of its conjuncts, Miller's argument depends upon the false claim that the part of the content of the premise that goes wholly beyond the content of the conclusion can be expressed by a material conditional of the form 'premise-if-conclusion.'

So, Miller offers four arguments intended to show that there are no insufficient good reasons. The *first* argument is unsound because it depends upon the false claim that every valid deductive argument is circular or question-begging. The *second* argument, which depends upon the sceptical concern about whether an uncertain reason can support a proposition, seems doubtful, as Miller concedes, since insufficient reasons are supposed only to make their conclusions reasonable. The *fourth* argument is complex and breaks down at two separate points. However, the *third* argument seems sound: an insufficient reason for accepting a proposition as true says nothing about the truth of that proposition. Thus, there are no probative insufficient reasons. The argument generalises to all good reasons: an insufficient reason for accepting a proposition as having a specific virtue does not say whether or not the proposition has that virtue. There are no good insufficient reasons: insufficient reasons are no good.

4. Doing Without Reasons?

We have agreed with Miller, despite rejecting most of his arguments, that there are neither probative sufficient reasons nor probative insufficient reasons. Supposed probative sufficient reasons do not survive sceptical doubt and supposed probative insufficient reasons are nugatory. How then can we proceed epistemically *in a rational way*?

Miller contends that no reason at all is needed for classifying a proposition as true. With regard to action, Miller affirms, all we need is a true prediction; there is no need or use for a good reason to think that it is true (1994, pp. 64-66).

The obvious objection is that, while it may be true that all we need is true propositions or true predictions, that is of no help to us unless we can discover which propositions or predictions are true. Probative sufficient or, failing those, insufficient reasons, were intended to help with that task. In their absence what can Miller offer?

Miller says that we may propose any hypothesis we like so long as, if it is false, it can be overthrown and rejected. The role that logic plays is a negative or critical one: it is used to derive from hypotheses propositions that can be tested by experience, or by other means; and if those propositions turn out to be false, the hypotheses are rejected (1994, p. 67).

Miller considers the objection that, if h implies e, and e turns out to be false, it seems that **not-e** is a reason against h, and thus a reason for **not-h**. But, then, on Miller's view, **not-e** must beg the question of **not-h**, since it implies it; and if there is no good reason for **not-e**, then there is none for **not-h** either, and thus no reason to reject h (1994, pp. 67-68). All refutations and rejections seem ultimately arbitrary. Miller is here turning on his own view the circularity and sceptical objections that he made against probative reasons. His responses to the objections are as follows.

First, with regard to circularity, he says that, although **not-e** may beg the question of **not-h**, it does not beg the question of h, which is the question at issue (1994, p. 68). But that seems false. If h is the question at issue, then the question is *whether* **h**, which is to say that the question is whether **h** or **not-h**; so if **h** is the question at issue, so is **not-h**. Therefore, if **not-e** *does* beg the question of **not-h**, it also begs the question of **h**. So, Miller's rebuttal of the circularity objection fails; but since the circularity objection fails anyway, that does not matter.

Second, with regard to the sceptical objection, Miller says that a chain of justification for **h** will always stop at something doubtful and thus leave **h** open to question, so **h** is always at issue. But advance along a critical chain leads us to new questions. For instance, I propose **h**; you derive from it **e** and propose **not-e**; I derive **k** from **not-e** and claim **not-k**. Since **k** need not be **not-h**, my assertion that **not-k** may be quite a different issue from whether **h** is true (1994, pp. 68-70).

It is not clear how that contrast is supposed to answer the charge that critical reasons are just as doubtful as justificatory ones. In any case, the contrast seems not to hold, because a similar dialectic can happen in the case of attempted justification. For instance, I question **h**; you deduce **h** from **j**; I doubt **j**; you derive the unappealing **m** from **not-j**; I provide an argument for **m**; you derive the negation of one of my premises from **n**, and we are now discussing a question quite different from the **h** with which we started. So Miller fails to rebut the sceptical objection or to offer a legitimate (and illuminating) contrast between justificatory and critical strategies.

Miller recognises that these defences may seem casuistic (1994, p. 70). A better response, he thinks is to reject negative reasons as well as positive ones.

> We do not need reasons against a hypothesis in order to classify it as false (nor against a course of conduct in order to classify it as foolish). All we need is a false consequence of it; not... a reason to suppose that we have identified a false consequence... It follows... that we are in permanent peril of classifying statements incorrectly and of doing things wrongly... It does not follow that we do not often get things right...
>
> ...And it is because we are aiming at truth that our classifications are not arbitrary, even though they may well be wrong... [For,] we shall test [a] hypothesis, perhaps showing that it has consequences that contradict other statements that are classified as true. These other statements will not supply us with a reason for rejecting [the hypotheses]. But if we are concerned about truth we shall not persevere with them all... ; we shall have to decide which one of them to reject. We may do this wrongly (1994, pp. 70-71; the ellipses show where

merely redundant passages have been removed).

I guess that people in general will find puzzling what Miller says there. On his view, we make conjectures and we reject a conjecture if it has a false consequence. How do we tell whether we have a false consequence? We need no reason to classify a consequence as false, he says. That sounds wholly arbitrary. He admits that we may make the classification wrongly; but, he claims, we often get things right. "Truth and falsehood do get separated" (1994, p. 71) But he does not explain how that claim can be anything but arbitrary in the absence of any reasons to classify a statement one way rather than another. He says that classification without reasons is not arbitrary because our aim is truth, which means that we can reject a statement that contradicts another statement that is classified as true. But that assumes that we have already classified some statements as true, independently of any reason for doing so, which still leaves it all ultimately arbitrary. The only clue we get as to how arbitrariness is to be avoided is his cursory reference to *testing* a hypothesis, given that he said earlier (1994, p. 67) that we may test a proposition "by experience, or by other means." But testing a hypothesis by experience means comparing it against observation statements; and if we are to end up classifying a hypothesis as false by this means, then we need an observation statement that is classified as true; and since there are no good reasons for classifying a statement as true, this still leaves things entirely arbitrary.

That is all very unsatisfactory. Having rejected good reasons, Miller seems left with 'anything goes.' We can avoid following Miller into that quagmire by recognising that there are good, and thus sufficient, epistemic reasons that are not probative.

5. Non-Probative Sufficient Reasons

Here is my attempt to say what Miller *should* have said. It is taken from Popper (1957b, 1959).

The game of science is defined by its aim and by a set of rules specifying which moves in the game are permissible, or impermissible, or obligatory, under specified circumstances. The rules are subservient to the aim: they are designed to help players to achieve the aim of the game and to prevent them from undermining the achievement of the aim. So long as we are playing the game, the rules specifying impermissible or obligatory moves give *sufficient reasons* for not making a particular move or for making a particular move, respectively. Those reasons are reasons of instrumental rationality: he who wills the end wills the necessary means. The reasons are therefore sufficient relative to the aim; they are not sufficient reasons for a person who does not have the aim. A rough specification of the game of science follows.

The aim of the game is to obtain explanations that are better than those that we currently have. In this game, one explanation, $E2$, counts as better than another explanation, $E1$, *other things being equal,* if one of the following hold:

(b1) $E2$ is falsifiable but $E1$ is not;
(b2) $E2$ explains what $E1$ explains and some other things besides;
(b3) $E2$ provides a unified solution to problems that were explained in different ways by $E1$;
(b4) $E2$ generates surprising falsifiable predictions that are not derivable from $E1$ and those predictions survive testing;
(b5) $E2$ corrects $E1$, that is, it shows that some falsifiable predictions of $E1$ that were thought to be successful were actually not successful and $E2$ explains why they *seemed* successful.

An explanation is *falsifiable* if and only if it is inconsistent with an observation statement, that is, a statement describing a situation we could *conceivably* observe with our actual powers of observation; and it is *falsified* if and only if it is inconsistent with an *accepted* observation statement.

Rules specifying permissible moves include:

(R1)   anyone may join the game of science (there is no limit on the number of players);
(R2)   any player may identify a problem to be solved;
(R3)   any player may propose a new explanatory theory to solve an identified problem;
(R3)   any player may criticise any identified problem or any explanatory theory;
(R4)   any player may carry out observations to try to falsify any explanatory theory or any accepted observation statement;
(R5)   any player may try to rescue a falsified theory or observation statement from falsification.

Rules specifying obligatory moves include:

(R6)   if a player makes an observation which he describes with the observation statement $s1$, and other players make observations which they describe with the statements $s2$, ...sn, and the statements $s1$-sn differ, if at all, only with respect to space-time co-ordinates, then all players *must* accept $s1$, that is, $s1$ counts as an accepted observation statement (for example, the statement made by use of the sentence 'here is a black swan' in a particular time and place);

(R7)   if a player derives a contradiction from the conjunction of an accepted observation statement and an explanatory theory, $E1$, and other players check and accept the derivation, then all players *must* accept that $E1$ is falsified, that is, $E1$ counts as a falsified theory;

(R8)   if a player compares an explanatory theory, $E1$, with an explanatory theory, $E2$, with regard to the properties (b1)-(b5) and infers that $E1$ is a better explanation than $E2$, and other players check his assessment and very few dispute it, then all players *must* accept that $E1$ is a better explanation than $E2$;

(R9)   if, by rule (R8), sufficient players have accepted that explanatory theory, $E1$, is a better explanation than explanatory theories $E2$-En, where all currently available rivals to theory $E1$ are among theories $E2$-En, then all players *must* accept that $E1$ is the currently best theory in its field, that is, $E1$ counts as the currently best theory in its field;

(R10)   any theory that has at any time been the currently best theory in its field, and that has also passed a severe test, counts as knowledge.

Rules specifying impermissible moves prohibit pseudo-scientific stratagems, including the following:

(R11)   a player may accept that an explanatory theory has been rescued from falsification only if the inconsistency between theory and observation statement is removed in such a way that

- a theory, $E1$, in the set of theories that generated the inconsistency is replaced by another theory $E2$ and
- $E2$ is better than $E1$ in at least one of the ways (b1)-(b5) without also being worse than $E1$ in some other way.

Thus, the rules of the game of science specify sufficient reasons for accepting an observation statement, for accepting a theory as falsified, for accepting one theory as a better explanation than another, for accepting a theory as the currently best available in its field, and for rejecting an attempt to rescue a theory from falsification. None of these sufficient reasons are probative sufficient reasons: they are not sufficient reasons for accepting a proposition as true or as false. But they are sufficient reasons, *within the game of science*, for accepting particular classifications of propositions. To play the game of science is to abide by its rules (cheats are only pretending to play the game). So one who is playing the game of science is *required*, on pain of inconsistency, to accept a proposition as an accepted observation statement, or as a falsified theory, or as the currently best theory in its field, and so on, when the rules of the game decree such a move. Of course, no one is required to play the game of science; and sufficient reasons for moves within the game of science are not sufficient reasons for people who are not playing the game of science. They are relative sufficient reasons, that is, reasons that are sufficient relative to the game of science.

Reasons that are sufficient relative to the game of science, though not probative, are *epistemic*. Unfortunately, philosophers generally still insist that a proposition cannot be a part of knowledge unless it is known to be true or unless it is true. But as science education shows, many theories that are regarded as false are yet regarded as components of scientific knowledge (recall the example of Newton's theory, given in section 1). So, reasons for accepting a theory as knowledge, or for making other important moves in the game of science, need have no connection with truth; in fact, none of the sufficient reasons within the game of science is a reason for accepting any proposition as true. As we saw in sections 2 and 3, there are no probative reasons. What makes a theory scientific knowledge (as specified by the rules of the game of science) is that it survived a severe test and that it is, or was at one time, the best theory in its field.

A proposition P is an epistemic sufficient reason for a proposition Q to have a specific epistemic status S if and only if the conjunction of P with a statement of the rules of the game of science logically implies that Q has S. Consequently, if P is true and we are playing the game of science, then we are required, by the rules of the game, to accept that Q has S. I have stated this so that we do not have to be aware that P is true or even to accept that P is true in order to be required to make a move in the game of science. If I am playing a particular board game, for instance, I may be required to make a particular move even though I have taken my eye off the board.

There is no sufficient reason for playing the game of science. If we are not interested in obtaining better explanations and we do not find playing the game of science fun, it seems we will have no reason to play the game (barring unusual circumstances, such as wishing to irritate someone who hates it when people play the game of science). Even if we are interested in obtaining better explanations, playing the game of science is no guarantee that we will get them. The fact that people have in the past made epistemic progress by playing the game of science is no guarantee that continued play will lead to the same result. The rules of the game prevent us from getting *worse* explanations (we retain the explanations we have until we find a better one); but so does not playing the game. It seems that (again, barring unusual circumstances) the only reasons we may have for playing the game of science is that we enjoy it and that we *hope* by playing to get better explanations. But these are, presumably, what Miller meant by "subjective reasons." They may be sufficient reasons for some people but not for others.

There are, then, epistemic sufficient reasons, but only relative to the game of science. There are no epistemic sufficient reasons that are absolute. Perhaps this is what Miller means when he denies the possibility of epistemic sufficient reasons, since a reason is not truly sufficient unless it is absolute and thus 'stands on its own two feet.' We may find sufficient reasons for playing the game of science; but again, these are not absolute sufficient reasons; they are sufficient reasons only relative to the ends or desires of specific individuals. So there are no absolute epistemic sufficient reasons. The only absolute sufficient reasons that we have noticed are non-epistemic, ontological ones (see section 2).

6. Conclusion

Miller argues that there are no good reasons for or against any proposition. He considers both sufficient and insufficient reasons. He rejects the possibility of probative sufficient reasons on the ground of the claim that every deductively valid argument is circular. But that claim is false. He rightly rejects the possibility of probative sufficient reasons on the ground of sceptical doubt. He offers four arguments against the possibility of probative insufficient reasons. Two of the arguments depend upon the false claim that every deductively valid argument is circular and one of those arguments depends on a further false claim. An argument based upon sceptical doubt he later casts doubt upon. But a simple argument pointing out that an insufficient reason for a proposition says nothing about that proposition's truth seems successful. Thus, there are neither probative sufficient reasons nor probative insufficient reasons. Miller concludes that, apart from subjective reasons (concerned with satisfying desires or achieving ends), the absence of probative reasons means that there are no good reasons at all, either sufficient or insufficient.

I have argued that Miller leaves out something essential, as a result of which his account of our knowledge is baffling because, in the absence of reasons, propositions appear to be classified arbitrarily, and we seem to end up with 'anything goes.' In rectification, I distinguish epistemic reasons from probative reasons. Given that insufficient reasons are useless, I make no use of epistemic insufficient reasons. But epistemic sufficient reasons can be defined in terms of the game of science which is designed to encourage players to come up with new explanations and to ensure that we retain good explanations until we can replace them with better ones; so progress is possible, and encouraged, while regress is not permitted within the game. Epistemic sufficient reasons explain why our classifications of propositions are not arbitrary: they are governed by the rules of the game of science. But such reasons are sufficient only *relative* to the game of science. They are not probative reasons, which would be absolute, if there were any.

Epistemic sufficient reasons, being defined within the game of science, are not reasons for playing that game. The only reasons for playing the game of science are subjective.

Appendix: Miller's Fourth Argument Against the Notion of Support

It is often maintained that a hypothesis h that entails a proposition e which is an accepted statement of some particular fact, may be made probable by e. Miller argues as follows (1994, pp. 62-63):

(x) h entails e;
therefore,
(xi) e is part of the content of h;
(xii) the positive support that e gives to h is explained entirely by (xi);
(xiii) e cannot be a reason for itself;
therefore,
(xiv) citing e as a reason for h begs part of the question at issue;
(xv) given (x), h is logically equivalent to e-&-(h-if-e), where the conditional in parentheses is a material conditional;
therefore,
(xvi) the part of the content of h that goes wholly beyond e can be expressed by h-if-e;
(xvii) a proposition e provides positive support for a proposition k only when e and k overlap in content;
(xviii) except in trivial cases, e countersupports k, if e and k have no content in common;
therefore,
(xix) e countersupports any part of h that goes wholly beyond e, such as h-if-e;
therefore,
(xx) it is not the case that e can provide a good reason in favour of h when e offers h probabilistic support.

Proposition (xi) introduces the notion of *content* again. Given that Miller defines the content of a proposition as the set of its logical consequences, (xi) follows from (x) by definition. But all that (xi) means is that e is a logical consequence of h. Propositions (xii) and (xiii) seem unobjectionable. But (xiv) seems not to follow. It would, perhaps, follow if it were true that a logical consequence of h is a component part of h; but, as we saw in Chapter 6, propositions are not composed of other propositions. From the fact that e is a logical consequence of h it does not follow that e is a component part of h, and thus it does not follow that citing e as a reason for *h* is question-begging.

We might consider whether the argument would work in the special case in which *h* *does* assert *e* because *e* is a *conjunct* of *h*. Unfortunately, it does not. We can see that by substituting '*a-&-e*' for '*h*' in Miller's argument down to proposition (xvi), which is where the argument breaks down. The modified argument is as follows.

(x*)   *a-&-e* entails *e*;
therefore,
(xi*)   *e* is part of the content of *a-&-e*;
(xii*)   the positive support that *e* gives to *a-&-e* is explained entirely by (xi*);
(xiii*) *e* cannot be a reason for itself;
therefore,
(xiv*)   citing *e* as a reason for *a-&-e* begs part of the question at issue;
(xv*)   given (x*), *a-&-e* is logically equivalent to *e-&-((a-&-e)-if-e)*, where the 'if' signifies a material conditional;
therefore,
(xvi*)   the part of the content of *a-&-e* that goes wholly beyond *e* can be expressed by the material conditional *(a-&-e)-if-e*.

Premise (x*) is true so is (xi*); also (xii*) and (xiii*) seem true. Further, (xiv*) does now seem to follow. The truth of (xv*) can be seen from the following truth-table, in which, for perspicuity, the material conditional, *(a-&-e)-if-e*, is replaced by the logically equivalent inclusive disjunction **(not-e)-or-(a-&-e)**.

e	&	[not-*e*	or	(*a*	&	*e*)]
T	**T**	F	**T**	T	**T**	T
T	**F**	F	**F**	F	**F**	T
F	**F**	T	**T**	T	**F**	F
F	**F**	T	**T**	F	**F**	F

which shows *e-&-((a-&-e)-if-e)* to be true just if *a-&-e* is true.

But (xvi*) is false. It says that the part of the content of *a-&-e* that goes wholly beyond *e* can be expressed by the material conditional *(a-&-e)-if-e*. What Miller means by that is that *e* and *(a-&-e)-if-e* share no logical consequences (other than the logical truths) and every logical consequence of *a-&-e* that is not a logical consequence of *e* is a logical consequence of *(a-&-e)-if-e* (1994, p. 62; see also 'Technical Note b,' p. 73). In other words, (xvi*) says that every logical consequence of *a-&-e* that is not a logical consequence of e, is a logical consequence of **not-e-or-(a-&-e)**. That entails that a is a logical consequence of **not-e-or-(a-&-e)**. But that is false: if a and e are both false, then **not-e-or-(a-&-e)** is true but a is false; so a is not a logical consequence of **not-e-or-(a-&-e)**. So, not only is a restricted case of Miller's argument invalid at that point but, as a consequence, Miller's original argument is also invalid at that point. Thus, Miller's argument is invalid on at least two counts: (xiv) does not follow; and (xvi) does not follow. Informally, the argument fails because:

- it depends upon the claim, which we saw in Chapter 7 to be false, that every valid deductive argument is circular or question-begging;
- even in the case of arguments that *are* circular because the premise is a conjunction and the conclusion is one of its conjuncts, the argument depends upon the false claim that the part of the content of the premise that goes wholly beyond the content of the conclusion can be expressed by a material conditional of the form 'premise-if-conclusion.'

9 SOME SPURIOUS LIMITS TO REASONING

Abstract. Two common claims in philosophy are that there are some 'deep' disagreements that cannot, in principle, be resolved by rational people using rational argument, and that there are some situations in which it is not possible for rational persons to disagree. I argue that both claims are false. The first fails to take account of refutations. The second fails to recognise the role of conjectures in the dynamics of the growth of knowledge. There seems to be no type of disagreement such that it is impossible for rational parties to reach agreement by rational argument; but it is also seems that there is no situation in which persons are rationally required to reach agreement. Given the same evidence, it may be rational for one person to believe a specific proposition and another to believe its negation.

Keywords. Agreement; argument; belief; conjecture; deep disagreement; growth of knowledge; refutation.

1. Introduction

People often disagree about some factual matter and they often try to resolve the disagreement by rational argument. They may, or may not, succeed. Some philosophers claim that there are some situations in which rational persons who disagree will, in principle, be unable to reach *agreement* through rational argument. Further, some philosophers claim that there are some situations in which it is not possible for rational persons to *disagree*. I argue that both claims are mistaken.

In qualifying an argument as 'rational' I mean to exclude rhetorical tricks in which arguments are used to persuade, not in virtue of the logical connections that they exhibit, but in virtue of some other character that they have, such as a play on ambiguity, an appeal to emotion, a threat, or a lively delivery. Rational argument includes empirical testing, the argument from experience, in which a proposition is shown to be inconsistent with an agreed observation statement.

By qualifying the participants in a debate as 'rational' I mean that their behaviour in the debate is appropriate to the aim of improving our knowledge; that is, the persons are *epistemically* rational. So, a party to a debate does what is rationally *impermissible*, and thereby acts irrationally, if he acts in a way that frustrates the attempt to find the best answer to the question being discussed. Instances of such rationally impermissible behaviour include avoiding, ignoring or dismissing relevant arguments, employing sophistry, failing to scrutinise critically, lying, making *ad hominem* attacks, using terms ambiguously, begging the question, treating the premises of an empirical theory as a set of implicit definitions, explaining away counter-evidence in an ad hoc way, using threats, bribes or stirring musical themes, and many others. Such activities may be deliberate, accidental, negligent or incompetent.

In section 2, I relate the circumstances in which it is maintained by some philosophers that rational persons who disagree will, in principle, be unable to reach agreement through rational argument. I show in each case how agreement could, in principle, be reached by means of rational arguments employed by persons behaving rationally. In section 3, I describe the circumstances in which it is maintained by some philosophers that rational persons will be bound to agree if they are aware of the relevant arguments. I explain why, even in such situations, disagreement between rational persons is still possible. In section 4, I conclude. Throughout I use italicised, standalone '*p*' and '*q*' as schematic letters for sentences when I am talking about a proposition but it does not matter for my purpose *which* proposition; and I abbreviate 'it is not the case that *p*' to 'not-*p*.'

2. Deep Disagreement

Robert Fogelin argues that deep disagreements cannot be resolved by means of argument (1985, pp. 3-5). He makes the following claims, all of which are false:

(i)   "Arguing is the process of producing … compelling grounds … [that are] true or at least thought to be true and [which], together with other accepted propositions, lend adequate support to the claim to be established" (1985, p. 3);

(ii)   the possibility of a genuine argumentative exchange "presupposes a background of shared commitments," that is, "beliefs and

preferences," along with "shared procedures for resolving disagreements" (1985, p. 3);
(iii)   in normal disagreement, for example, concerning past athletic achievements, any challenge to the privileged status of official record books "would be so bizarre that we would dismiss it rather than attempting to answer it" (1985, p. 3);
(iv)   in contrast, a deep disagreement, one which "proceeds from a clash in underlying principles," "cannot be resolved through the use of argument" (1985, p. 5).

Often, arguing is an attempt, not to establish a claim but, rather, to undermine a claim, by deriving from it consequences that are taken to be false or otherwise unacceptable. In some cases we may undermine a claim by arguing that it entails a contradiction. For example, Aristotle claimed that, in the absence of interference, heavier bodies fall more rapidly than lighter bodies dropped from the same height. Galileo drew the following inferences from that claim. Since a heavy ball will fall more quickly than a light ball, then, if we join the heavy ball and the light ball together, the slower rate of fall of the light ball will act as a drag on the rate of fall of the heavy ball, so the combined object will fall at a slower rate than the heavy ball. However, the combined object is heavier than the heavy ball by itself, so it will fall more quickly than the heavy ball. Therefore, the combined ball will fall less quickly, and more quickly, than the heavy ball (Galileo 1638, 301-302).

Galileo was trying to establish that the rate of fall of freely falling bodies is independent of their weight, so it might be objected that an attempt to undermine a claim is an attempt to establish its negation. But that is not so. We may argue that a claim entails a consequence that is *taken to be* unacceptable without attempting to *establish* that the consequence is unacceptable, and thus without attempting to establish the negation of the claim. For instance, someone may claim that we ought to be vegetarian because eating meat takes away the lives of many animals. An objector may point out that the vast majority of animals that are slaughtered for food would not have existed at all if they had not been bred for their meat; and, on the better farms, animals live comfortably among their natural companions, are well-fed, protected from predators, cared for when disease afflicts them and, ultimately, killed humanely, so they live better lives than animals living in the wild (Scruton 1996, pp. 36-38, 71-75). So, if we all became vegetarian, we would *deny* good lives to billions of animals. That consequence of vegetarianism is unwelcome to the person who advocates vegetarianism for the sake of animals; and it thereby undermines her claim. But the objector need not be trying to establish either that the consequence is unacceptable or that vegetarianism is: the objector may, in Socratic fashion, leave the ethics of animal welfare and of vegetarianism an open question. The Socratic objector is not even trying to establish that those questions are open, since she can admit that there may be additional considerations on either side.

Further, even if we offer a formal derivation of a contradiction from a claim, we need not thereby provide "compelling grounds" that the claim is false, given that adoption of a deviant logic may be able either to avoid the contradiction, by modifying relevant rules of inference, or to reconcile it with the premises, as in dialetheism, which accepts that some, but not all, contradictions are true. For each of these reasons, Fogelin's (i) is false.

Suppose that Alf affirms that p but Betty disagrees. It is true that an argument to the conclusion that not-p will be ineffective in moving toward agreement if Alf does not accept its premises. If Alf and Betty share very few relevant beliefs or preferences, then it might not be possible to construct an argument that not-p using premises that both Alf and Betty accept. Still, Betty may, like Galileo or a Socratic objector, be able to construct an argument that not-p from premises that Alf accepts (even though she does not accept them). She may persuade Alf that not-p by showing that the conjunction of the proposition that p with other propositions that Alf accepts entails a proposition that q that Alf is reluctant to accept. Thus, Fogelin's (ii) and (iv) are false.

We can imagine a discussion of past athletic achievements in which one of the parties challenges the use of official record books to settle a question. She may argue, for instance, that with regard to the particular matter being discussed the record books are all wrong because of some special circumstances that led to a systematic mistake. Or, as Richard Feldman points out (2005, p. 17) it may be that the record books disagree with each other over the matter in question. Thus, Fogelin's (iii) is false.

Fogelin's examples of deep disagreement concern abortion, which he says rests on a disagreement over whether immortal souls enter newly fertilised eggs, and affirmative action, which he says turns on differences over whether groups, in addition to individuals, have moral status (1985, pp. 5-7). Andrew Lugg points out that people *do* argue about these issues and that the debaters do in fact share extensive frameworks of beliefs and preferences. He argues that deep disagreements can progress by means of argument, albeit slowly, to a resolution step by step. The resolution might be achieved by the parties coming to suspend judgment; but other times it may result in shared belief because debate is an opportunity for learning, thus moving away from the beliefs and preferences with which one started. A debate is not an argument in the sense of a logical progression from premises to conclusion; it is a goal-directed activity in which people make use of arguments to answer a question (Lugg 1986, pp. 47-50).

Fogelin's discussion of deep disagreements draws on Wittgenstein's view that there are "hinge" or "framework" propositions that are beyond rational debate (Fogelin 1985, pp. 3-4, 6). But Feldman (2005, pp. 18-21), following Lugg, argues that any such propositions may be debated, criticised and amended. Harvey Siegel (2013, sections 8-9) concurs and reinforces the point by criticising Wittgenstein's candidates for "hinge" propositions. For example, 'every human being has parents' may turn out to be false given developments in genetic engineering, and 'there are physical objects' is a recurrent topic of rational debate amongst philosophers in which progress has been made despite persistent disagreement.

Another attempt at identifying disagreements that are, in principle, irresolvable by argument between rational people is made by Michael Lynch, who focuses on disagreements concerning what epistemic principles are most likely to lead us to true answers to our questions (2010, pp. 264-65). Such a disagreement is *deep*, he says (2010, p. 265), if it is such that:

(a)   the parties to the disagreement share common epistemic goals (say, truth);

(b)   if the parties affirm distinct principles with regard to a given domain, those principles pronounce different methods to be the most reliable in that domain, and those methods are capable of producing incompatible beliefs about that domain;

(c)   there is no further epistemic principle, accepted by both parties, which would settle the disagreement;

(d)   the epistemic principles in question can be justified only by means of an epistemically circular argument.

Lynch gives an example. With respect to the most reliable method of ascertaining the truth about the distant past, Abel affirms that it is reading the Holy Book, while Cain affirms that it is 'inference to the best explanation' of the historical and fossil record. Since the two methods give different answers, and assuming that neither Abel nor Cain thinks that time travel is an option, there appears to be no shared principle that will settle the matter (2010, pp. 265-66).

However, Lynch says that the epistemic method of deduction applies to questions of any sort (2010, p. 265). In that case, there *is* a shared principle that may settle the matter. For instance, Cain could look at Abel's answers with a view to deriving from them, by deduction, something that Abel is reluctant to accept, perhaps even a contradiction, in which case Abel may give up the answers to which his epistemic principle has led him, and perhaps give up or amend that principle too. Even if, with regard to matters about the distant past, Abel's answers appear to entail nothing that Abel would find untoward, conjunction of those answers with propositions held by Abel in other domains may entail something that Abel would be unwilling to accept. Since deduction is applicable to any subject-matter, it seems that there can be no deep disagreements concerning epistemic principles of the sort that Lynch posits, because his condition (c) will never be met (compare Popper 1976, pp. 59-60).

Suppose that Abel rejects deduction as a method of ascertaining the truth about the distant past. That would make him what Karl Popper calls an "irrationalist" with regard to such questions. An irrationalist is someone who refuses to be swayed by argument, thinking that solutions to problems are best found by appeal to emotions, passions, instincts, impulses or tradition (Popper 1945, vol. 2, pp. 224-28). A person may be an irrationalist with respect to every proposition or, more commonly, she may be an irrationalist with respect to some subset of propositions (some 'hinge' propositions, for example), being prepared to be swayed by argument with respect to propositions outside of that subset. Abel, we are now supposing, is an irrationalist with regard to propositions about the distant past, refusing to be swayed by argument from the propositions enunciated in the traditional Holy Book. Needless to say, such irrationalism frustrates the attempt to use argument to find the best answer to the question, so it is rationally impermissible. Is it now impossible for Cain and Abel to reach agreement? No, because Cain accepts that deduction is applicable to such questions, so Abel may be able to use deduction to derive from the propositions that Cain accepts a proposition that Cain is unwilling to accept, thereby refuting Cain's position (Popper 1945, vol. 2, pp. 227-28, 231, 240). Notice that Abel still denies that deduction may be used to discover answers to questions about the distant past; but he knows that Cain favours it, so he can use it to show an inconsistency or other weakness in Cain's position, using the tool of the rationalist against the rationalist, while disdaining the tool for his own use.

Suppose, now, that Abel is adept at inferring from Cain's assertions about the distant past, perhaps in conjunction with claims Cain makes about other topics, propositions that Cain is unwilling to accept, including some contradictions, and that as a result Cain, like some others before him (Popper 1945, vol. 2, pp. 231, 356 note 9), abandons reason and becomes an across-the-board irrationalist. He still adheres to the same propositions about the distant past, but now as an emotional attachment rather than as a result of 'inference to the best explanation.' Since neither Cain nor Abel is prepared to be swayed by argument concerning their dispute about the distant past, no rational resolution of the dispute is available to them. But that does not entail that the dispute cannot be resolved rationally by others. People who are prepared to be swayed by argument may still discuss the matter, they may find reasonable means to avoid the errors and contradictions into which Cain fell, and they may eventually be able to agree concerning which propositions about the distant past are most plausibly true.

Lynch contends that, while a deep dispute about epistemic principles cannot be resolved by theoretical[11] arguments, it may be resolved by *practical* arguments concerning what the disputants want or value, specifically their own good (2010, pp. 268-77). However, that seems to be mistaken. First, as we have seen, so long as one of the parties to the dispute accepts the applicability of deduction, a resolution by means of theoretical argument is, in principle, available to them. Second, if both parties reject the applicability of deduction to the dispute, they will not be able to resolve the matter by means of argument, whether that argument is theoretical *or* practical. But a resolution of the dispute by means of argument will, in principle, be available to rational others. Even the dispute as to whether we should be irrationalists is resolvable by means of argument. Popper (1945, II, pp. 232-47) offered the practical or moral argument that being prepared to revise one's views in response to argument is superior to irrationalism, because it enables one to make better decisions, it makes peaceable resolution of disputes more likely, and it is more favourable to equal rights, humanitarianism, impartiality, humility, and freedom of thought. Of course, such an argument will not persuade an irrationalist to give up irrationalism, because the irrationalist will not be swayed by argument; but it does show that the dispute is, in principle, resolvable by argument between rational people.

There are, then, no deep disagreements that, in principle, cannot be resolved by argument, if the parties to the disagreement are rational. Even where the parties to a dispute are unable to resolve it because both of them are irrationalists who reject argument, the dispute is, in principle, resolvable by means of argument by rational people. That is not to say that every dispute will end in agreement if the parties to it argue rationally; it is to say only that agreement is possible between rational people so long as argument proceeds, particularly when, over time, the growth of our knowledge enables new considerations to be brought into play.

3. Radical Disagreement

Fogelin contends that in a normal (non-deep) argumentative exchange there are shared procedures for resolving disagreements (1985, p. 3). Consequently, he says, the use of argument will bring rational parties to agreement, so long as they are, competent, unbiased and not pig-headed (1985, pp. 3-4). Feldman concedes that in every normal argumentative

---

[11] Lynch speaks here of "epistemic" arguments, which is confusing, since there is practical knowledge as well as theoretical knowledge.

exchange the use of argument rationally *ought* to end in agreement; but he adds that, in cases in which the available evidence does not support one side or the other, the parties rationally ought to *agree* to suspend judgment rather than to agree to the disputed proposition or to its negation (2005, pp. 14-18, 20). Either the overall argument supports the proposition or it goes against the proposition or it is neutral; the "epistemically appropriate responses" are, in the first case, belief, in the second case, disbelief, and in the third case, suspension of judgment. A rational resolution of the *disagreement* need not be a resolution of the *issue* (Feldman 2005, pp. 16-19).

Feldman is an 'evidentialist' who maintains that beliefs should follow the evidence (2000, p. 678). That position appears to be self-refuting because it implies that the belief that beliefs should follow the evidence should follow the evidence, but it offers no evidence for that belief (see also Frederick 2019a, p. 35). Feldman's talk of "epistemically appropriate responses" indicates that he is speaking of epistemic rationality. But he is mistaken in maintaining that rational parties to a disagreement ought, if they share all their evidence, to end in agreement, either both believing that *p*, or both believing that not-*p*, or both suspending judgment whether *p*. His mistake seems to result from a failure to recognise the role of conjectures in the social dynamics of the growth of knowledge.

It seems that evidentialism would be epistemically rational if we gained new knowledge by gathering evidence and then adjusting our beliefs accordingly. In fact, we proceed by studying and criticising theories which are articulated in articles, books and so on. That enables us to discover implications and problems that were unknown to the authors of the theories and that spur us on to develop new conjectures to solve those problems (Kuhn 1970; Popper 1959, preface to 1934 edition; 1968a; 1968b). The new conjectures are typically *counter-intuitive* in that they *contradict* accepted theories and observation statements, so they cannot be inferred from what we previously took ourselves to know. However, they may imply *unexpected* predictions which can be *tested* by means of observation, and they may survive attempts to refute them, in which case they may *overturn* previously accepted theories with which they conflict, and engender a *reinterpretation* of past evidence, thereby replacing previously accepted observation statements with new ones (Kuhn 1970, pp. 6-7 and passim; Popper 1957b; 1975, esp. pp. 12-22). Consider an example based on the history of science.

Toward the end of the seventeenth century, Isaac Newton put forward a new theory according to which space and time are infinite, physical space is Euclidean, simultaneity is absolute, and all particles of matter attract each other by means of a force of gravity which appears to act instantaneously at a distance across empty space. By the mid-nineteenth century, Newton's theory had enjoyed a century-and-a-half of unparalleled success. It was far and away the best explanation of the phenomena in its domain (Kuhn 1957, pp. 256-62) and scientists believed the theory to be true (Kuhn 1957, pp. 259-60). Unfortunately, improved telescopic technology revealed that the observed motions of Uranus were not as predicted by the theory (Kuhn 1957, pp. 261-62). Now imagine that the following debate occurs.

Emma Empiric is a physicist who claims that, despite its past success, Newton's theory is now refuted. She admits that it is still by far the best explanation in its domain; but, she says, if Uranus is not where the theory says it is, then the theory is false. She applies herself to the task of replacing Newton's theory with a better one. Donald Dogmatic is a physicist who maintains that, because Newton's theory is still easily the best explanation in its domain, the *overall* evidence supports Newton's theory, so we should believe it. He suggests that the counter-evidence concerning Uranus's erratic behaviour is best ignored. Angela Agnostic is a biologist who suspends judgment on the truth or falsity of Newton's theory because her theoretical preoccupations lie elsewhere; but she insists that the counter-evidence should be highlighted as a problem to be resolved. Urbain Leverrier points out that the predictions of the motions of Uranus were not derived from Newton's theory by itself; rather, in order to obtain any predictions about the motions of Uranus, Newton's theory had to be conjoined with a number of statements describing how the world is. Newton's theory is true, he says, but we were mistaken in thinking that there are just seven planets: there is an eighth planet the gravitational force from which causes the unexpected deviations of Uranus's motions. He says that he has used Newton's theory to calculate what the size and orbit of the eighth planet must be if it is to account for the unexpected motions of Uranus. Empiric complains that no one has seen the supposed eighth planet: there is no evidence for it; it is a mere conjecture. Leverrier agrees; but he adds that his hypothesis of the eighth planet will, if it survives testing, as he expects it to do, supply new evidence, namely, sightings of the planet that will be evidence that the planet exists. Furthermore, the new state of the total evidence will favour Newton's theory because it will be shown that the peculiar motions of Uranus are consistent with that theory.

This is a rational disagreement to the extent that the responses of the participants are rationally permissible, that is, to the extent that the responses could realistically eventuate in a contribution to the growth of knowledge. Empiric's response seems clearly to be rationally permissible. Even if her alternative to Newton's theory, assuming she can come up with one, is not successful, we know that she *might* have been successful. For, seven decades later, when Newton's theory was still the best explanation in its domain, Albert Einstein propounded a new theory according to which the space and time are not absolute, physical space is not Euclidean, simultaneity is not absolute, and there is no force of gravity (Einstein 1920), and this new theory implied predictions of motion that contradicted the predictions of Newton's theory but which turned out to be more accurate (Zahar 1973, pp. 249-50, 256-59).

Dogmatic's response is not rationally permissible. The clash between accepted theory and accepted observation statements is an opportunity for learning that ought to be acknowledged. Simply ignoring the counter-evidence would frustrate the growth of knowledge. Another dogmatic and rationally impermissible response would be to declare that there is no clash between accepted theory and accepted observation statements because the axioms of Newton's theory are implicit definitions: the theory's key terms, such as 'mass' and 'force,' have whatever meaning renders Newton's theory true. That also obstructs the growth of knowledge: it weakens accepted theory to avoid clashes with accepted observation statements rather than seeking better theories that explain more. If Dogmatic had claimed that Empiric's obsession with trivial discrepancies testified to her incompetence, that *ad hominem* attack would also have been rationally impermissible (Popper 1959, sections 19-20). In contrast, while Agnostic's response involves no attempt to contribute to the growth of knowledge, it is rationally permissible because it does not frustrate the growth of knowledge.

Leverrier's response is also rationally permissible; indeed, it is laudable because his conjecture about the eighth planet is sufficiently detailed that it can be tested. Given the size and orbit that he ascribes to the planet it would be visible on a clear night if telescopes were pointed in appropriate directions at specific times. The tests were later carried out and the eighth planet was observed and named 'Neptune' (Kuhn 1957, pp. 261-62). Newton's theory was saved, for the time being.

Thus, Feldman's principle that, if the overall evidence indicates that p, one is rationally required to believe that p, is mistaken. It makes Empiric's and Agnostic's rationally permissible responses rationally impermissible and Dogmatic's rationally impermissible response rationally permissible. It does make Leverrier's rationally permissible response rationally permissible, but for a wrong reason, namely, that it is belief in the currently best theory, rather than that it is a proposal of a testable amendment to accepted theory that, if it survives testing, will provide surprising new evidence.

Feldman might object that although *overall* the evidence favoured Newton's theory, there was nevertheless a conflict, given that some of the evidence seemed to point the other way. It is, he might say, only when *all* the evidence indicates that p that one rationally ought to believe that p.

It must, however, be doubtful that such a situation ever obtains. Even after Newton's theory had supplanted the previously successful theories of Galileo and Kepler, Newton had reservations about it because its posited force of gravity, acting at a distance, seemed 'occult.' Since Newton and his contemporaries were generally mechanists in scientific matters, the apparent dependence of Newton's theory on an occult force was taken by many as evidence of its falsity (though not by Newton, who took it as evidence of God's immanence). It was only the continued empirical successes of the theory after Newton's death that persuaded later scientists to ignore the apparent absurdity of action-at-a-distance and re-categorise the occult property as a natural one (Kuhn 1957, pp. 258-59; Koyré 1957, chapters vii-xii); but by then improvements in methods of observation were starting to produce empirical counter-evidence. After the discovery of Neptune, Leverrier turned his attention to some irregularities in the motion of Mercury that were inconsistent with predictions derived from Newton's theory. He conjectured that there is a ninth planet and he used Newton's theory to calculate its size and orbit. He even gave the planet a name, 'Vulcan.' Unfortunately, that time, Leverrier's conjecture failed the empirical test: Vulcan did not exist. Leverrier then conjectured that what made Mercury's orbit erratic was a gravitational force from an asteroid cloud. That conjecture also failed the empirical test. He still believed that Newton's theory is true; but he died before coming up with another conjecture that might save it. Before anyone did save it, Einstein's theory of general relativity supplanted it. Einstein's theory accounted serendipitously for the motions of Mercury and implied novel predictions that survived testing (Zahar 1973, pp. 249-50, 256-59); but there appears to be counter-evidence to Einstein's theory, too, not least its inconsistency with quantum theory.

However, even if we were ever in a situation in which *all* the current evidence in a given domain indicates that p, it would still be possible that we or someone else could come up with a rival theory that better explains that evidence and explains or predicts other things besides. So, one would be rationally permitted to affirm that not-p if one had a conjecture that entailed that not-p and a proposal for research that promised to develop the conjecture into a sophisticated theory and also promised to generate evidence that the new theory is better than the theory that p.

It might be said that, given that the currently best solution may be false, one ought rationally to suspend judgment about it. Similarly, the person proposing a new, untested, solution should suspend judgment on that solution. In the earlier example I said that Leverrier believed that Newton's theory is true, which seems to have been the case, and that Empiric believed that Newton's theory is false; though, since Empiric is fictional, that is just a stipulation. The question is: was it rationally permissible in this situation for Leverrier to *believe* that p and for Empiric to *believe* that not-p, or were the two of them rationally required to *suspend judgment* whether p? Suppose that a non-scientist witnesses and understands the disagreement between Leverrier and Empiric. It would be natural for her, as it was for

Agnostic, to suspend judgment about Newton's theory, to wait and see how the debate turns out. But for Leverrier and Empiric, who are engaged in the debate on opposing sides, opposed *beliefs* seem more natural. Perhaps Empiric *could* have started the daunting creative work of finding a replacement for Newton's theory without actually believing that Newton's theory is false; and perhaps Leverrier *could* have undertaken the mathematically demanding work of calculating the size and orbit of the required eighth planet if he had not believed that Newton's theory is true. But it seems that, at least in some cases (perhaps in many cases), it is easier for people to devote considerable efforts to a challenging theoretical task if they *believe* that they are on to the truth. Further, such belief may have sustained their *tenacity* in defending and developing their own view and in criticising its rival, thereby helping to expose hidden strengths and weaknesses in the opposing views, and thus to give clearer guidance for future contributions to the growth of knowledge. Since belief, rather than suspension of judgment, will aid rather than undermine the growth of knowledge, at least for some, and plausibly for many, potential contributors, it is rationally permissible. Therefore, Empiric and Leverrier may rationally agree to disagree, rather than agreeing to suspend judgment.

It might be interjected that it may be enough to sustain Empiric and Leverrier in their respective intellectual endeavours if the former *suspected* rather than *believed* that Newton's theory were false and if the latter *suspected* rather than *believed* that Newton's theory were true (compare Carter 2018). Perhaps so; perhaps not. It is sufficient for belief to be rationally permissible that there be some people for whom belief would be required to bring forth the substantial efforts involved in making groundbreaking contributions to the growth of knowledge.

The general points illustrated by the example may be stated as follows. In any rational argumentative exchange, we are trying to discover a solution to a problem; and whatever solutions we consider, some of which may have been proposed by others, some of which we may have invented ourselves, it is always possible that we or someone else could come up with a better solution (compare Stanford 2006, pp. 17-23). Consequently, even if we agree that the current state of the argument indicates that p, we must remain open to the possibility that some alternative to the proposition that p may provide a better solution. So, our purpose in improving our knowledge will be served if people are at liberty to seek alternatives to the proposition that p and to argue about the merits and demerits of those alternatives compared to the other available options. Such argument will generally be more productive if each of the solutions in contention has its own advocate(s) who will be tenacious in exploring the strengths of their solution and the weaknesses of its rivals; and such tenacity may depend upon belief. So, when it is agreed that the best explanation available is that p, that the current state of the argument indicates that p, that the overall or total evidence indicates that p, it is rationally permissible for a person to believe that p, at least if he has promising ideas for how any counter-evidence may be explained away; but it is also rationally permissible for a person to believe that not-p, provided that he has a conjecture that entails that not-p and has ideas that he thinks can be developed in such a way that the state of the argument will then indicate that not-p. An action or a stance is epistemically rational if it is appropriate to the aim of improving our knowledge. Thus, contra evidentialism, it can be rational to believe a proposition for which there currently exists no evidence at all.

Similarly, if the current state of the argument *leaves it open* whether p, two people who are behaving rationally may disagree whether p, rather than suspending judgment whether p, if one has a conjecture that entails that p, while the other has a conjecture that entails that not-p, and each has ideas that he thinks can be developed in such a way that the state of the argument will then indicate that his conjecture is better than any others available. Thus, whatever the state of the argument, people may always rationally disagree because "the growth of knowledge depends entirely on the existence of disagreement" (Popper 1976, p. 34).

4. Conclusion

Two claims often made in contemporary philosophy are that:

- there are some situations in which rational persons who disagree will, in principle, be unable to reach agreement through rational argument;
- there are some situations in which it is not possible for rational persons to *disagree*.

I have argued that both claims are false.

The idea of rationally irresolvable disagreement is suggested by the idea that people reason by trying to establish conclusions by deriving them from accepted premises. On that view, if two people share few or no premises, the prospects for agreement seem slim. However, even where the parties share no premises, they can attempt to derive propositions that are unacceptable to their opponent from the opponent's own premises. Arguments can be used to refute. Indeed, even an irrationalist who refuses to be swayed by argument can use arguments to refute his opponent's views if his opponent accepts the use of argument. And even a dispute between two irrationalists may be resolvable by argument by rational people, even though the irrationalists themselves will not make use of the resolution.

The contention that rationality *requires* agreement in some situations appears to overlook the role of conjectures in the dynamics of the growth of knowledge. The best explanation, however successful, is still a conjecture that may be replaced with something better; and a so far unsubstantiated conjecture may stimulate research that changes the total evidence. Even where the parties to a discussion all agree that the current state of the argument indicates that p, it is rationally permissible for any of them to defend a proposition that q which is inconsistent with the proposition that p if they have an idea for how it may be shown that the proposition that q is a better solution to the problems being discussed than is the proposition that p. Indeed, agreement that the current state of the argument indicates that p will be, for some people, a spur either to find new arguments against the proposition that p or to find new alternatives to the proposition that p that may turn out to be better. Further, even if agreement is reached that p, one of the parties to the debate (or someone else) may later come forward with a new argument that not-p.

There is no rational requirement to believe the currently best solution even if all the available evidence points that way. It may be rationally permissible to believe that solution. But it is also rationally permitted to believe the negation of that solution if one is making a serious attempt to provide a better solution. Such belief may be a help, even an indispensable help, in generating innovative contributions to the growth of knowledge.

Consequently, it seems that any disagreement between rational people is in principle resolvable by argument, but no disagreement between rational people is *conclusively* resolvable by argument, since further progress in the growth of knowledge is always a possibility.

III ECONOMICS

10 ECONOMICS DOES NOT NEED VALUE SUBJECTIVISM

Abstract The subjective theory of value is acclaimed as a major advance in economics. That theory is nowadays usually taken to imply value subjectivism. I suggest instead that the theory be viewed as an evolution of thought with four stages: the substitution of relational for intrinsic theories of objective value; the recognition that social-scientific explanations refer to the theories about value that agents accept; the rejection of objective values; the substitution of preferences or evaluations for theories of value. I explain that the first two developments were progressive, the latter two regressive.

Keywords. Economics; Stanley Jevons; Carl Menger; objective value; preference; relational property; subjective value; theories of value; value subjectivism; Leon Walras.

1. Introduction

It is commonly claimed that a major advance in economics was made when the value of a good ceased to be regarded as an objective property of it, such as its cost of production or the quantity of labour expended in producing it, and was instead regarded as subjective, a property of valuing agents.

> If one were looking for a single criterion by which to distinguish modern economic theory from its classical precursors he would probably decide that this is to be found in the introduction of the so called subjective theory of value

into economic theory (Samuelson 1947, p. 90).

The triumvirate of the marginalist revolution – Jevons, Walras, and Menger – rejected the objective cost-of-production theories of value and focused instead upon the subjective principle of utility and consumer demand as the keystone of a new approach to economics (Skousen 2001, p. 170).

The subjective theory of value is commonly thought to imply value subjectivism. If values are objective, then a good may be valuable to an agent independently of whether the agent desires or prefers it or regards it as valuable. Value subjectivism denies that values are objective. It has weaker and stronger versions. A weaker version affirms:

(s)   value is not an objective property of things: there are only various agents' desires or preferences.

The same applies to the cost of a thing, which is the value of the most valuable option foregone in order to obtain the thing.

Value consists of the subjective valuations of individual users (Skousen 2001, p. 170).

Goodness and badness are qualities that are assigned to physical things, to commodities or services, by personal evaluations (Buchanan 1982, 12).

Cost is subjective; it exists in the mind of the decision-maker and nowhere else (Buchanan 1969, 41).

A stronger version of value subjectivism was more popular a century and more ago than it is today. It affirms the conjunction of (s) with:

(m)   what an agent desires is always a mental state of satisfaction and what an agent prefers is always one mental state over another.

For example:

A unit of pleasure or of pain is difficult even to conceive; but it is the amount of these feelings which is continually prompting us to buying and selling, borrowing and lending, labouring and resting, producing and consuming (Jevons 1871, p. 11); the object of Economics is to maximise happiness by purchasing pleasure, as it were, at the lowest cost of pain (Jevons 1871, p. 23).

However, (m) is implausible, it has been criticised in Robert Nozick's thought experiment of 'the experience machine' (Nozick 1974, pp. 42-45), and it seems no longer to be generally held by economists. Nowadays, it is customary to affirm that talk about satisfaction or utility should be regarded as a way of talking about preferences for goods or services or for outcomes in general, not just for mental states (Hausman 1992, p. 18; Luce and Raiffa 1957, pp. 15-17; Samuelson and Nordhaus 1998, pp. 80, 83, 96-101). But contemporary economists usually retain the value subjectivism of (s):

> There are no right or wrong answers to these [normative] questions because they involve ethics and values rather than facts (Samuelson and Nordhaus 1998, p. 8).

I argue that what is labelled 'the subjective theory of value' is a jumble of four ideas:

(i)   a relational theory of objective value;
(ii)   the insight that explanations of rational action invoke agents' accepted theories rather than facts;
(iii)   the idea that value is not objective but is projected onto the world by the mind;
(iv)   the assumption that explanations of rational action can dispense with agents' theories of value in favour of agents' preferences.

The third idea, value subjectivism, is incompatible with the first idea, that values are objective but relational, yet it may have been arrived at from the first idea by a progression of thought that passed through the second idea; or, at least, I suggest that the so-called subjective theory of value can be viewed as such a development. The fourth idea is incompatible with the second idea and independent of the other two. It belongs to the subjective theory of value only because, historically, it was held by theorists who advocated the third idea (value subjectivism). However, economics needs only the second of the four ideas, which means that it must reject the fourth: but it need take no stand on the issue of whether values are objective.

In a discussion of the objectivity of values it should be borne in mind that there may be evaluative facts as well as non-evaluative facts; but in what follows I sometimes contrast values and facts, simply to avoid circumlocution.

2. Intrinsic versus Relational Properties

The first idea that constitutes the so-called subjective theory of value is that value is not, as on classical theories, an intrinsic property of goods; it is a relation of goods to human well-being. Thus, Carl Menger, says:

> The value of goods arises from their relationship to our needs, and is not inherent in the goods themselves (1871, p. 120); a good can have great value to one economizing individual, little value to another, and no value at all to a third, depending upon the differences in their requirements and available amounts (1871, p. 146).

Similarly, Stanley Jevons affirms:

> utility, though a quality of things, is *no inherent quality*. It is better described as *a circumstance of things* arising out of their relation to man's requirements (1871, p. 43); the very same articles vary in utility according as we already possess more or less of the same article (1871, p. 44).

This relativity of value to an agent in a set of circumstances is quite consistent with its objectivity. A thing may be objectively valuable to a person in a set of circumstances at a particular time. A unit of good, g_1 (even the same unit of good g_1), can have each of the following objective properties:

(1)   at time t_1, it is of greater value to Albert than is a unit of good g_2;
(2)   at time t_2, it is of less value to Albert than is a unit of good g_2;
(3)   at time t_2, it is of greater value to Bridget than is a unit of good g_2;
(4)   at time t_2, it is of no value to Clive.

There are many such objective relational properties. For example, physical distance in space is one of them. If at 2.00 p.m. Doreen starts walking from King's Cross to Euston, then King's Cross has each of the following objective properties:

(1a)   just after 2.00 p.m. it is closer to Doreen than is Euston;
(2a)   at 2.10 p.m. it is farther from Doreen than is Euston;
(3a)   at 2.10 p.m. it is closer to Eric (who is at the Angel) than is Euston;
(4a)   at 2.10 p.m. it is no distance from Fiona (who is at King's Cross).

If the value of a good for a person in specific circumstances is not a *physical* relational property of the good, it may nevertheless be an *objective* relational property of it.

Thus, the 'triumvirate of the marginalist revolution' point out that classical theories that made value an intrinsic property of goods, like the labour theory of value, are mistaken:

> *labour once spent has no influence on the future value of any article*…we are always starting clear at each moment, judging the values of things with a view to future utility… I hold labour to be *essentially variable,* so that *its value must be determined by the value of the produce, not the value of the produce by that of the labour* (Jevons 1871, pp. 164-65).

> Whether a diamond was found accidentally or was obtained from a diamond pit with the employment of a thousand days of labor is completely irrelevant for its value… Goods on which much labor has been expended often have no value, while others, on which little or no labor was expended, have a very high value (Menger 1871, p. 146).

> why is labor worth anything and why is labor exchanged?... it is because it is both useful and limited in quantity (Walras 1896, p. 180).

If value is an objective relation between a good and a person in a set of circumstances, we can explain what classical economists regarded as a paradox. Water is necessary for life; diamonds are not. Yet, normally, one can obtain a great deal in exchange for diamonds but very little in exchange for water. The reason is that, generally, people have plenty of water, so an additional amount is of little value to them, but they have few, if any, diamonds, so an additional unit is of great value to them. However, in a desert, where people have very little water, a person may be willing to exchange diamonds for a small quantity of water (Jevons 1871, pp. 78-79; Menger 1871, pp. 140-41; Walras 1896, p. 182). This is an illustration of the law of diminishing marginal value: ceteris paribus, the more of something a person has, the less value to that person is an additional unit of it.

As we will see shortly, Menger was only a wavering adherent of a relational theory of objective value. Jevons was a value subjectivist, so his talk of utility being relative to a person's (contextual) *requirements* should be interpreted as the claim that there are objective relational facts concerning goods and the subjective satisfactions of agents in particular circumstances. The same goes for Leon Walras:

value is an essentially relative thing. Undoubtedly, behind relative value there is something absolute, namely the intensities of the last wants satisfied…But these…are subjective or personal and not at all part of external reality or objective. They are within us, and not within the things (1896, p. 164).

3. Facts versus Theories

The second idea that constitutes the so-called subjective theory of value is that it is not the objective values of goods that are important in explaining people's choices but, rather, the *theories that people accept* about the values of goods. Economics explains social phenomena by reference to the choices that people make, and it explains those choices by reference to the values that people *think* options have, rather than by reference to the actual values of the options (though the two may sometimes coincide). Economic explanations of action are rational, or teleological: they render an agent's actions intelligible given her accepted theories about fact and value.

For example, if Doreen believes that Eric is offering her a unit of good g_1 for one of her units of good g_2, and if she is of the opinion that an additional unit of g_1 is more valuable to her than is a unit of g_2, it is understandable that Doreen hands over to Eric a unit of g_2. Doreen's action can be explained by her accepted theories of fact and value. Indeed, her action can be explained by those theories even if the theories are false, even if an additional unit of g_1 is *not* more valuable to her than is a unit of g_2, and even if Eric was simply waving around his unit of g_1 and had no intention of trading it for a unit of g_2. In contrast, if Eric *is* offering Doreen a unit of g_1 for one of her units of g_2, and if an additional unit of g_1 is *objectively* of greater value to Doreen than is a unit of g_2, the conjunction of those two facts gives no explanation for why Doreen hands over to Eric a unit of g_2, because Doreen may be ignorant of those two facts.

Further, some things that people think are valuable to them are actually of no value to them. Lucky charms, love potions, divining rods, and quack medicines are of no objective value to the people who use them because those things do not have the properties ascribed to them in the theories that those people accept; and implements, statues and buildings used by pagans for the worship of idols are of no objective value to those people because the need they are intended to satisfy exists not in those people but only in the theories about themselves that they accept (Menger 1871, p. 53).

The value of goods is therefore nothing arbitrary, but always the necessary consequence of human knowledge that the maintenance of life, of well-being, or of some ever so insignificant part of them, depends upon control of a good or a quantity of goods.

Regarding this *knowledge*, however, men can be in error about the value of goods just as they can be in error with respect to all other objects of human knowledge. Hence they may attribute value to things that do not, according to economic considerations, possess it in reality…In cases of this sort we observe the phenomenon of *imaginary* value (Menger 1871, p. 120).

That passage contains the first three ideas of the subjective theory of value. The idea that value is an objective relational property figures in the first paragraph, where Menger says that value is non-arbitrary and a relation between goods and the well-being of agents; and also in the second paragraph when he says that an agent's knowledge of value may be mistaken. The idea that it is not actual values, but people's *accepted theories* of value, that explain their behaviour is expressed in the second paragraph with the talk of mistaken knowledge and 'imaginary value.' An element of value subjectivism also enters the picture in the first paragraph, in that value is said to be a consequence of agents' knowledge, which may be false knowledge. In the second paragraph, Menger seems torn between saying that it is *theorised* values that matter for economic explanations and that economics is concerned only with *objective* values.

Insofar as Menger holds that values are objective relational properties of objects about which people's accepted theories may be mistaken, the law of diminishing marginal value is still in the picture and it would exercise a constraint on people's theorising about value. For instance, if Fiona thinks that she will obtain as much value from a tenth chocolate as she obtained from the first, she may learn after she eats her tenth chocolate that her theory of value is false (and, one hopes, revise it). Thus, while explanation of a particular choice may refer to an agent's accepted theories of value and say nothing about objective values, laws of objective value may be invoked to explain why the theories of value that people accept tend to have some recurring features (for instance, they may tend to include a version of the law of diminishing marginal value).

4. Value Subjectivism

The third idea that constitutes the so-called subjective theory of value is that values are not objective properties of things at all but are merely projections of our theories of value, or of our desires or preferences, onto external things. Thus, after noting that it is people's accepted theories about the values of things, rather than the objective or actual values of things, that are invoked in economic explanations of action, Menger goes on to affirm not merely that economic explanations of action can ignore objective values but that there are no objective values:

> Value is thus nothing inherent in goods, no property of them, nor an independent thing existing by itself. It is a judgment economizing men make about the importance of the goods at their disposal for the maintenance of their lives and well-being. Hence value does not exist outside the consciousness of men (1871, pp. 120-21). The importance that goods have for us and which we call value is merely imputed. Basically, only satisfactions have importance for us, because the maintenance of our lives and well-being depend on them. But we logically impute this importance to the goods on whose availability we are conscious of being dependent for these satisfactions (1871, p. 139).

However, the fact that we explain choices by referring to agents' *accepted theories* about values rather than by referring to objective values does not imply that there are no objective values. At most it means that we do not need to hold an opinion about whether values exist objectively in order to explain how people behave. Similarly, we can explain some of the behaviour of religious people by referring to their accepted theories about God, rather than by referring to God, but that does not commit us to denying the existence of God: we need take no view on that matter. Of course, if we reject the existence of objective values, we reject thereby also the law of diminishing marginal value; but we can replace it with a psychological counterpart, perhaps appropriately labelled the 'law of diminishing marginal utility' (where 'utility' may be cashed out in terms of preferences).

I have been speaking of agents' *accepted theories* of value, rather than following Menger in speaking of agents' possibly false *knowledge* of value, because 'false knowledge' sounds discordant to some people's ears. A theory accepted by an agent about a topic is just a proposition about that topic that the agent accepts, where acceptance of a proposition need not amount to believing it, since the proposition may be accepted provisionally, and where the proposition may be compound, that is, a conjunction of several propositions. However, even talk of agents' accepted theories of value is not altogether happy. It is unobjectionable when we are speaking about agents who think that values are objective, whether intrinsic or relational. In the case of those agents we can explain their actions truly in terms of the theories they accept about the values of the options they choose or decline. On the other hand, it may seem false, or at least misleading, to explain the choice of an agent who is a value subjectivist in terms of the theories he accepts about the values of the relevant options, given that the value subjectivist himself might object that he accepts no theories about the values of the relevant options, except the theory that they have no values, because there are, so far as he is concerned, only his and other agents' *valuations* of those options. It might therefore be proposed that we follow the practice of contemporary economists in speaking, not of agents' accepted theories of value, but of agents' *preferences*; for, it may be said, even agents who are value objectivists should concede that when they choose the option that they deem most valuable they are choosing the option that they prefer.

5. Preferences versus Theories

The fourth idea that constitutes the so-called subjective theory of value is that explanations of rational action can dispense with agents' accepted theories of value in favour of agents' preferences. However, explanations of actions in terms of agents' preferences will not do, for the same reason that, as we saw in section 3, explanations of actions in terms of the values of options will not do. An agent may be ignorant of her actual preferences between options, just as she may be ignorant of the actual values of the options. Thus, what explains an agent's choices is not her preferences, but her *accepted theories* about what her preferences are.

For example, Albert is attracted to Bridget but it is not clear to him why. He does not know which of the following options he prefers:

(a)　　to have a sexual relationship with Bridget;
(b)　　to protect Bridget in a fatherly way;
(c)　　to observe Bridget from a distance and imitate her in secret.

To put it another way, Albert does not know which of the following propositions is true:

(a')　　that he prefers to have a sexual relationship with Bridget;
(b')　　that he prefers to protect Bridget in a fatherly way;
(c')　　that he prefers to observe Bridget from a distance and imitate her in secret.

He may make a mistake as to which option he prefers, that is, as to which proposition about his preference is true. His choice of action will depend not upon the preference that he has, but upon the preference that he *takes himself* to have. The explanation of Albert's actions must refer to his accepted theory about his preference, not to his actual preference. We should note in passing that, because Albert is unclear which of the three theories about his preference is correct, if he acts on the one he accepts as most plausible, he is not acting on a belief (he believes none of them).

Adherents of the subjective theory of value often talk about what an agent *values*; but that is ambiguous as between what an agent actually values and what she thinks or hypothesises that she values; it thus obscures the distinction between them. For example, suppose that Albert begins a sexual relationship with Bridget because he (thinks that he) values that more than the options that he has to forego in order to achieve it. He may in time be disappointed to discover that all along it was an avuncular relationship with Bridget that he (in fact) valued more highly, and that sort of relationship with her is no longer possible. Albert's accepted theory of what he values was mistaken; but it was that theory, not his actual values, that explained his action.

An advocate of preferences (or valuations), rather than of accepted theories of them, might suggest that, even if there are some occasions when agents are mistaken about their preferences, it is plausible that, *normally*, agents are not so mistaken; so explaining actions in terms of preferences will, normally, not lead one astray. There are two problems with that suggestion. First, unless there is a strong reason to do so, it would be perverse to accept one type of explanation rather than a rival type when the former type explains only a proper subclass of the cases that can be explained by the latter type. Explanations in terms of an agent's *accepted theories* about her preferences can explain cases of action in which the agent's accepted theories about her preferences are false *as well as* cases of action in which the agent's accepted theories about her preferences are true. Second, explanations in terms of an agent's *preferences* cannot explain even the latter cases. For example, suppose that we know the following about Clive:

(I)   he thinks (truly) that he is offered a coffee;
(II)   he prefers having a coffee to not having one.

If Clive mistakenly thinks that he would prefer to forgo the coffee, we cannot explain the fact that he declines the offer of coffee by referring to the conjunction of (I) and (II), but we can explain it by referring to the conjunction of (I) and Clive's mistaken theory that he would prefer to forgo the coffee. On the other hand, if Clive correctly thinks that he would prefer to accept the coffee, we can explain the fact that he accepts the coffee by referring to (I) and his correct theory about his preference; but we cannot explain it by referring to the conjunction of (I) and (II), because that conjunction is compatible with Clive mistakenly thinking that he would prefer to forgo the coffee. Given that Clive thinks (truly) that he is offered a coffee, his preference for having a coffee is neither necessary nor sufficient to explain his choice (Schueler 2009, pp. 110-117). I guess that everyone has at some time declined a coffee (or other beverage) only to realise shortly afterward that she really preferred to have one, and at some other time accepted a coffee (or other beverage) only to realise shortly afterward that she really preferred not to have one; so the example of Clive is hardly far-fetched.

It might be thought that there is a danger of a vicious infinite process in shifting explanations of rational action from preferences to accepted theories about preferences. After all, an agent may be mistaken about which theories she accepts. If the possibility of an agent being mistaken about her preferences commands the explanatory shift from preferences to accepted theories about preferences, then the possibility of an agent being mistaken about her accepted theories about her preferences commands an explanatory shift from accepted theories about preferences to accepted theories about accepted theories about preferences; and so on ad infinitum.

That thought is confused. What commands the explanatory shift from preferences to theories about preferences is not that an agent can be mistaken about her preferences. It is rather that, as we just noted, preferences do no work in explanations of rational action. What does the explanatory work is the agent's fallible knowledge, the theories she accepts, about her preferences, not the preferences themselves. The agent's accepted theories about her preferences, in combination with her accepted theories about the other facts of her situation, constitute her view of her situation and make intelligible the choices that she makes. The agent's accepted theories about her situation, including her accepted theories about her preferences, can explain her choices without her having accepted any second-order theories about those accepted first-order theories; so explanations in terms of her accepted first-order theories do not lead us on to an infinite hierarchy of accepted theories. The explanation of Clive's choice of coffee that invokes his accepted theory that he is offered a coffee, and his accepted theory that he prefers a coffee to no coffee, does not require Clive to have accepted any second-order theories about his theories. In fact, it seems unlikely that Clive will have accepted any such second-order theories. In the case in which an agent does accept second-order theories about her relevant accepted first-order theories, it will be the accepted second-order theories that need to be invoked in explaining her action; but there will be no need there to invoke any accepted third-order theories, and it seems it would be rare for agents to have such things.

It might be protested that an explanation of an action in terms of the theories that the agent accepts is missing the vital ingredient of motivation, and that it is desire, or preference, that supplies the motivational push to action. However, as we saw above, in cases of rational action, a desire or preference does not motivate unless the agent accepts a theory about it; and an agent who lacks a particular desire or preference for a specific option may nevertheless be motivated to take that option if she accepts a theory that she has that desire or preference. Perhaps what underlies the protest is a picture of the agent as acting only when some desire *makes* her act. But that picture is faulty: an agent acts only if it is *up to her* whether she acts (Alvarez 2009, 2013; Frederick 2013b; Steward 2012).[12]

Ironically, explanations in terms of agents' preferences or desires, rather than agents' accepted theories of preferences or desires, may have a use outside of economics. It is generally accepted that people sometimes act irrationally. Sigmund Freud, and other psycho-analysts, invoke sub-conscious desires to explain actions of agents that are contrary to the theories of fact and value that the agents accept (Peters 1960, pp. 53-71). Whatever the value of such explanations, they fall outside of economics, which explains actions, and the phenomena which they engender, on the assumption that agents act rationally.

To forestall a possible confusion, I am not claiming that desire is a kind of belief, for example, that to desire that p is to believe that it is desirable that p, or to believe that one prefers that p. In the example given above, Albert desires that he has an avuncular relationship with Bridget, but he does not believe that it is desirable that he has such a relationship, and he does not believe that he prefers that he has such a relationship. He does not even accept the theory that it is desirable that he has such a relationship, or the theory that he prefers that he has such a relationship. Further, the explanation of Albert's commencement of a sexual relationship with Bridget invoked his *acceptance of the theory* that he preferred a sexual relationship with Bridget, not a *belief* that he preferred such a relationship, nor a belief that such a relationship is desirable. He accepted the theory because it was the most plausible of the hypotheses available, not because he believed it. In some cases an agent will believe an accepted theory; but the acceptance of the theory does the explanatory work whether or not the agent believes the theory. Thus, while desires are irrelevant for rational explanations, relevant beliefs are not always available and they are dispensable even when they are available.

It might be thought that there is an infinite regress here: explanation of rational action invokes acceptance of a theory; but acceptance of a theory is itself a rational act. However, acceptance of a theory is not always a rational act. The bulk of the theories about fact and value that we accept are ones

---

[12] Additional criticism of the 'Humean' desire theory of motivation is provided by G. F. Schueler (2009).

that we inherit culturally or biologically, either not by means of acts or by means of acts that are non-rational (rather than irrational), so there is no infinite regress (Popper 1949a; 1957, pp. 49-52; 1994c, pp. 134-39; also Hayek 1963, pp. 60-63; 1970).

6. Conclusion

Classical theories of value were mistaken in viewing value as an intrinsic objective property of things. The movement of economics away from those classical theories involved two steps forward and two steps back. The first step forward was to see that objective value (if there is such a thing) is relational: the objective value of a good is relative to an agent in a set of circumstances. The second step forward was to see that explanations of rational choices invoke, not objective values, but agents' accepted theories about values. Agents' accepted theories about value may be true or false; they may be about objective values or simply about preferences. The first step back was to affirm or assume that economics entails the denial of the existence objective values, rather than being agnostic about the matter. The second step back involved eschewing talk of agents' accepted theories of value in favour of talk of agents' preferences or values. That step was regressive because an agent's actual preferences, as opposed to his accepted theories about his preferences, are explanatorily inert (except perhaps in explaining psychopathology).

Finally, there was also a third step back, which involved supplanting the notion of preference with the notion of revealed, or demonstrated, preference. I have not discussed that retrograde step here, as it went out of favour with the abandonment of behaviourism and its manifold inadequacies have been indicated by others (Hausman 1992, pp. 19-22, 156-58; Nozick 1977, pp. 126-35).

11 ENTREPRENEURSHIP: ALERTNESS, JUDGMENT, AND CONJECTURE

Abstract. I criticise, from a critical rationalist perspective, Israel Kirzner's notion of entrepreneurial alertness and Matthew McCaffrey's endorsement of Joseph Salerno's rival account of entrepreneurial judgment.

Keywords. Alertness; conjecture; entrepreneur; judgment; Israel Kirzner; Matthew McCaffrey; Joseph Salerno.

Matthew McCaffrey (2015) argues that the account of entrepreneurial alertness advanced by Israel Kirzner is unsatisfactory and faces serious difficulties when it tries to explain the effects of public policy on entrepreneurship. He suggests that more satisfactory answers to questions of policy can be found by considering intervention through the framework of entrepreneurial calculation and judgment. I focus here on alertness and judgment as accounts of entrepreneurial discovery.

Kirzner attributes to Lionel Robbins an account of entrepreneurial decision-making in terms of maximising which involves individuals perceiving and reacting to incentives. Kirzner criticises this account because incentives must be known to an actor in order to be incorporated into standard utility calculus. But pure profit opportunities are unknown: they are waiting to be discovered. Alertness to opportunities must therefore be explained by factors other than conventional economic incentives. Unfortunately, Kirzner does not offer an explanation. Indeed, he finds it paradoxical that previously unseen opportunities can cause their own discovery: "How can an *unnoticed* potential outcome, no matter how attractive, affect behavior?" (1985, pp. 108-109).

Kirzner's approach seems mystical. In his view, it seems, new opportunities are already there to be seen and the entrepreneur is a person who is alert to noticing them. But in fact, new opportunities are not simply there waiting to be noticed. As they are as yet unrealised possibilities, they cannot be perceived at all. There can be no people, entrepreneurs or others, whose perception is sufficiently acute to perceive them.

McCaffrey seems to accept this. He proposes substituting entrepreneurial *judgment* for entrepreneurial *alertness*. It is not, however, clear what McCaffrey means by 'judgment.'

From a critical rationalist perspective it seems clear that what the entrepreneur actually does is to make a guess. In an act of creative imagination he conceives of an activity that is not currently performed and that would solve a problem he is pondering. He then makes a conjecture about whether that activity is likely to be profitable and he subjects that conjecture to criticism by gathering information about technical possibilities for realising the activity and their likely costs, and about potential demand at various prices for the output of the activity. The information he gathers will be full of holes, so he has to decide whether to gamble on pursuing the activity in question. If he does gamble and he is lucky, he makes a profit; otherwise he breaks even or makes a loss. This account applies equally to the sorts of 'arbitrage' opportunities on which Kirzner focuses and to the 'creative destruction' opportunities that Schumpeter highlights.

In places it seems as if McCaffrey is proposing this sort of solution. He says:

> entrepreneurs make speculative judgments about the future state of the market. Eventually, consumer demand will reveal whether particular uses of capital were justified. If his initial judgments were correct, the entrepreneur earns profits, and if not, he incurs losses. The entrepreneur therefore bears the uncertainty of the future in exchange for the chance to reap profits (2015, p. 191).

"Speculative judgments" sound like guesses. However, McCaffrey immediately goes on: "The key point, however, is that in order to do this entrepreneurs must exercise judgment about the allocation of resources." It seems that exercising judgment is something different to a guess; perhaps it is supposed to be some mysterious process of intuition or 'tacit knowledge' through which some people can know things not knowable in any other way. That sort of view is propounded by some contemporary philosophers, including Thomas Nagel (1979, pp. 134-35), where "judgment" is identified with "the faculty Aristotle described as practical wisdom." Some of the things that McCaffrey says seem to be open to interpretation along those lines. He says that in deciding whether or not to proceed, the entrepreneur must calculate to compare costs and benefits of alternative options; then, quoting Joseph Salerno (1990, p. 60), he says:

> Calculation consists in entrepreneurs appraising the future prices of the factors of production through their "'experience' of past prices and … their 'understanding' of what transformations will take place in the present configuration of the qualitative economic data" (2015, p. 192).

But what does such 'experience' and 'understanding' (in quotation marks) amount to? How is one supposed to appraise future prices in terms one's 'experience' of past prices and 'understanding' of future changes? There is no known connection between the past and future prices in question: it all depends upon innumerable possibilities that might or might not occur in future. And who can antecedently 'understand' which of the myriad possible transformations of qualitative data will be realised? It sounds as if McCaffrey and Salerno think that entrepreneurs have some kind of mystical insight into all of this. Why do they not just admit that the entrepreneur makes a guess which is informed, but by no means determined, and perhaps only slightly influenced, by the very scanty information that he currently has? After critical appraisal of his guess, he then takes a gamble which might, or might not, pay off.

McCaffrey says that "calculation provides, among other things, a basis for entrepreneurs' judgment regarding the direction of the factors" (2015, p. 192). But calculation, enables entrepreneurs to appraise rival conjectures about future courses of action: it is used in *criticising* conjectures already proposed. It is not a 'basis' for those conjectures or 'judgments.' McCaffrey speaks as if the entrepreneur's 'judgments' are somehow derived from, or imposed upon him by, his current information, rather than being speculative conjectures about possible new profitable activities that are in need of criticism and testing.

It might be suggested that the view that McCaffrey and Salerno articulate agrees with the 'conjecture and refutation' position I have expressed. However, if that were the case, it would be puzzling why they expound that position in an obscure and, indeed, misleading way. For, what they say suggests that guessing is not up to the entrepreneurial job, which requires a special faculty of knowing (labelled 'judgment,' but which no one has been able to explain). As well as Salerno, McCaffrey (2015, p. 191) refers approvingly to the work of Nicolai Foss and Peter Klein. But here is what the latter say:

> the Knightian (and, we would argue, Misesian) entrepreneur

> who owns capital and bears uncertainty – acting in calendar time – may possess the characteristics of the Kirznerian entrepreneur (i.e., being alert to potential, imagined opportunities for gain) but in addition must also possess the special faculty of exercising judgment... (2010, pp. 153-54).

The ability to make a more or less informed guess is one that every one has and one that everyone regularly utilises. It is surely not a "special faculty of exercising judgment." If all these authors do subscribe to the 'conjecture and refutation' view, they should be criticised for expressing it so poorly.

On the matter of public policy, what government intervention does is to alter the evaluation of opportunities. It may do this by regulation, including taxing, which makes many conjectured forms of activity that would have appeared profitable appear decidedly unprofitable, thus making it unlikely that they are pursued, even though, in many cases, they would have been profitable and increased welfare but for the government intervention. It may do it by nationalisation, through which government alters the evaluation of many conjectured forms of activity by making some of them impossible to evaluate, even after they have been pursued, with the result that some such activities that would have been profitable and would have increased welfare are not pursued, while others which are unprofitable and decrease welfare are pursued.

In conclusion, it seems that the reluctance of contemporary theorists to acknowledge that our knowledge grows by conjecture, criticism and empirical testing, leads them to posit, or at least to fall back on, some mystical faculties through which knowledge is acquired, such as entrepreneurial alertness or entrepreneurial judgment. In fact, there are no such 'faculties.' Entrepreneurship is guesswork tempered by calculation and empirical testing.

MISCELLANY

12 HAACK'S DEFECTIVE DISCUSSION OF POPPER AND THE COURTS

Abstract. Susan Haack criticises the US courts' use of Karl Popper's epistemology in discriminating acceptable scientific testimony. She claims that acceptable testimony should be reliable and that Popper's epistemology is useless in discriminating reliability. She says that Popper's views have been found acceptable only because they have been misunderstood and she indicates an alternative epistemology which she says can discriminate reliable theories. However, her account of Popper's views is a gross misrepresentation and her alternative epistemology cannot do what she claims for it. The courts should not be concerned with reliability and, insofar as they use the term 'reliability,' it should be construed in a procedural rather than a substantive sense. Since Popper's epistemology gives something like a characterisation of science at its best, the courts should continue to invoke Popper's theories in their discrimination of acceptable testimony.

Keywords. Ad hoc; basic statement; courts; cumulative growth; falsifiability; Susan Haack; induction; justification; misrepresentation; objective knowledge; observations; Karl Popper; reliability; scepticism; test.

1. Introduction

Susan Haack, in her draft paper, 'Popper on Trial: A Brief History of a Big Muddle' (2009), discusses the use that US courts have made of Karl Popper's philosophy in judgments related to scientific status. She says (2009, p. 2) that her aims are to show that:

(1)   legal players have systematically misunderstood Popper;
(2)   Popper's philosophy of science is no help in determining reliability;
(3)   courts' concern to determine reliability is both legally essential and philosophically legitimate;
(4)   the picture that legal players have mistakenly attributed to Popper is closer to the mark than the account Popper actually offers.

I agree that Haack's (1) and (2) are correct, but I argue that her (3) and (4) are false. More centrally, I highlight a number of ways in which Haack seriously misrepresents Popper's views.

Haack's draft paper (2009) has been superseded by two published papers of hers (2010 and 2013). I discuss it because it is still available online and the two later papers very largely repeat what is said in the draft paper and treat Popper in the same hostile and polemical style. I will note, in passing, discrepancies between the later papers and the draft paper, though I ignore some additional small errors in the later papers as well as the personal attack on Popper in her 2010 (p. 397, including footnote 14).

2. Karl Popper

Haack distinguishes the "authentic Popper" from the "shadow Popper," who is "a kinder, gentler, and feebler Popper who doesn't really offer anything that one could dignify by calling it a 'theory of science'" (2009, p. 3). The "authentic Popper," she says, subscribes to the following views (2009, pp. 3-4):

(i)   what distinguishes science is that its statements are falsifiable;
(ii)   a statement is falsifiable if and only if it is incompatible with a statement reporting the occurrence of an observable event at a specified place and time (a 'basic statement');
(iii)   a scientific statement is falsified when a basic statement with which it is incompatible is accepted;
(iv)   the acceptance of a basic statement can be neither justified nor impugned, but is a matter for decision on the part of the relevant scientific community, though their decision may be prompted by what they observe;
(v)   the method of science is not inductive but a matter of making bold, falsifiable conjectures, testing them as severely as possible and, should they be falsified when they are tested, dropping them and starting again rather than making *ad hoc* adjustments to save them;
(vi)   theories which have been tested but not (yet) falsified have been 'corroborated,' to a degree depending on the severity of the tests

passed, but there is no reason to believe a corroborated theory, as it is not shown to be true or probable or reliable.

Haack's (i) is curiously incomplete. When Popper introduces his falsifiability criterion of demarcation, in the very section of his book which Haack cites in support of her claim (i), he makes it clear that there are *two* components to the demarcation of science, one logical and one methodological, the latter presupposing the former. Thus, a scientific statement is falsifiable; but the empirical method of science requires in addition procedures that exclude attempts to save a falsifiable statement from falsification by means of ad hoc manoeuvres (1959, section 6, pp. 40-42; section 9, pp. 49-50).[13] This second, methodological, component to Popper's demarcation of science is essential for distinguishing science from pseudo-science, and it was, Popper says (1974a, p. 29, pp. 31-33), his appreciation of it that led him to his falsificationist account of science. It is astonishing that so important, and so prominently stated, a part of Popper's theory of science is neglected in Haack's exposition of the 'authentic Popper' and that when she does mention it (see below) she attributes it to 'shadow Popper.'

Haack's (iv) is mistaken. Of course, Popper does insist that acceptance of a basic statement cannot be justified: all basic statements are implicit with theories which go far beyond the content of any observation (1959, sections 25, 27 and 30, including footnote *3 and Appendix *x, (1), pp. 420-422). So we decide to accept a basic statement even though it is not justified; but, says Popper

> The decisions are reached in accordance with a procedure governed by rules (1959, section 30, p. 106).

That means that, contrary to Haack's (iv), if the acceptance of a basic statement violates the rules in question, then it can be impugned. One rule

> tells us that we should not accept *stray basic statements* – i.e., logically disconnected ones – but that we should accept basic statements in the course of testing *theories* (1959, section 30, p. 106)

which means that we should impugn the acceptance of stray basic statements. Unfortunately, Popper is not very explicit about the other rules. He does say, though, in the very section that Haack cites for her faulty

---

[13] In my references to Popper's works I usually include section numbers as well as page numbers, because there are different editions of his books.

interpretation, that a basic statement is one about which investigators are likely to reach agreement because it describes an observable event which motivates the decision to accept it (1959, section 29, pp. 104-5). Thus, acceptance of a basic statement can also be impugned if it is not agreed by investigators in the light of their observations. In her later papers (2010, p. 401; 2013, p. 6),[14] Haack corrects (iv), dropping the claim that basic statements cannot be impugned.

Haack's (v) is also mistaken. Popper does not say that falsification generates just one acceptable option, namely, rejection, and one unacceptable option, namely, ad hoc adjustment. He explicitly recognises the acceptable option of independently-testable adjustment, that is, adjustment which increases the falsifiability of the theory by yielding new falsifiable predictions, and he emphasises its importance by giving historical examples of progress made in that way (1959, section 20, pp. 82-83; 1974a, p. 33 (e)). Indeed, he says this in the very section of his 1959 which Haack cites for her mistaken interpretation. In her later papers (2010, p. 405; 2013, p. 11), Haack notes that Popper permits non-ad-hoc adjustment but she represents this as some kind of confused afterthought. However, the confusion is not in Popper; though his use of the same term, 'falsifiability,' to cover both logical and methodological components of demarcation seems, with hindsight, to have been unhelpful.

Haack complains that Popper is guilty of 'covert skepticism' (2009, p. 5; 2010, p. 404; 2013, p. 9) because, if the acceptance of basic statements is not justified by observations, then there is no guarantee that a scientific statement that has been falsified is actually false, which implies that scientific claims can no more be shown to be false than they can be shown to be true. However, Popper explicitly recognises that fact:

> no conclusive disproof of a theory can ever be produced; for it is always possible to say that the experimental results are not reliable, or... (1959, section 9, p. 50)

and in footnote *1 to that passage he complains that he has

> been constantly misinterpreted as upholding a criterion...based upon a doctrine of 'complete' or 'conclusive' falsifiability.

Indeed, his recognition of the fact that accepted basic statements may be false (see also 1957a, section iii, pp. 41-42, footnote 8) is one of the things

---

[14] Page references to Haack's 2013 are to the online copy, not to the book which contains it.

that lies behind his acceptable option, mentioned in our previous paragraph, of independently-testable adjustment of a falsified hypothesis. That is the option that Haack suppressed in her (v), above. It is *her misrepresentation* of Popper's view that makes the scepticism covert, so her complaint against Popper is really a complaint against the straw-man "authentic Popper" that she fabricates.

That is not to deny that there are other places in which Popper talks as if falsification established falsity; but that simplistic view is not his considered view. Popper's lapse into the simplistic view appears often to be a function simply of the need to avoid unnecessary complications, where the point he is making would in all essentials stand if the complications were taken into account but would then need to be made in a long-winded fashion (for example, 1971, pp. 13-14). All theorists make use of that recourse, thankfully. On some occasions, though, Popper's lapse into the simplistic view seems to be the result of his momentarily forgetting his considered view (for example, 1974b, p. 1110). That is a type of frailty to which every thinker is subject; and it is an accepted academic standard of exposition and criticism that such lapses are noted and dismissed so that a thinker is presented and criticised at his best. As we have seen, Haack's exposition of Popper's views falls short of normal academic standards not only in that respect, but also in misrepresenting Popper grossly and also gratuitously in that the correctives to her gross misrepresentations are contained in the very passages she cites.

Haack contrasts "shadow Popper" with "authentic Popper" as follows (2009, pp. 5-6):

Authentic Popper	**Shadow Popper**
(a) science is demarcated by the falsifiability of its statements	(a') science is demarcated methodologically, in terms of the procedures that (good) scientists follow
(b) science is like an endless building site in which, each day, the previous day's work is demolished and building begins anew	(b') science is like a medieval cathedral, gradually erected over many generations, which suggests a more or less cumulative picture of scientific progress

Authentic Popper	**Shadow Popper**
(c) knowing subjects and their experiences are epistemologically irrelevant	(c') the 'empirical basis' of science is like piles driven into a swamp, which suggests that basic statements are partially but not fully justified by what scientists observe
(d) corroboration is only a measure of what the verisimilitude of a theory *appears* to be, relative to other theories, at a given time	(d') the process of conjecture and refutation might yield an increment of verisimilitude
(e) we can never have reason to think a corroborated theory true, probable, or closer to the truth than other theories	(e') it is rational to prefer a corroborated theory as the basis for action

We have already seen that the first contrast, (a)/(a'), involves a serious misrepresentation of Popper's view: (a'), far from being a view of a spurious Popper, is an integral and very important part of Popper's account of science which was there from the beginning. Each of the other contrasts is also more or less objectionable. I discuss them in turn.

Neither (b) nor (b') gives a satisfactory description of Popper's view: the truth is somewhere between the two. On Popper's view, (b') is unsatisfactory because the growth of knowledge is not cumulative. First, it is not the case that we begin by collecting and arranging our experiences, or accepting stray basic statements, and then generalising from them to obtain scientific theories; rather, we propose a new theory and then test it (1959, sections 1-3, pp. 27-34, section 30, p. 106, section 85, pp. 278-81, Appendix *x, (1), pp. 420-422). Second, successful new theories are not simply added to successful old theories; rather, the new theories typically contradict their predecessors and replace them, as Newton's theory *corrected* the theories of both Kepler and Galileo (1957b).

> The growth of knowledge…is not a repetitive or a cumulative process but one of error-elimination (Popper 1968a, p. 144).

However, that does not entail (b), because new theories are proposed as solutions to problems which arise from prior theories, so new knowledge builds upon past achievements in the sense that new theories depend upon the *problems* discovered by the study, criticism and testing of prior theories

(1949a; 1949b, section iv, pp. 344-47; 1959, preface to 1934 edition, p. 13, section 85, p. 277; 1968a, pp. 118-26, 142-46; 1968b, 162-80).

> In science we want to make progress, and this means that we must stand on the shoulders of our predecessors...[T]he scientific tradition...only tells us where and how other people started and where they got to...We use it by checking it over, and by criticising it (1949a, p. 129).

Thus, Popper's conception of human knowledge is *historical* but not *cumulative* because, while later knowledge depends upon earlier knowledge, it also typically *revises* it.

That Haack's (c) misrepresents Popper's view should be clear from the fact that it contradicts Popper's affirmation that basic statements are accepted if they can be agreed in view of observations (see the discussion of Haack's misstatement of Popper's view in her (iv), above). As Popper puts it elsewhere:

> science is impossible without experience...it is observation rather than perception which plays the decisive part. But observation is a process in which we play an intensely *active* part. An observation is a perception, but one which is planned and prepared (1949b, sections i-ii, p. 342).

In support of (c), Haack refers to Popper 1968a, but without giving any page references. Perhaps the passage she has in mind is the following:

> Traditional epistemology has studied knowledge or thought in the subjective sense – in the sense of the ordinary usage of the words 'I know' or 'I am thinking'. This, I assert, has led students of epistemology into irrelevances: while intending to study scientific knowledge, they studied in fact something which is of no relevance to scientific knowledge. For...scientific knowledge belongs...to the world of objective theories, objective problems, and objective arguments (1968a, p. 108).

Popper is not there saying that experiences are irrelevant to scientific knowledge; he is rather contrasting epistemology, which he says is concerned with linguistically formulated and publicly accessible theories, with a concern with individuals' private states of thought or belief, which is perhaps a more appropriate subject-matter for a psychologist. When he talks of objective theories, problems and arguments, Popper means ones which have been given physical expression in language (spoken, signed or, especially, written). When we objectify our theories, we distance ourselves from them, which enables us to examine and criticise them more dispassionately, so that we can learn from ourselves. Such objectified knowledge can also be accessed and criticised inter-subjectively so that we can learn from each other even across the generations. It is objectified knowledge that enables the spectacular growth of knowledge that we have seen in the history of science (1968a, pp. 106-22; 1968b, pp. 160-61). In Haack's 2010 and 2013, the attribution of (c) to Popper is not repeated.

Haack's (c') is best dismissed quickly. Popper's metaphor of basic statements being like piles driven into a swamp is unfortunate if it suggests that basic statements are partially justified, since Popper maintains explicitly that basic statements are not justified at all. It would therefore be appropriate for an expositor to point out the ways in which the metaphor is ill-chosen. It is another thing entirely for an expositor to propose that the metaphor's unfortunate suggestions indicate that Popper surreptitiously held an alternative view to the one he explicitly affirmed.

Popper's theory of verisimilitude presents a large and complex topic that I will not discuss here, except to say that it appears to me that Popper was mistaken in propounding that theory, which seems inconsistent with his account of scientific knowledge. I can therefore appreciate the attempt to distinguish different, and conflicting, strands in that theory, such as Haack's (d) and (d'). It does, though, seem objectionable to present Popper's difficulties with the idea of verisimilitude as evidence that Popper had two different theories, one official and one underhand.

Haack's contrast between (e) and (e') does highlight a real difficulty in Popper's position. Given (e), that we never have reason to think a corroborated theory true, probable, or closer to the truth than other theories, it follows that we cannot be *rationally required* to prefer the best-corroborated theory as the basis for action. Yet Popper does seem to say the that we are rationally required to prefer the best-corroborated theory as the basis for action (1971, pp. 21-22; 1974a, p. 82; and elsewhere). Sometimes, however, he says only that it is *reasonable* or *rational* to act on the best-corroborated theory (1957a, p. 56; 1959, p. 282). That could mean that it is *rationally permitted*, rather than rationally required, to so act, which is consistent with it being also rationally permitted to act *against* the best-corroborated theory (1957a, p. 56 comes close to saying that). In other words, we are rationally permitted to *choose* whether or not to act on the best-corroborated theory. That position is not only consistent with Popper's epistemology, it is also a defensible position (see my 2013a, section 3, and my Forthcoming, for discussion). One might expect a charitable interpretation to point that out.

In her contrast of 'authentic Popper' with 'shadow Popper,' then,

Haack's exposition is not only uncharitable but is also seriously distorting. Further, when she lights upon passages which seem to conflict with each other, she immediately presents them as inconsistencies or as evidence that Popper had an official and an unofficial theory. Instead of trying to disclose the systematic thought that lies behind the apparent conflicts, which it is not difficult to do, as I have just shown, she simply throws up her hands (2009, pp. 5-6; 2010, pp. 404-7; 2013, pp. 10-13).

Haack also complains (2009, p. 6, 2013) of some of Popper's verbal quirks which facilitate an interpretation along the lines of her 'shadow Popper,' such as:

- using words like 'knowledge' and 'discovery' without their usual connotation of truth;
- using 'falsified' without its usual connotation of falsehood;
- having at one time used the word 'confirmation' instead of 'corroboration.'

The third complaint seems peevish, given that, as Haack herself notes (2009, p. 6), Popper soon desisted from using the term 'confirmation' when he realised how misleading it was. I have some sympathy for her first two complaints: the terms 'knowledge' and 'falsified' (and perhaps even 'discovery') do seem, with hindsight at least, to be somewhat unsuitable. We can agree that Popper's choice of terms could have been better; but a similar complaint can reasonably be made of probably all significant thinkers. Anyone proposing a new approach faces the problem of finding appropriate expression and usually resorts to using some old terms in somewhat novel ways. The duty of the exegete is to interpret sympathetically, being careful to note the verbal quirks and to take steps to try to avoid misunderstanding. Simply complaining that the quirks lead to misunderstanding seems to fall short of that.

In summary, then, there are serious deficiencies in Haack's critical exposition of Popper's views. It is unsympathetic and uncharitable, polemical rather than scholarly, journalistic rather than academic. Further, her misrepresentations are not only gross, but also gratuitous, given that the correctives to her caricatures are contained in the very segments of Popper's work that she cites for her misrepresentations.

3. Legal Confusion

Having cooked up a bifurcated Popper, Haack goes on to say that the views of 'shadow' Popper are responsible for a systematic misinterpretation of 'authentic' Popper according to which a claim that has been tested but not falsified is thereby confirmed, that is, shown to be probable, warranted, valid, or reliable. It is that misinterpretation, she says, that seduces some people into thinking that Popper's philosophy of science will be helpful to courts needing to determine whether scientific testimony is reliable (2009, p. 7).

Haack discusses the US Supreme Court case, *Daubert v. Merrell Dow Pharmaceuticals, Inc* (1993), in which, she says, the majority opinion was that judges are required to screen expert testimony not only for relevance but also for reliability; and in the case of scientific testimony, this requires courts to determine whether proffered scientific evidence really is scientific knowledge (2009, p. 8). The problem, she says, was that Justice Blackmun, speaking for the Court, and quoting Popper, said that what distinguishes science is the method of generating hypotheses and testing them to see if they can be falsified. Justice Blackmun, she says, was apparently unaware that Popper "expressly disavows any interest in the reliability of scientific theories" (2009, pp. 8-9). The confusion, she says, goes well beyond Blackmun. She cites a brief submitted by the American Medical Association which avers that "[a]n opinion is only based upon scientific knowledge if it is developed in accordance with the scientific method" and, citing Popper, goes on to say that "[i]f a hypothesis is repeatedly corroborated by empirical testing, it is ... *generally accepted as valid*" and that, while "no scientific theory is ever definitively confirmed...[a]s a practical matter..., some theories are *so thoroughly tested that they become virtually incontrovertible*" (2009, pp. 10-11, emphasis added by Haack). She quotes similar misconstruals of Popper in other amicus briefs, one of which she describes as an "exegetical travesty" (2009, p. 11), somewhat ironically, given her own exegetical travesty of Popper discussed above. She also cites further misconstruals along the same lines in the law reviews (209, pp. 12-13). She goes on to exhibit various alleged confusions, some of them gross, but some not clearly confused, that have arisen in court cases with respect to testability (2009, pp. 14-20).

4. Reliability

In her concluding section, Haack says:

> in any case involving scientific testimony the question of reliability is bound to arise, and must be determined *somehow*; and unless there is such a thing as (objectively) supportive evidence, such determinations could only be arbitrary. If Popper's account of what science is and how it works were true, *the legal system's interest in the question of the reliability of scientific testimony would be simply misconceived* (2009, p. 20).

Thus, she says, Popper's account of science would have radical implications for any legal system (2009, p. 21). She thinks that the legal system's interest in determining reliability is not misconceived because there is available a more plausible epistemology than Popper's.

Haack suggests that a better epistemology will affirm that a claim that has been tested but not falsified is thereby shown to be to some degree reliable (2009, p. 21). Such an epistemology would:

- be holistic;
- acknowledge the articulated, ramifying complexity of the evidence with respect to any serious scientific claim;
- recognise that while there is such a thing as genuinely supportive evidence, the relation of supportiveness is not purely formal, not a matter of logic in the narrow sense;
- acknowledge that scientific knowledge, like all empirical knowledge, ultimately depends on our interactions with the world;
- start with an individual conception of warrant – the degree to which a claim is warranted for an individual – and proceed from there to a social and eventually to an impersonal conception;
- focus on the difference between well- and poorly-conducted inquiry rather than remaining obsessed with rooting out 'pseudo-science.'

For the development of such a view she refers us to her book, *Defending Science* (2003).

I have not consulted the cited book; but there appears to be nothing in her list of points that could do anything to solve the problem of induction in a way which would show that testing a theory could reveal it to be reliable. In the third bullet-point, "recognise that…there is such a thing as genuinely supportive evidence" simply begs the question. The simple fact is that all the regularities that appear to obtain in the world, against which our theories have been tested, could, for all we can ever know, cease to obtain in the next instant, perhaps because they are just a temporary blip in a long-term chaos, or perhaps because they are simple time slices of regularities which, outside of those time slices, are so massively complex that it is beyond our powers to comprehend them, or perhaps for some other reason. Thus, supposed evidence that a regularity has obtained through human history is no evidence that it will continue to obtain in future (or even that it obtained at times in the remote past). *We can have no way of determining whether a theory is reliable.*

Does this have radical implications for any legal system, as Haack says it does? It would if, as Haack thinks, the functioning of the courts depends upon their ability to determine which theories are reliable. However, the fact that the courts have been functioning for centuries without being able to determine whether a theory is reliable seems to show that Haack's thought is false. It seems that, when reference to reliability is made in the courts and such reference is important for the functioning of the system, it need be the case only that the courts are using 'reliability' in a sense different to that in which Popper and Haack use it. How, then, should 'reliability' be interpreted when it is used indispensably in legal cases? Here is a sketch of an answer.

The courts are concerned with due process, which implies that their decisions should be arrived at only through approved procedures. One set of approved procedures concerns which testimony is admissible; and in the case of scientific testimony, courts need a way of distinguishing acceptable from unacceptable kinds. The way this distinction is made by the courts needs to make sense to the wider society; and that implies that, ceteris paribus, the distinction ought to be made in a way which is, broadly, in line with the way that the distinction would be made by those people who are acknowledged in the society to be scientists. Thus, if Popper's account of science delivers a rating of scientific theories which is broadly in line with the way that most or leading scientists would rate the same theories, as Popper claims (1949b, p. 356; 1957b; 1974b, pp. 977-87; and elsewhere) and as his positive reception amongst scientists suggests (despite his being reviled by philosophers), then the appeal of the courts to Popper's account of science would assist the courts to discharge their functions. This remains so even though Popper's account entails that scientific theories cannot be known to be reliable; and it remains so even if the courts use the *term* 'reliable' in a way which picks out theories that are well-rated by Popper's standards; and it remains so even if lawyers and others make very mistaken or misleading statements about verification, reliability, evidential support, and so on, so long as these confusions do not adversely affect their ability to discriminate falsifiable and well-tested theories from others.

5. Conclusion

Haack's aims, recall, were to show that:

(1)   legal players have systematically misunderstood Popper;
(2)   Popper's philosophy of science is no help in determining reliability;
(3)   courts' concern to determine reliability is both legally essential and philosophically legitimate;
(4)   the picture that legal players have mistakenly attributed to Popper is closer to the mark than the account Popper actually offers.

We can concede (1) given Haack's discussion which was reported in section 3, above. We must readily affirm (2) in light of the summary account of Popper's views that I gave in section 2. However, (3) is false. For, while courts must distinguish between good and bad kinds of scientific testimony, they need not make the distinction in terms of reliability. Indeed, since the claim that it is possible to determine reliability is philosophically illegitimate, the courts *cannot* distinguish between scientific theories or testimonies in terms of reliability. If, nevertheless, the courts do *talk* of determining reliability it would be charitable to interpret the term 'reliability' in a procedural rather than a substantive sense; indeed, such an interpretation would comport with other familiar practices of the courts. Finally, (4) is plain false because of the problem of induction, for which Haack neither offers nor suggests a tenable positive solution.

Haack therefore fails to achieve what she set out to do. However, what is more striking than that failure is her unsympathetic, polemical, uncharitable and gross misrepresentation of the views of Karl Popper.

13 GETTIER'S CLASSIC IRRELEVANCE

Abstract. Edmund Gettier's three-page article 'Is Justified True Belief Knowledge?' is generally regarded as a classic of epistemology. I argue that Gettier cases depend upon three assumptions, two of which are false and the third of which seems to generate a paradox for the ordinary-language epistemology that Gettier practises. I show that there are other problems with the definition of knowledge as justified true belief. I suggest that we follow Karl Popper in abandoning individual and subjective epistemologies of justification in favour of theories of social, objective and conjectural knowledge.

Keywords. Epistemology; Edmund Gettier; justified true belief; objective knowledge; Karl Popper.

1. Introduction

Edmund Gettier argues that accounts of knowledge as justified true belief are false. His paper is a staple of contemporary epistemology and many attempts have been made to respond to its challenge. I argue that his paper – and, by implication, contemporary epistemology – is misconceived. In section 2, I summarise Gettier's argument. In section 3, I show that his argument rests upon three assumptions, two of which are false and the third of which seems to generate a paradox for the ordinary-language epistemology that Gettier practises. I also explain briefly why knowledge cannot be justified true belief. In section 4, I suggest that we should abandon contemporary epistemology and follow the lead of Karl Popper's exploration of social, objective and conjectural knowledge. Throughout, when I speak of 'justified belief' I mean *epistemically justified belief* (non-epistemic kinds of justification, such as prudential justification, are ignored).

2. Gettier's Argument

Gettier (1963, p. 121) accepts that:

(a) person, S, may be justified in believing a false proposition;

(b) if S is justified in believing P, and P entails Q, and S deduces Q from P, and he accepts Q as a result of this deduction, then S is justified in believing Q.

Gettier then proposes two counterexamples (pp. 122-23) to refute the following claim (p. 121):

(c) S knows that P if and only if (i) P is true,
(ii) S believes that P,
(iii) S is justified in believing that P.

Counterexample 1
Smith and Jones have applied for the same job. The president of the company has assured Smith that Jones will be selected. Smith has just counted ten coins in Jones's pocket. Smith therefore has strong evidence for:

(1) Jones is the man who will get the job, and Jones has ten coins in his pocket.

Smith sees that (1) entails,

(2) The man who will get the job has ten coins in his pocket,

and he believes (2) on that ground. Therefore, Smith is justified in believing that (2) is true; that is, (ii) and (iii) hold with regard to Smith and (2). But, in fact, Smith will get the job. Also, unknown to Smith, he himself has ten coins in his pocket. So (2) is true; that is, (i) holds with regard to Smith and (2). So, according to (c), Smith knows that (2) is true.

But *Smith does not know that (2) is true*. The reason is that (2) is true in virtue of the number of coins in Smith's pocket, while Smith does not know how many coins are in Smith's pocket, and bases his belief in (2) on a count of the coins in Jones's pocket, whom he falsely believes to be the man who will get the job.

Counterexample 2:
Jones has at all times in the past within Smith's memory owned a car, and always a Ford, and Jones has just offered Smith a ride while driving a Ford. So, Smith has strong evidence for:

(3)   Jones owns a Ford.

Smith is totally ignorant of the whereabouts of Brown. He selects three place-names quite at random, and constructs the following three propositions:

(4)   Either Jones owns a Ford, or Brown is in Boston;
(5)   Either Jones owns a Ford, or Brown is in Barcelona;
(6)   Either Jones owns a Ford, or Brown is in Brest-Litovsk.

Smith realises that each of these propositions is entailed by (3) so he believes them for that reason. He is therefore completely justified in believing each of these three propositions. So with regard to Smith and (5), (ii) and (iii) hold.

As it happens, Jones does not own a Ford (he is at present driving a rented car) and, entirely unknown to Smith, Brown is in Barcelona. Therefore, *Smith does not know that (5) is true.* Yet, (5) is true; that is, with regard to Smith and (5), (i) holds as well as (ii) and (iii); so, according to (c), Smith knows that (5) is true.

3. Critique

Gettier's (a), (b) and (c) articulate propositions that seem acceptable to his contemporary epistemologists. He appears himself to accept (a) and (b). His counterexamples are therefore intended to show that (c) is false.

Gettier's counterexamples depend upon three assumptions, one of which is implicit.

Assumption 1 is that Smith has strong evidence for a belief, P.

Assumption 2, which is implicit, is that if someone has strong evidence for something that he believes, then he is justified in believing it.

Assumption 3 is that a person, S, does not know that P is true, if: P is true in virtue of a fact that S does not know, and S believes P because it is a logical consequence of a false belief of S for which S has strong evidence.

Gettier offers no arguments for these assumptions. He seems to think that these assumptions are what 'the plain man' would say or what we would say 'pre-philosophically.' The trouble is, the plain man is often ignorant and confused. So a philosopher ought to subject the assumptions to a critical examination. Upon such examination, the first two assumptions appear to be false and the third seems to generate a paradox for ordinary-language epistemology.

As we saw in Chapter 5, Section 2, there is no such thing as evidence for the *truth* of an empirical proposition, because of the problem of induction. There was strong evidence for Kepler's astronomy, there was strong evidence for Galileo's law of free fall, for about two centuries there was very impressive evidence for Newton's theory; but we now take all of those theories to be false. Strong evidence for a proposition consists only in the fact that the proposition has survived severe critical evaluation more successfully than its available rivals (see Chapter 5, Section 3).

In Gettier's counterexample 1, Smith's evidence for the first conjunct of (1) is that the president of the company has assured him that Jones will get the job. But what sort of person is the president of the company? If he is someone like Donald Trump, it seems doubtful that what he says should be taken as strong evidence for anything. Even if the president of the company is not like Donald Trump, is it *he* who makes the selection or is he merely reporting what he has been told about what the personnel manager has decided? We must presume that Smith does not know. And so on and so forth. In short, Smith's evidence is weak. Similarly, in counterexample 2, it is false that Smith has strong evidence for (3). Smith has not subjected (3) to severe tests of any sort. He simply notes that (3) is consistent with remembered facts about Jones owning or driving a Ford in the past. He has made no attempt to falsify (3). Gettier's *Assumption 1* is therefore false.

Gettier's *Assumption 2* also appears to be false because there is no connection between strong evidence and truth. Once we acknowledge that a proposition for which we have strong evidence may be false, how can we maintain that we are justified in believing it?

It seems that Gettier's *Assumption 3* will lead him into self-contradiction. In the nineteenth-century Newton's theory was the leading scientific theory and the paradigm of knowledge. On numerous occasions scientists derived from that theory a successful prediction concerning the occurrence of a total solar eclipse and the ranges of places in which the eclipse would be visible. Take just one of those successful predictions. Would 'the plain man,' if asked, say that the scientists knew that the prediction was true? I suspect it would be difficult to find an educated person who denied it. On Gettier's ordinary-language epistemology, then, the scientists knew that the prediction was true. However, according to Gettier's *Assumption 3*, the scientists did not know. The prediction was true in virtue of a fact that the scientists did not know, namely, the curvature of space-time; but the scientists believed the prediction because it was a logical consequence of a false belief of theirs for which they had strong evidence, namely, that the movements of the celestial bodies are due to a force of gravity which acts instantaneously at a distance (such a force does not exist, according to general relativity). So, Gettier's *Assumption 3* lands him in paradox.

Thus, neither of Gettier's counterexamples is cogent. But that does not mean that we have rescued the claim that knowledge is justified true belief. We have already noted that strong evidence is insufficient for justified belief; and it seems obvious that weak evidence or no evidence is also insufficient for it. We should therefore reject the notion of justified belief. That leaves open the possibility that knowledge is *true belief for which there is strong evidence*, where we interpret 'strong evidence' for a proposition as meaning that the proposition has survived severe critical evaluation more successfully than its available rivals. Gettier's counterexamples are irrelevant to that claim because they are not examples involving strong evidence. However, the switch from justification to strong evidence so understood is unlikely to appeal to contemporary epistemologists because it will not certify as knowledge the prejudices of 'the plain man.' Like Gettier, they must, to pursue their dogmatic project, permit any old memories or random statements or incidental observations to count as strong evidence. In any case, there are reasons to consider a more radical alternative.

4. A Popperian Alternative

Concern with the question of when 'plain men' consider it correct to say of a person that she knows that p has led epistemologists to focus on trivia, such as whether Smith knows that the man who will get the job has ten coins in his pocket. It also diverts attention from the epistemologically important matter of the *growth* of knowledge, which takes place through co-operative activity within an appropriate institutional context. For such reasons, Karl Popper (1945, chapter 23; 1959; 1972b) recommends that epistemology should focus instead on published conjectures that are subjected to inter-subjective criticism, including empirical testing. We may summarise, and simplify, his approach as follows.

A published theory counts as objective knowledge if and only if it has been severely criticised and it has stood up to severe criticism better than any rival published theories. A theory that counts as objective knowledge may be refuted the next time it is tested. So, objective knowledge is always conjectural; that is, so far as we can know, it might be false. Even a thoroughly tested and successful theory may be refuted the next time it is tested, as happened when Newton's theory, which was published in 1687, was refuted by Eddington's eclipse experiment in 1919. Consequently, belief that an item of objective knowledge is true is never justified; and a theory's status as objective knowledge is entirely independent of whether anyone believes it.

Thus, Popper rejects Gettier's (a) and (b) because no belief can be justified, but he accepts the following counterparts:

(a')   a false theory may be a part of objective knowledge;
(b')   if P is a part of objective knowledge, and P entails Q, then Q is a part of objective knowledge.

Popper concurs with Gettier in rejecting (c); and he holds no counterpart of it.

14 WHY NEIL LEVY IS WRONG TO ENDORSE NO-PLATFORMING

Consider two contrasting views of human knowledge.

Indoctrination. There are experts who know what is true. The rest of us should defer to them. The experts must decide whether any person is permitted to publish an opinion, so that false or damaging views are suppressed. A view can be effectively rebutted by impugning the expertise of the person expounding it.

Inquiry. Any supposed expert may be mistaken even in her own field of research. Novel discoveries can, and often are, made by people outside of official circles. Anyone should be allowed to put forward her opinion; and all opinions, whether of experts or others, should be open to criticism from all quarters to enable mistakes to be discovered. A view can be effectively rebutted only by arguments against it.

Defenders of free speech usually accept a version of the second view. It is that view that is consistent with – even suggested by – the history of science. Kepler was an expert in astronomy but he was wrong about the planetary motions. Newton, another expert, did better than Kepler, but he turned out to be wrong too. Edison's production of his electric light refuted the unanimous scientific opinion that such a light was impossible. The special theory of relativity was propounded by a man working in the Swiss Patent Office.

Neil Levy (2019), on the other hand, appears to accept a version of the first view. That is a view espoused by religious sects and totalitarian regimes. It assumes that the truth can be known independently of critical debate.

Levy argues in favour of no-platforming, which prevents a person from contributing to a public debate on the grounds that her contribution is dangerous or unacceptable. Defenders of free speech reject no-platforming: they contend that what appear to be dangerous or unacceptable views should be criticised, not suppressed, so that mutual learning can take place under the stimulus of open debate.

Levy's concern is that dangerous or unacceptable views can acquire indirect ("higher order") evidence in their favour by being aired on a respectable platform. An invitation to speak at a university campus or a prestigious event, or to write an opinion piece for a newspaper, selects someone from among the large crowd of potential speakers. It thereby typically certifies *expertise* and *sincerity*, which in turn show that the speaker's opinion should be given particular weight. Being invited to speak at a university confers much credibility, he says. Therefore, inviting someone to a university to expound a view that is bad or false generates *misleading* indirect evidence in favour of that view; and we should avoid generating misleading evidence.

Levy seems unaware of the low regard in which the press, and also university humanities departments, are held in society at large, including large parts of university-educated society. That makes it doubtful that speaking at a university campus could generate indirect evidence for the views expressed. But we can leave that thought on one side because it is the mission of a university to promote the growth of knowledge, which requires a critical comparison of competing views. Since competing views cannot all be true, the fact that a view is expounded by a speaker at a university cannot be evidence in favour of it and against the rival views that also get expressed there.

Curiously, Levy adds that the supposed indirect evidence is extremely difficult to rebut. If a university gives a platform to a climate-change sceptic, he says, the indirect evidence it provides in favour of her view is not rebutted by the university inviting another speaker later to 'balance' her, or if she is subject to a devastating response from the floor. "We can rebut her claim *that global warming isn't occurring*, but we cannot rebut her claim *that the invitation certifies my expertise*" (2019).

But, if the platform for the climate-change sceptic generates indirect evidence for *her* view, the platform for the speaker with the opposing view generates indirect evidence for *his* view. As we just noted, if the same thing (the platform) generates indirect evidence for two contradictory views, it generates indirect evidence for neither over the other. Further, if a speaker is subject to a devastating response from the floor, then her view is rebutted, as Levy admits. Why does it matter that it does not rebut her claim that the invitation certifies her expertise? Experts are often wrong. What matters is that her view is refuted.

Levy continues that the invitation is only *prima facie* indirect evidence. If we discover that a speaker was invited only because he made a big donation to the school, or because he is the dean's cousin, that evidence is considerably weakened. It is this kind of consideration – not rational argument – says Levy, that rebuts such indirect evidence. Such *ad hominem* attacks (he's funded by the oil industry; he's a racist) or attacks on the credibility of those who provided him with a platform do not address his views, but they are, says Levy, often appropriate responses to indirect evidence.

However, such personal attacks seem entirely inappropriate. Even if the person is not an expert, what he says may still be a worthwhile contribution to the debate; and that is so even if we think it is false. If we try to explain why it is false we may understand better the position we take to be true; we might even find some truth in the contribution, if not directly, then indirectly, perhaps in the sort of way that Newton's explanation of the tides by reference to the moon's influence endorsed a contention made in astrological lore.

No-platforming, by stifling debate, hampers the growth of knowledge. Where there is free debate, as should be the case in any university, being invited to speak generates no evidence, direct or indirect, for what is said. Some people are experts, or more expert than others, but expertise is no guarantee of truth. Challenging a participant's expertise is a diversion from the business of the debate, which should be concerned with which of the rival views stands up best to criticism.

I develop the points I make in this note in more detail in my 2016c.

178

AGAINST THE PHILOSOPHICAL TIDE

15 WE SHOULD NOT SHIELD OURSELVES FROM ABHORRENT BELIEFS

John Schwenkler (2018) asks whether we should shield ourselves from others' abhorrent beliefs. He says that there seem to be circumstances in which it is good sense to shield oneself from abhorrent beliefs and other circumstances in which to do so is closed-minded. His attempt to distinguish the two circumstances involves him in another problem which he does not attempt to solve. I explain why a rational person who wants to improve his knowledge should not shield himself from abhorrent beliefs.

Schwenkler says that some of our choices have the potential to alter our cognitive perspective in ways that we regard as a loss. He gives an example of Russian spies in the 1980s living in the United States who spend a lot of time in close relationships with US citizens, thereby exposing themselves to theories they find abhorrent and often acting as if they hold those theories themselves. They may therefore worry about becoming more sympathetic to those abhorrent theories, not because they have *learned* that the theories are true, but because their familiarity with and pretended embrace of, those theories might cause them to *unlearn* some of what they presently understand about the world. He suggests some other examples:

(i)   a documentary that a friend invites you to watch puts forward a message that you think is dangerously false;

(ii) a discipline you are thinking of studying involves ideological presuppositions you reject.

In such cases, he says, a choice is seen as altering one's cognitive perspective for the worse, though the choice may have other things in favour of it.

Schwenkler considers the objection that it would be *dogmatic, ideological, closed-minded,* or *fearful of the truth* to refrain from a course of action because one might thereby come to have a belief that one currently deems abhorrent. His example is a climate-change sceptic who eschews an oceanography course out of fear that it will incline him to believe in climate change, which he regards as a hoax. Schwenkler concedes that such closed-mindedness is a vice but he makes a distinction. The climate-change sceptic is closed-minded because he *believes falsely* that climate change is a hoax; but if he *knew* it was a hoax, then his behaviour would not be closed-minded. Thus, if a spy is asked to infiltrate a group of hateful extremists and she *knows* that the extremists' views are false and abhorrent, she has a good reason for rejecting the assignment, namely, that she would risk becoming more sympathetic to those hateful views.

Unfortunately, says Schwenkler, that will not do. The person who acts non-knowingly and from a mere belief might still *believe that she knows* the thing in question: that climate change is a hoax, say. "What could assure us, when we exercise cognitive caution in order to avoid what we take to be a potential impairment of our understanding or a loss of our grip on the facts, that we aren't in that situation as well?"

Let us summarise. Schwenkler's problem is: how do we avoid being misled by abhorrent theories without being closed-minded? Schwenkler's solution is: we refuse to engage with the abhorrent theories when we know that they are false. Schwenkler's new problem is: how can we *really* know that such theories are false rather than merely *thinking* that we know that they are false?

Schwenkler's new problem seems insoluble, as sceptics have argued for millennia. Since his solution to the first problem depends upon a solution to the second, his solution to the first problem is useless. Can we do better?

It seems that to *avoid being closed-minded*, we must be prepared, in principle, to consider *any* theory that is a rival to one of our favoured views (Mill 1859, chapter 2). Since the theories are rivals, at most one of them can be true (they might all be false, since the true theory might not yet have been discovered). So, how do we *avoid being misled* by a false theory? We criticise it. Wherever we have rival views we should attempt to criticise each of them (including our own pet theory, if we have one), and then evaluate the theories according to how well they stand up to criticism. The criticisms will usually reveal new problems which are likely to prompt us to invent new theories to solve them, so we may end up, if we are lucky, with a theory that is different to any of those with which we began and better than all of them. Of course, we can never be sure that we have eliminated all the false theories: even the theory that is currently the best of all those so far considered may later be rejected as false. But we may often find that, through open-mindedness and criticism, we have been able to discover which theories are better and which worse (Popper 1976).

Let us go back to Schwenkler's spies immersing themselves into a foreign and distasteful culture. They espouse a set of theories when with the natives; but they may subject those theories to criticism when on their own or when back with their own people. So long as they retain their critical faculties, they can avoid 'going native' even while giving the *appearance of being native*. Through criticism they achieve detachment. Of course, one might expect that the spies would come to have sympathy for the native views the better they come to understand them; but such appreciative sympathy is quite compatible with acknowledgement that the views in question are false. There is a risk of the spies *going native*, switching from one 'paradigm' to another, only insofar as they suspend their critical faculties – or insofar as they *learn through criticism* that the native views are actually better than their own.

Our current theories may be mistaken. If we are rational and we want to improve our theories, we will welcome criticism of them. The strongest and most enlightening criticism often comes from considering radically different, perhaps even abhorrent, theories. The rival theories can be evaluated; and from their strengths and weaknesses we may not only be able to rate one as better than the other but we may also see more deeply into the heart of our problems and thereby be able to come up with better theories.

In short, insofar as we seek knowledge, we should retain an open mind and thus we should never shield ourselves from abhorrent beliefs. We can avoid being bewitched by abhorrent beliefs (or alluring beliefs) by subjecting all available theories to criticism.

16 HOW NOT TO DEFEND HOMOSEXUAL EQUALITY

Paul Russell (2017) maintains that identities such as race, gender and sexual orientation have equal ethical standing because:

(a)   such identities are not constituted by beliefs, values or practices;
(b)   such identities cannot be discarded.

He says: "What 'tolerance' requires in this context is recognising and acknowledging *differences* and *diversities* with respect to significant (natural) features that shape the experience, interests and needs of various groups within society… The force of tolerance in these contexts … is to insist on *the equal worth and value* of these various identities…" Therefore, says Russell, we should resist attempts to present those who identify as gay as making a choice and affirming certain values and practices that they are capable of shedding.

Unfortunately for Russell, (a) and (b) are false. Fortunately for us all, the equal ethical standing of people of different races, sexes, genders and sexual orientations does not depend on either (a) or (b).

Someone who is strictly heterosexual may be repelled at the prospect of having sex with a person of the same sex, whereas a homosexual may find the same prospect alluring. That is a difference of values. Similarly, men and women typically have different values in that, typically, different things are important to them; they also seem typically to have different beliefs and expectations, in that, typically, they take interest in different features of the surrounding world and find different practices attractive. Accordingly, sex and sexual orientation do seem to be in part constituted by beliefs, values and practices. So, (a) is false.

In this age of transgenderism it seems ludicrous to claim that gender is an identity that cannot be discarded. However, Russell seems to mean by 'gender' not a *social-sexual role*, such as masculine or feminine (which is what is usually meant by the term), but a *sex*, that is, male or female. But people do change their sex too, with surgery and hormones. Perhaps Russell would insist that such changes are not really changes of sex because the chromosomes (XX or XY) remain unchanged. But the relative importance of chromosomes versus genitalia in determining sex is debatable. Even with regard to changing one's *race* there is scope for debate, given the case of Rachel Dolezal who claims to be culturally black though she was born white. For gender and perhaps race, then, (b) is false. It also seems to be false for homosexuality.

We may distinguish sexual orientation as *an inclination* from sexual orientation as *an aspect of a lifestyle*. The latter is clearly a matter of choice which involves a set of beliefs, values and practices. In past ages in which homosexual practices were suppressed, there were many people who had a strong inclination for homosexuality but who lived as heterosexuals, married, had children and exhibited no sexual interest in persons of the same sex. In choosing a heterosexual lifestyle they adopted a set of practices with accompanying values and beliefs. Indeed, some of them may have chosen that lifestyle because they accepted the prevailing beliefs and values in their society according to which homosexuality is wrong. Their chosen heterosexual identity was in part constituted by practices, beliefs and values. Other people in those societies who also had a strong inclination for homosexuality chose a homosexual lifestyle, more or less secretly. They might have chosen that lifestyle and its associated practices because they believed that homosexuality is not wrong and that same-sex relationships are healthy. Their chosen homosexual identity was in part constituted by practices, beliefs and values. Contrary to Russell's claim, then, those who identify as gay *are* making a choice and *are* affirming particular beliefs, values and practices.

Political suppressions of homosexuality are attempts to curtail the rights of people to engage in homosexual activity, and then to ensure that people are punished if they do what they no longer have a legal right to do. Such suppressions are *not* attempts to discover, punish or eliminate people who have a strong *inclination* for homosexuality but who never engage in homosexual activity. It is homosexuality as *an aspect of lifestyle*, with its associated practices, beliefs and values, that is the target of suppression. So, Russell's demand for equal treatment for people who have a strong *inclination* for homosexuality, rather than for those who *choose* a homosexual lifestyle, is pointless; and it offers no defence for the latter.

The demand for homosexual equality should be the demand that those who *choose to engage in homosexual practices* have rights equal to those of people who choose not to engage in such practices. The reason for the demand is twofold:

(i)   all people have equal rights in virtue of being people, so long as they do not violate the rights of others;
(ii)   people who engage in homosexual practices do not thereby violate the rights of others.

Spelling out in any detail what 'equal rights' amounts to is notoriously difficult, but that is not my concern here.

Whether a strong *inclination* for homosexuality is an unchangeable product of nature (as Russell maintains), a product of upbringing or environment, or a product of some combination of those, is an interesting question for scientists to investigate in the spirit of free enquiry. It is of no concern for politics.

Contrary to Russell's claim, therefore, there is no need to resist attempts to present those who identify as gay as making a choice and as affirming particular beliefs, values and practices that they are capable of shedding. It seems that Russell claims that those who identify as gay are *not* making a choice because he wants to say that gays are not to *blame* for having a strong inclination for homosexuality. He can then insist that it is wrong to punish people for having that inclination. But that insistence is consistent with maintaining that an inclination for homosexuality is unfortunate; that anyone so unfortunate as to have such an inclination should not give in to it but should rather try to live as a heterosexual or else give up sex altogether; and even that, to help them to avoid blameworthy behaviour, people who are so unfortunate as to have a homosexual inclination should be prohibited from choosing homosexual activity.

Instead of claiming that gays are not to blame for having a homosexual *inclination* (which may be false, for all we know so far), Russell should have argued that gays are not to blame for *choosing* a homosexual lifestyle that suits them, *because it is not wrong to make such a choice.*

186

17 PAUL RUSSELL'S CONFUSION ABOUT TOLERANCE

Paul Russell (2017) contends that the Left misunderstand what tolerance requires. Tolerance, he says, is not just a matter of recognising 'diversity' and 'difference.' It is, crucially, a matter of acknowledging and accepting disagreement and ideological conflict. Criticism, condemnation and even ridicule should not be confused with intolerance. Thus,

(1)   tolerance means that people are entitled to hold and express views that others regard as mistaken, foolish, objectionable or pernicious, and that others are entitled to criticise those views, so long as no one resorts to coercive measures that violate the rights of others.

There is, for example, a significant difference between a Sunday preacher condemning atheists as 'Godless, wicked fools', and a fanatic threatening to murder 'blasphemers.' The former is a form of (objectionable) ignorance and dogmatism; but the latter is a plain case of intolerance. Tolerance does not, therefore, involve a commitment to affirming the equal worth and value of all doctrines and practices that fall within the scope and bounds of tolerance.

The identity politics of the Left, Russell says, goes awry in paying too little attention to the following distinction.

Ideological identities, such as a person's religious identity, are legitimate targets of criticism and debate because they are optional and are constituted by doctrines, beliefs and values that have implications for our social and ethical practices and institutions.

> *Non-ideological identities*, such as race, gender and sexual orientation, are inappropriate targets for praise or blame because they involve no ideological *content* but instead turn on unchosen natural qualities and features that cannot be discarded in light of critical scrutiny or reflection of any kind.

Tolerance, he says, means that divergent groups are required to accept the equal worth and value of non-ideological identities. A just society rejects all forms of criticism of these groups as unacceptable forms of bigotry, prejudice and hate. In consequence, all criticism of ideological views must be formed and presented in a manner that pays due respect to the most important and essential identity that others in our community and society have – the identity of being rational beings with equal ethical standing and worth. Thus,

(2)   tolerance requires suppressing any view that implies that people of different non-ideological identities have unequal ethical standing.

The Left goes wrong, he says, in assimilating objections against a religion's ideology to forms of bigotry and prejudice directed against non-ideological identities, and dismissing both as racist or xenophobic.

Russell's position is at variance with a traditional understanding of what tolerance requires. Consider Aristotle's theory, expressed in his *Ethics* and *Politics*, that barbarians are naturally less rational than Greeks and in consequence have an inferior set of rights. Tolerant societies permit the expression of Aristotle's view and they also permit criticism of it; but, according to (2), in a tolerant society Aristotle's view would be outlawed.

Indeed, Russell's position is self-contradictory. His (ideological) liberal identity is optional and is constituted in part by the belief that all people have an equal ethical standing no matter what their non-ideological identity is. That belief should be open to criticism, according to (1); but, according to (2), all criticism of that belief should be suppressed.

If we are genuinely in favour of tolerance, we should resolve the conflict between (1) and (2) by rejecting (2). We should insist that all views are open to criticism (including that one).

How did Russell, who champions (1), come to accept the intolerant (2) and thereby contradict himself? In his defence of (2) he slides from the proposition that people cannot be *blamed* (or praised) for their non-ideological identities ("There is no ideological *content* to their identity to assess or debate – the relevant identity is an inappropriate target for praise or blame") to the proposition that people may not be criticised in virtue of their non-ideological identities ("Since any proposed non-ideological identity will lack ideological content, it cannot serve as a basis for legitimate criticism or evaluation of any kind").

But the latter proposition does not follow from the former. Aristotle did not blame barbarians for being less rational than Greeks but he did criticise them as falling short of a desirable standard. The distinction will be familiar to anyone who has held a position of responsibility in an organisation. In carrying out performance appraisals or job interviews, for instance, we often criticise people's shortcomings, which may be due to natural (in)abilities, without implying that they are to blame for them. Within an organisation, a person's natural (non-ideological) abilities make him suitable, or unsuitable, for a particular position to which sought-after rights attach.

However, I suspect that confusion between blame and criticism is only part of the explanation for Russell's self-contradiction. Indeed, it may be a product of the underlying explanation, namely, that Russell has set out to defend the indefensible, namely, laws against 'hate speech.' Such laws are an execrable violation of freedom of expression, and freedom of expression is essential for human flourishing, as I explain in my 2016c and my 2020, chapter 6, section 6.4.

18 HÁJEK'S FAULTY DISCUSSION OF PHILOSOPHICAL HEURISTICS

Alan Hájek (2017) discusses philosophical heuristics; but his discussion of arguments and their logical properties is somewhat remiss. He says,

> For our purposes, an *argument* is a number of premises followed by a conclusion, where the premises are intended to lend support to the conclusion.

But that is a very narrow view of what an argument is. For instance, in the classic form of argument known as a 'reductio ad absurdum,' the conclusion is a self-contradiction. Far from it being intended that the premises lend support to the conclusion, the insupportable conclusion is intended to refute the premises. Similarly, an argument may be intended to show that two propositions, P and Q, are inconsistent with each other, by showing that if P is true, then Q is false, and if Q is true, then P is false, without any intention to lend support to the conclusion that Q is false or to the conclusion that P is false. Or an argument may be used to show that Q follows from P without it being intended that P lends support to Q (for example, P may be known to be false).

Hájek goes on:

> A *sound* argument is one that is valid and whose premises are true (and so its conclusion is true, too). An *unsound* argument is one that is either invalid or that has at least one false premise.

That is indeed an established terminology. Yet a valid reductio ad absurdum is a very powerful form of argument despite having at least one false premise. It is at least infelicitous to label it 'unsound.'

Hájek does recognize the power of reductio ad absurdum arguments, but he also misstates it:

> if you are not sure how to prove some claim, perhaps because it seems so obvious, try *reductio ad absurdum* reasoning. That is, suppose that the claim is false, and show that this leads to a contradiction. This provides a *proof* of the claim, one in which the claim is established conclusively by that reasoning.

That is false. Consider the set of all sets that are not elements of themselves. Suppose that we want to prove the claim:

(a)   the set of all sets that are not elements of themselves is an element of itself.

Following Hájek's advice, we suppose that (a) is false. That would be so if

(b)   the set of all sets that are not elements of themselves is not an element of itself.

But if (b) is true, then that set, as it is not an element of itself, belongs to the set of all sets that are not elements of themselves; but it is that set, so it is an element of itself. So, it both is and is not an element of itself. Our supposition that (a) is false therefore leads to a contradiction. According to Hájek that provides a *proof* of (a). But it does no such thing because we can also show that if (a) is true, then the set of all sets that are not elements of themselves is both an element of itself and not an element of itself. This, of course, is Russell's Paradox which, ironically, Hájek himself had mentioned four paragraphs earlier.

It is not sufficient, to prove a claim by reductio ad absurdum, to show that the falsity of the claim implies a contradiction. One has to show that the *negation* of the claim implies a contradiction. It is impossible for a claim and its negation to be true together or to be false together. But (a) and (b) each imply that the set of all sets that are not elements of themselves exists; so they can be false together if there is no such set. The fact that (a) and (b) both lead to self-contradiction shows the falsity of their common assumption:

(c)   there is a set of all sets that are not elements of themselves.

The supposition that (c) is true leads to a contradiction; therefore we can infer the negation of (c):

(d)   there is no set of all sets that are not elements of themselves.

Thus, the negation of (a) is not (b) but:

(e)   it is not the case that the set of all sets that are not elements of themselves is an element of itself

which is true if and only if either (b) or (d) is true. We obtain the negation of (a) by applying the negation operator to the whole sentence, which is known as a 'wide-scope negation,' rather than applying it only to the predicate of (a), as in (b), which is known as a 'narrow-scope negation.'

The distinction between wide-scope and narrow-scope negations applies not only to sentences containing definite descriptions, such as (a) and (b), but also to sentences containing proper names and other singular terms, such as,

(f)   Socrates is wise,

which has the narrow-scope negation,

(g)   Socrates is not wise,

which implies the existence of Socrates, and the wide-scope negation,

(h)   it is not the case that Socrates is wise

which would be true if either Socrates was not wise or Socrates did not exist. Thus, the logical form of (f) may be shown perspicuously as follows:

(i)   something is Socrates and it is wise.

Just as observation statements are theory-laden and thus implicitly general (recall chapters 1, 2, 3 and 5), so singular statements are quantifier-laden and thus implicitly general. Recognition of this point scuppers the empiricist insistence (Strawson 1956) that the meaning of quantified sentences is to be explained by reference to singular predications.

19 WINNING THE ARGUMENT?

Some interactions are *win-lose*: a person gains at the expense of another. For example, in theft, the thief benefits at the expense of the victim. Some interactions are *lose-lose*: no-one comes out better off. Nobody wins a war. Some interactions are *win-win*: everyone gains. Trade is the standard example: Anne wants Bob's apple more than she wants her orange, and Bob wants Anne's orange more than he wants his apple, so they exchange and both are better off.

In logic, an argument consists of a set of propositions, one of which is the conclusion, the rest of which are the premises. The argument is valid if and only if the conclusion follows from the premises. In that case, necessarily, if all the premises are true, the conclusion is true; alternatively, necessarily, if the conclusion is false, at least one of the premises is false. In this note, I use 'argument' as it is used in logic.

Debates and altercations are often called 'arguments' but they are not arguments in the logician's sense. In an *altercation* people may shout, accuse, decry and insult; they might make use of some arguments, but they often do not. No one wins an altercation: it is lose-lose.

In a *debate*, people try to get a good answer to a question by using arguments to find the week spots in alternative answers. When a person talks about 'winning the argument,' she is talking about winning a *debate* and she sees debate as a win-lose interaction. She enters the debate with her own answer to the question and her aim is to leave the debate with her own answer intact and all the rival answers demolished. She is thereby vindicated and her opponents are humiliated. Such a person is a dogmatist; she has a closed mind; she is not prepared to consider that her current view may be in need of improvement or replacement.

A critical, or open-minded, person sees debate as win-win. She seeks out criticisms of her own current views, as well as criticising alternative views, in the hope that every party to the debate can learn something new. The aim is to gather and generate different answers to the question and then to rate those answers in the light of the critical arguments that have been discussed. An open-minded debater accepts that her current view may, at the end of the debate, be discovered to be inferior to some other view.

Open-minded debaters need not end up in agreement. It might turn out to be unclear which of the answers considered is best. Even if it is clear to all that one particular answer has withstood criticism better than all the alternatives, some open-minded debaters may reasonably be reluctant to accept that answer if they suspect that:

(i)   new information may come in that undermines it;
(ii)   one of the alternative answers could be modified and strengthened;
(iii)   a new and better answer may be proposed;
(iv)   some of the arguments accepted may in future be found to be invalid.

So, everyone may have learned something from the debate even if they all still disagree at the end of it. All of them win in that they come away from the debate with a better understanding of the question than they had at the start of it.

We engage in debate not only to find better answers to theoretical questions. Often we need an answer to a practical question about what to do. A person trying to decide what he shall do may engage in debate with others to improve upon his current answer to his practical question. He need not end up agreeing with any of those others in order to find the debate to have been worthwhile.

Agreement is, however, necessary when a group of people has to decide what they shall do *together*. In that case, if agreement cannot be reached through debate, it has to be reached by some other means, such as a majority vote or flipping a coin.

"An argument is a connected series of statements to establish a definite proposition," says Michael Palin in Monty Python's *Argument Room*. If he is talking about an argument in the logician's sense, he is wrong: if an argument is valid, the truth of all the propositions constituting the premises guarantees the truth of the proposition constituting the conclusion, and the falsity of the conclusion-proposition guarantees the falsity of at least one of the propositions that make up the premises. There is nothing there about establishing a definite proposition. If Palin is talking about a *debate*, his comment is appropriate for a dogmatist who sees debate as win-lose, rather than an open-minded person who sees debate as win-win.

Contemporary philosophers, it seems, would feel at home in a Monty Python sketch. For example, Alan Hájek (2017), repeating what has been said by innumerable contemporary philosophers, says: "an *argument* is a number of premises followed by a conclusion, where the premises are intended to lend support to the conclusion." Inconsistently, he recognises as a powerful form of argument the *reductio ad absurdum*, in which the self-contradictory conclusion in insupportable and is taken to refute the premises. Similarly, contemporary epistemologists are preoccupied with the dogmatist's question of how beliefs can be justified rather than with the question of how, through criticism, currently accepted theories can be improved or replaced.

I expand upon this criticism of contemporary philosophy in my 2015 and 2016b; also, specifically in relation to Michael Huemer, in my 2016a.

BIBLIOGRAPHY

Alvarez, Maria. 2009. 'Actions, Thought-Experiments and the "Principle of Alternate Possibilities".' *Australasian Journal of Philosophy* 87 (1): 61–81.

———. 2013. 'Agency and Two-way Powers.' *Proceedings of the Aristotelian Society* 113 (1pt1): 101–21.

Arnauld, Antoine and Nicole, Pierre. 1662. *Logic or the Art of Thinking*, James Dickoff and Patricia James (trans.). Indianapolis: Bobbs-Merrill (1964).

Ayer, A. J. 1946. 'Introduction.' In his *Language, Truth and Logic*, second edition (pp. 7-35). Harmondsworth: Penguin.

Beaney, Michael. 2014. 'Analysis.' *The Stanford Encyclopedia of Philosophy* (Summer 2014 Edition), ed. Edward N. Zalta. Downloaded 1 October 2014 from:

https://plato.stanford.edu/archives/sum2014/entries/analysis/

Bolzano, Bernard. 1837. *Theory of Science*, Jan Berg (ed.), Burnham Terrell (tr.). Dordrecht: Reidel (1973).

Bratman, Michael. 1987. *Intention, Plans, and Practical Reason*. Cambridge, MA.: Harvard University Press.

Broome, John. 2002. 'Practical Reasoning.' In *Reason and Nature: Essays in the Theory of Rationality*, ed. J. Bermùdez and A. Millar (pp. 85-111). Oxford: Oxford University Press.

Buchanan, James. 1969. *Cost and Choice*. Volume 6 of *The Collected Works of James M. Buchanan*. Indianapolis: Liberty Fund (1999).

———. 1982. 'The Domain of Subjective Economics.' In Israel Kirzner (ed.), *Method, Process, and Austrian Economics* (pp. 7-20). Lexington, MA: D. C. Heath & Co.

Carroll, John. 1994. *Laws of Nature*. Cambridge: Cambridge University Press.

Carter, Adam. 2018. 'On Behalf of Controversial View Agnosticism.' *European Journal of Philosophy* 26 (4): 1358-70.

Cohen, Morris and Nagel, Ernest. 1934. *Introduction to Logic and Scientific Method*. London: Routledge.

De Morgan, Augustus. 1847. *Formal Logic*. London: Taylor and Walton.

Duhem, Pierre. 1954. *The Aim and Structure of Physical Theory*, second edition, translated by P. P. Wiener. Princeton: Princeton University Press.

Dummett, Michael. 1973. 'The Justification of Deduction.' In his *Truth and Other Enigmas* (pp. 290-318). London: Duckworth (1978).

——————. 1981. *The Interpretation of Frege's Philosophy*. London: Duckworth.

Earman, John and Roberts, John. 1999. '*Ceteris Paribus*, There is no Problem of Provisos.' *Synthese* 118 (3): 439-78.

Earman, John, Roberts, John and Smith, Sheldon. 2002. '*Ceteris Paribus* Lost.' *Erkenntnis* 57 (3): 281-301.

Einstein, Albert. 1920. *Relativity*. London: Methuen (1962 enlarged edition).

Feldman, Richard. 2000. 'The Ethics of Belief.' *Philosophy and Phenomenological Research*, 60 (3): 667-695.

——————. 2005. 'Deep Disagreement, Rational Resolutions, and Critical Thinking.' *Informal Logic* 25 (1): 13-23.

Feyerabend, Paul. 1960. 'On the Interpretation of Scientific Theories.' In his *Realism, Rationalism and Scientific Method*. New York: Cambridge University Press (1981).

——————. 1975. *Against Method*. London: New Left Books.

Findlay, J. N. 1962. 'The Teaching of Meaning.' In his *Ascent to the Absolute*. London: George Allen & Unwin (1970).

Fogelin, Robert. 1985. 'The Logic of Deep Disagreement.' *Informal Logic* 7 (1): 1-8.

Foss, Nicolai and Klein, Peter. 2010. 'Alertness, Action, and the Antecedents of Entrepreneurship.' *Journal of Private Enterprise* 25 (2): 145-64.

Frederick, Danny. 2010. 'Two Concepts of Rationality.' *Libertarian Papers* 2/5. Available here:
https://www.academia.edu/213888/Two_Concepts_of_Rationality

——————. 2013a. 'Popper, Rationality and the Possibility of Social Science.' *THEORIA, An International Journal for Theory, History and Foundations of Science* 28 (1): 61-75. Available here:
https://www.academia.edu/1202022/Popper_Rationality_and_the_Possibility_of_Social_Science

——————. 2013b. 'Free Will and Probability.' *Canadian Journal of Philosophy* 43 (1): 60-77.

——————. 2014. 'Voluntary Slavery.' *Las Torres de Lucca* 4: 115-37. Available here:
https://www.academia.edu/4555466/Voluntary_Slavery

——————. 2015. 'The Contrast Between Dogmatic and Critical

Arguments.' *Organon F* 22(1): 9-20. Available here:
https://www.academia.edu/7457820/The_Contrast_Between_Dogmati
c_and_Critical_Arguments

__________. 2016a. 'Ethical Intuitionism: A Structural Critique.' *Journal of Value Inquiry* 50 (3): 631-47. Available here:
http://link.springer.com/article/10.1007/s10790-016-9547-8

__________. 2016b. 'Defective Equilibrium.' *Organon F* 23 (4): 443-59. Available here:
https://www.academia.edu/11159849/Defective_Equilibrium

__________. 2016c. 'Freedom: Positive, Negative Expressive.' Reason Papers 38 (2): 39-63. Available here:
https://www.academia.edu/20435616/Freedom_Positive_Negative_Ex
pressive

__________. 2017. 'The Unsatisfactoriness of Unsaturatedness.' In Piotr Stalmaszczyk (ed.), *Philosophy and Logic of Predication* (pp. 145-65). Bern: Peter Lang GmbH.

__________. 2019a. 'The Relevance of Karl Popper's *Open Society*.' *Cosmos + Taxis* 6 (6+7): 33-42.

__________. 2019b. 'A Regimented and Concise Exposition of Karl Popper's Critical Rationalist Epistemology.' *Cosmos + Taxis* 6 (6+7): 49-54. Available here:
https://www.academia.edu/12378320/A_Regimented_and_Concise_E
xposition_of_Karl_Popper_s_Critical_Rationalist_Epistemology

__________. 2020. *Freedom, Indeterminism, and Fallibilism*. New York: Palgrave Macmillan.

__________. Forthcoming. 'Falsificationism and the Pragmatic Problem of Induction.' *Organon F*.

Frege, Gottlob. 1892. 'On Concept and Object.' In Peter Geach and Max Black (ed. and tr.), *Translations from the Philosophical Writings of Gottlob Frege* (pp. 42-55). Oxford: Blackwell (1980).

__________. 1914. 'Logic in Mathematics.' In H. Hermes, F. Kambartel and F. Kaulbach (eds.), P. Long and R. White (trans.) *Posthumous Writings* (pp. 203-50). Oxford: Blackwell (1979).

Galileo Galilei. 1638. *Dialogues Concerning Two New Sciences*, excerpts in *The Essential Galileo*, ed. and tr. Maurice Finocchiaro (pp. 295-367). Indianapolis: Hackett Publishing (2008).

Gassendi, Pierre. 1658. *The Syntagma*. Selections in his *Selected Work*, ed. and tr. Craig Brush (pp. 279-434). New York: Johnson Reprint Corporation (1972).

Gettier, Edmund. 1963. 'Is Justified True Belief Knowledge?' *Analysis* 23 (6): 121-23.

Goodman, Nelson. 1954. *Fact, Fiction, and Forecast*, fourth edition. Cambridge, MA: Harvard University Press (1983).

Grice, Paul. 2001. *Aspects of Reason*. Oxford: Clarendon Press.

Haack, Susan. 1993. *Evidence and Inquiry*. Oxford: Blackwell.

__________. 2003. *Defending Science - Within Reason*. New York: Prometheus.

__________. 2009. 'Popper on Trial: A Brief History of a Big Muddle.' MS. Downloaded on 17 August 2014 from: http://www.eui.eu/documents/mwp/conferences/popper/haackpoppe rontrial.pdf

__________. 2010. 'Federal Philosophy of Science.' *New York University Journal of Law and Liberty* 5 (2): 394-435. Downloaded on 19 August 2014 from: http://migration.nyulaw.me/sites/default/files/ECM_PRO_066944.pd f

__________. 2013. 'Just Say "No" to Logical Negativism.' In her *Putting Philosophy to Work*, expanded paperback edition (pp. 179-94). New York: Prometheus. Downloaded on 19 August 2014 from: http://papers.ssrn.com/sol3/papers.cfm?abstract_id=2126805

Hájek, Alan. 2017. 'Philosophy Tool Kit.' *Aeon*, Newsletter, 3 April 2017, available here: https://aeon.co/essays/with-the-use-of-heuristics-anybody-can-think-like-a-philosopher

Harman, Gilbert. 1986. *Change in View*. Cambridge, MA.: MIT Press.

Hausman, Daniel. 1992. *The Inexact and Separate Science of Economics*. Cambridge: Cambridge University Press.

Hayek, Friedrich. 1963. 'Rules, Perception and Intelligibility.' In his *Studies in Philosophy, Politics and Economics* (pp.43-65). London: Routledge and Kegan Paul (1967).

__________. 1970. 'The Errors of Constructivism.' In his *New Studies in Philosophy, Politics, Economics and the History of Ideas* (pp. 3-22). London: Routledge and Kegan Paul (1978).

Hempel, Carl. 1988. 'Provisos: A Problem Concerning the Inferential Function of Scientific Theories.' In Adolf Grünbaum and Wesley Salmon (eds), *The Limitations of Deductivism* (pp. 19–36). Berkeley: University of California Press.

Huemer, Michael. 2005. *Ethical Intuitionism*. Basingstoke: Palgrave Macmillan.

Hume, David. 1739. *A Treatise of Human Nature*, Book I, ed. L. A. Selby-Bigge. Oxford: Clarendon (1888).

__________. 1740. *A Treatise of Human Nature*, Book III, ed. L. A. Selby-Bigge, Oxford: Clarendon Press (1888).

__________. 1748. *An Enquiry Concerning Human Understanding*. In David Hume, *Enquiries*, ed. L. A. Selby-Bigge (pp. 1-165), third edition. Oxford: Clarendon (1975).

Jevons, W. Stanley. 1871. *The Theory of Political Economy*. London: Macmillan

(1888).

Kant, Immanuel. 1781/1787. *Critique of Pure Reason*, first and second edition, Norman Kemp Smith (trans.). London: Macmillan (1933).

Kirzner, Israel. 1985. *Discovery and the Capitalist Process*. Chicago, IL: University of Chicago Press.

Kneale, William. 1949. *Probability and Induction*. Oxford: Clarendon Press.

Koertge, Noretta. 1980. 'Analysis as a Method of Discovery During the Scientific Revolution.' In T. Nickles (ed.), *Scientific Discovery, Logic, and Rationality* (pp. 139-57). Dordrecht: Reidel.

Kolodny, Niko and MacFarlane, John. 2010. 'Ifs and Oughts.' *Journal of Philosophy* 107 (3): 115–143.

Korsgaard, Christine. 1986. 'Skepticism about Practical Reason.' In her *Creating the Kingdom of Ends* (pp. 311-34). Cambridge: Cambridge University Press (1996).

Koyré, Alexandre. 1957. *From the Closed World to the Infinite Universe*. Baltimore: Johns Hopkins Press.

Kripke, Saul. 1980. *Naming and Necessity*, with addenda. Cambridge, MA.: Harvard University Press.

Kuhn, Thomas. 1957. *The Copernican Revolution*. Cambridge, MA: Harvard University Press.

__________. 1959. 'The Essential Tension.' In his 1977, pp. 225-39.

__________. 1970. *The Structure of Scientific Revolutions*, second enlarged edition. Chicago: University of Chicago Press.

__________. 1974. 'Second Thoughts on Paradigms.' In his 1977, pp. 293-319.

__________. 1977. *The Essential Tension*. Chicago: University of Chicago Press.

Lakatos, Imre. 1962. 'Infinite Regress and Foundations of Mathematics.' In his 1978b, pp. 3-23.

__________. 1967. 'A Renaissance of Empiricism in the Recent Philosophy of Mathematics?' In his 1978b, pp. 24-42.

__________. 1970. 'Falsification and the Methodology of Scientific Research Programmes.' In Imre Lakatos and Alan Musgrave, eds., *Criticism and the Growth of Knowledge* (pp. 91-196). Cambridge: Cambridge University Press.

__________. 1976. *Proofs and Refutations*. Cambridge: Cambridge University Press.

__________. 1978a. 'Newton's Effect on Scientific Standards.' In his *Philosophical Papers*, Volume 1, edited by John Worrall and Gregory Currie, pp. 193-222. Cambridge: Cambridge University Press.

__________. 1978b. *Philosophical Papers*, Volume 2, ed. J. Worrall & G. Currie. Cambridge: Cambridge University Press.

Lange, Marc. 1993. 'Natural Laws and the Problem of Provisos.' *Erkenntnis*

38 (2): 233–248.

Leibniz, Gottfried. 1679. 'Specimen Calculi Universalis.' In *Selections*, ed. Philip P. Wiener (pp. 98-99). New York: Charles Scribner's Sons.

__________. 1686. 'Identity in Individuals and True Propositions.' In *Selections*, ed. Philip P. Wiener (pp. 96-98). New York: Charles Scribner's Sons.

__________. 1765. *New Essays on Human Understanding*, P. Remnant & J. Bennett (trans. & ed.), corrected edition. Cambridge: Cambridge University Press (1982).

Levy, Neil. 2019. 'Why no-platforming is sometimes a justifiable position.' *Aeon*, Newsletter, 4 March 2019, available here: https://aeon.co/ideas/why-no-platforming-is-sometimes-a-justifiable-position?utm

Luce, Duncan and Raiffa, Howard. 1957. *Games and Decisions*. New York: Wiley and Sons.

Lugg, Andrew. 1986. 'Deep Disagreement and Informal Logic: No Cause for Alarm.' *Informal Logic* 8 (1): pp. 47-51.

Lynch, Michael. 2010. 'Epistemic Circularity and Epistemic Incommensurability.' In *Social Epistemology*, edited by Adrian Haddock, Alan Millar and Duncan Pritchard (pp. 262-77). Oxford: Oxford University Press.

McCaffrey, Matthew. 2015. 'Economic Policy and Entrepreneurship: Alertness or Judgment?' In *The Next Generation of Austrian Economics: Essays in Honor of Joseph T. Salerno*, ed. Per Bylund and David Howden, pp. 183-99. Aubern AL: Mises Institute.

Mendelssohn, Moses. 1763. *Philosophical Writings*, ed. and tr. Daniel O. Dahlstrom, Cambridge: Cambridge University Press (1997).

Menger, Carl. 1871. *Principles of Economics*, tr. James Dingwall and Bert Hoselitz. Auburn, AL: Ludwig von Mises Institute (2007).

Mill, John Stuart. 1843. *A System of Logic,* ed. J. M. Robson. Toronto: University of Toronto Press (1974).

__________. 1859. *On Liberty.* In Mary Warnock (ed.), *Utilitarianism and On Liberty*, second edition (pp. 88-180). Oxford: Blackwell (2003).

Miller, David. 1994. *Critical Rationalism*. Chicago: Open Court.

__________. 2005. 'Do We Reason When We Think We Reason, or Do We Think?' *Learning for Democracy* 1 (3): 57-71.

__________. 2006a. 'What Do Arguments Achieve?' In David Miller, 2006f, pp. 63-80.

__________. 2006b. 'Induction: A Problem Solved.' In David Miller, 2006f, pp. 111-32.

__________. 2006c. 'How Little Uniformity Need and Inductive Inference Presuppose?' In David Miller, 2006f, pp. 159-68.

__________. 2006d. 'Thirty Years of Language Dependence.' In David

Miller, 2006f, pp. 197-233.

__________. 2006e. 'In Memoriam.' In David Miller, 2006f, pp. 263-67.

__________. 2006f. *Out of Error*. London: Routledge.

__________. 2020. 'Logical Content and its Discontents.' Revised version of a paper presented at the colloquium, *Does Valid Reasoning Matter?* held at Congress centre ACADEMIA, Stará Lesná, The High Tatras, Slovakia, 13-16 September, 2018. https://warwick.ac.uk/fac/soc/philosophy/people/miller/slovakia.pdf

Musgrave, Alan. 2011. 'Interview with Alan Musgrave.' *The Reasoner* 5 (1): 2-4.

Nagel, Thomas. 1979. 'The Fragmentation of Value.' In his *Mortal Questions*. Cambridge: Cambridge University Press.

Nozick, Robert. 1974. *Anarchy, State, and Utopia*. Oxford: Blackwell (1980).

__________. 1977. 'On Austrian Methodology.' In his *Socratic Puzzles* (pp. 110-141). Cambridge, MA: Harvard University Press (1997).

Peters, R. S. 1960. *The Concept of Motivation*, second edition. London: Routledge and Kegan Paul.

Pietroski, Paul and Rey, Georges. 1995. 'When Other Things Aren't Equal: Saving *Ceteris Paribus* Laws from Vacuity.' *British Journal for the Philosophy of Science* 46 (1): 81-110.

Plato. 1956. *Meno*. In *Protagoras and Meno*, tr. W. K. C. Guthrie (pp. 115-57). Harmondsworth: Penguin.

Popper, Karl. 1945. *The Open Society and its Enemies*, volumes 1 and 2. London: Routledge and Kegan Paul (1966 fifth, revised edition).

__________. 1949a. 'Towards a Rational Theory of Tradition.' In his 1963b, pp. 120-35.

__________. 1949b. 'The Bucket and the Searchlight.' In his 1972b, pp. 341-61 (Appendix).

__________. 1957a. 'Science: Conjectures and Refutations.' In his 1963b, pp. 33-65.

__________. 1957b. 'The Aim of Science.' In his 1983, pp. 131-46.

__________. 1958. 'On the Status of Science and of Metaphysics.' In his 1963b, pp. 184-200.

__________. 1959. *The Logic of Scientific Discovery*. London: Hutchinson.

__________. 1961. 'Addendum I: Facts, Standards and Truth.' In his 1945, volume 2, pp. 369-396.

__________. 1963a. 'Truth, Rationality, and the Growth of Scientific Knowledge.' In his 1963b, pp. 215-50.

__________. 1963b. *Conjectures and Refutations*. London: Routledge and Kegan Paul (fourth edition, 1972).

__________. 1968a. 'Epistemology Without a Knowing Subject.' In his 1972b, pp. 106-52.

__________. 1968b. 'On the Theory of the Objective Mind.' In his 1972b, pp. 153-90.

__________. 1971. 'Conjectural Knowledge.' In his 1972b, pp. 1-31.

__________. 1972a. 'Two Faces of Commonsense.' In his 1972b, pp. 32-105.

__________. 1972b. *Objective Knowledge*. Oxford: Clarendon.

__________. 1974a. 'Intellectual Autobiography.' In Paul Arthur Schilpp (ed.), 1974, volume 1 (pp. 3-181).

__________. 1974b. 'Replies to My Critics.' In P. A. Schilpp, ed., *The Philosophy of Karl Popper*, volume 2 (pp. 961-1197). La Salle, IL: Open Court.

__________. 1975. 'The Rationality of Scientific Revolutions.' In his 1994 (1-32)

__________. 1976. 'The Myth of the Framework.' In his 1994, pp. 33-64.

__________. 1982. *Quantum Theory and the Schism in Physics*. Totowa, NJ: Rowman and Littlefield.

__________. 1983. *Realism and the Aim of Science*. London: Routledge.

__________. 1994a. 'Models, Instruments, and Truth.' In his 1994b, pp. 154-84 (London: Routledge).

__________. 1994b. *The Myth of the Framework*, London: Routledge.

__________. 1994c. *Knowledge and the Body-Mind Problem*. London: Routledge.

Popper, Karl and Eccles, John. 1977. *The Self and its Brain*. London: Springer-Verlag (1983 edition).

Prichard, H. A. 1932. 'Duty and Ignorance of Fact.' In his *Moral Writings* (pp. 84-101). Oxford: Clarendon Press (2002).

Priest, Graham. 2004. 'What's So Bad About Contradictions?' In *The Law of Non-Contradiction*, ed. G. Priest, J. C. Beal & B. Amour-Garb (pp. 23-38). Oxford: Clarendon Press.

Priest, Graham and Thomason, Neil. 2007. '60% Proof.' *Australasian Journal of Logic* 5: 89-100.

Quine, W. V. O. 1951. 'Two Dogmas of Empiricism.' In his *From a Logical Point of View* (pp. 20-46). Cambridge, MA: Harvard University Press (1953 edition).

Raz, Joseph. 2010. 'Reason, Reasons and Normativity.' In *Oxford Studies in Metaethics*, volume 5, ed. R. Shafer-Landau (pp. 5-23). Oxford: Oxford University Press.

Russell, Bertrand. 1903. *The Principles of Mathematics*. London: George Allen and Unwin.

__________. 1924. 'Logical Atomism.' In his *Logic and Knowledge*, ed. R. Marsh (pp. 321-43). London: George Allen and Unwin (1956).

__________. 1959. *My Philosophical Development*. London: George Allen & Unwin.

Russell, Paul. 2017. 'The Limits of Tolerance.' *Aeon*, Newsletter, 2 August

2017, available here:
https://aeon.co/essays/why-religious-identities-are-not-immune-to-robust-criticism

Ryle, Gilbert. 1949, *The Concept of Mind*, London: Penguin (1983).

Salerno, Joseph. 1990. 'Postscript: Why a Socialist Economy is "Impossible".' In Ludwig von Mises, *Economic Calculation in the Socialist Commonwealth*, tr. S. Adler, pp. 49-69. Auburn, AL: Mises Institute.

Samuelson, Paul. 1947. *The Foundations of Economic Analysis*. Cambridge, MA: Harvard University Press.

Samuelson, Paul and Nordhaus, William. 1998. *Economics*, sixteenth edition. Boston, MA: McGraw-Hill.

Schrödinger, Erwin. 1960. 'What is Real?' In his *My View of the World* (pp. 61-110). Cambridge: Cambridge University Press (1964).

Schueler, G. F. 2009. 'The Humean Theory of Motivation Rejected.' *Philosophy and Phenomenological Research* 78 (1): 103-22.

Schwenkler, John. 2018. 'Should You Shield Yourself From Others' Abhorrent Beliefs?' *Aeon*, Newsletter, 2 July 2018, available here: https://aeon.co/ideas/should-you-shield-yourself-from-others-abhorrent-beliefs

Scruton, Roger. 1996. *Animal Rights and Wrongs*. London: Demos.

Searle, John. 1969. *Speech Acts*. Cambridge: Cambridge University Press.

Sextus Empiricus. 2000. *Outlines of Scepticism*, ed. J. Annas and J. Barnes. Cambridge: Cambridge University Press.

Siegel, Harvey. 2013. 'Argumentation and the Epistemology of Deep Disagreement.' *Cogency* 5 (1): 135-70.

Skousen, Mark. 2001. *The Making of Modern Economics*. New York: M. E. Sharpe.

Smith, Sheldon. 2002. 'Violated Laws, Ceteris Paribus Clauses, and Capacities.' *Synthese* 130 (2): 235-64.

Stanford, Kyle. 2006. *Exceeding Our Grasp*. Oxford: Oxford University Press.

Steward, Helen. 2012. *A Metaphysics for Freedom*. Oxford: Oxford University Press.

Strawson, P. F. 1956. 'Singular Terms, Ontology and Identity.' *Mind* 65 (260): 433-54.

__________. 1959. *Individuals*. London: Methuen (1979).

__________. 1992. *Analysis and Metaphysics*. Oxford: Oxford University Press.

Wallace, R. J. 2014. 'Practical Reason.' *The Stanford Encyclopedia of Philosophy (Summer 2014 Edition)*, ed. E. N. Zalta, downloaded on 27 July 2014 from: http://plato.stanford.edu/archives/sum2014/entries/practical-reason/

Walras, Leon. 1896. *Elements of Theoretical Economics*, third edition, tr. Donald Walker and Jan van Daal. Cambridge: Cambridge University Press

(2014).

Watkins, John. 1958. 'Confirmable and Influential Metaphysics.' *Mind* 67 (267): 344-65.

——————. 1970. 'Imperfect Rationality.' In *Explanation in the Behavioural Sciences*, edited by Robert Borger and Frank Cioffi (pp. 167-217). Cambridge: Cambridge University Press.

——————. 1973. *Hobbes's System of Ideas*, second edition. London: Hutchinson.

——————. 1984. *Science and Scepticism*. Princeton: Princeton University Press.

Whately, Richard. 1853. *Elements of Logic*, eighth edition. New York: Harper and Brothers.

Whitehead, Alfred and Russell, Bertrand. 1927. *Principia Mathematica*, volume 1, second edition. Cambridge: Cambridge University Press.

Zahar, Elie. 1973. 'Why Did Einstein's Programme Supersede Lorentz's? (II)' *British Journal for the Philosophy of Science* 24 (3): 223-62.

INDEX

ABOUT THE AUTHOR

Danny Frederick was born in London. Until he was almost ten he lived at Latimer Road in the old Notting Hill slums (long since demolished). His family was then re-housed on a council estate in Shepherd's Bush. He went to the academically undistinguished Christopher Wren Comprehensive School in Shepherd's Bush where he did well enough at A level to obtain a place as an undergraduate at the London School of Economics (LSE). After his first year at the LSE he was shortlisted for a prestigious MacTaggart scholarship. He studied philosophy as an undergraduate at the LSE and as a postgraduate at Lancaster University and also at Birkbeck College London, where he obtained an M.Phil. During his final year at Birkbeck, he also taught philosophy to undergraduates and a postgraduate at King's College London. However, having become disillusioned with academic philosophy (as currently practised), he left academe to work in administration and management, eventually working as a chartered management accountant. He resigned from his job in 2006, having made sufficient money. Gradually he found himself being drawn back into academic philosophy. Since November 2009 he has had forty-five articles published, or accepted for publication, in peer-reviewed academic journals and books. His book, *Freedom, Indeterminism, and Fallibilism*, was published in 2020 in the Palgrave Studies in Classical Liberalism series. He has an academic webpage here: https://independent.academia.edu/DannyFrederick